Dymphna Callery

Dymphna Callery was a librarian before discovering drama as an undergraduate at Sheffield University. Her theatre credits include Ibsen's *A Doll's House* and Edna O'Brien's *Virginia* together with her first play *Olywyn: for One Woman and Cello*, and stage adaptations of *Thérèse Raquin* and *Women in Love*. She has a Masters Degree in Writing Studies, and her poetry collection *What She Said and What She Did* was published in 1996.

After a spell in community arts, she taught drama and writing at Liverpool John Moores University for twelve years, and is now Head of Drama at the University of Wolverhampton. She writes regularly for *Total Theatre* magazine and has participated in numerous workshops from a wide range of physical theatre practitioners, in addition to leading workshops in Britain and abroad. *Through the Body* is her first book.

DYMPHNA CALLERY

Through the Body

a practical guide
to physical theatre

Routledge
New York

Nick Hern Books
London
www.nickhernbooks.co.uk

100723165C

A Nick Hern Book

Through the Body first published in Great Britain in 2001
as a paperback original by Nick Hern Books Limited,
14 Larden Road, London W3 7ST
and in the United States of America by Routledge,
29 West 35 Street, New York, NY 10001

Reprinted 2002, 2003, 2004, 2005 (twice), 2006, 2007, 2009, 2010, 2011

British Library Cataloguing data for this book
is available from the British Library

ISBN 978-1-85459-630-7 (UK)

Library of Congress data available

ISBN 978-0-87830-124-9 (USA)

Cover design: Ned Hoste, 2H
Cover photograph: Simon Richardson

Typeset by Country Setting, Kingsdown, Kent CT14 8ES
Printed by the MPG Books Group in the UK

Contents

Preface

Someone once said that talking about music is like dancing architecture: I wonder what they would say about a book describing the process of physical theatre. It is incredibly hard to talk about a creative process whose medium of exchange is primarily the body: even when teaching the spoken word comes second to the physical exercise. Although language is used through the teaching and creative process it plays a secondary role, a supporting role. You can explain, encourage, describe, coach, suggest images, metaphors and similes, you can use language with all its powers of description and suggestion, but only to help the other person (student or colleague) perform the physical movement with the qualities that you had envisaged: but finally the rightness – dare one say 'truth'? – of the move or exercise is something that can only be felt, as Dymphna so aptly puts it, *through the body*.

This book is a mixture of three inter-related elements – it is a mapping of the field of physical theatre, a gathering of collective wisdom about the teaching and making of that work, and some forty or fifty really useful exercises and games. Putting these three together mean that this book is a long-overdue manifesto for physical theatre – which still remains marginal within the predominantly text-based theatre of Britain. New Theatre is often taken as being synonymous with New Writing, yet physical theatre, although 'New', is invisible to many theatre commentators because its performance text isn't written. Matters are made even worse because physical theatre isn't easy to define, which may explain why the first question of the book is 'What is physical theatre?' Her introduction answers this question with some common sense definitions and descriptions. Hopefully this will create a more general awareness of this dimension of theatre and thus broaden our understanding of the scope and possibility of the medium.

When one thinks of a physical approach to theatre the names Eugenio Barba, Jerze Grotowski and Jacques Lecoq, immediately spring to mind. No-one can doubt the huge influence that these men have had on how we teach and practise contemporary theatre, and Dymphna makes ample reference to their writings and thought, but, just as importantly, she brings to our notice a new generation of teachers and practitioners who are making their own researches and discoveries. While it has been my job as director of the International Workshop Festival (IWF) to be informed about the field of professional training, I have found much in this book that is completely new to me and have been obliged to revise my image of the state of physical theatre in Britain. It's not just the references to a wider body of work – she includes lesser-known figures such as Roy Hart and Moshe Feldenkrais – but her acknowledgement of young British practitioners like Lucy O'Rorke of Bouge-de-la, or Hayley Carmichael of Told By An Idiot. Of course it is important to know where the first ideas and impulses for this movement in theatre came from, but it is equally important for the British reader to know what is happening now, here in Britain. Scratch below the surface of West End and commercial theatre and you find a thriving culture of experiment and innovation.

I said that this book was a mixture of three things – tour d'horizon of the field, and a gathering of theoretical reflections and practical exercises. The breadth of her reading and research is reflected in the bibliography, but this doesn't account for her *feeling for practice*. A key to this lies in her references to some of the video-documentations produced by Peter Hulton's Arts Documentation Unit (notably, workshops given as part of the International Workshop Festival by Gennadi Bogdanov and Jos Houben in 1996). What her bibliography doesn't mention is that Dymphna has been a participant in many IWF workshops over the years: she may be an experienced teacher and now a published author but she still has the wisdom and humility to be open to new practices and approaches to theatre. Her book about practice is the result of experiences and understandings that have happened through her own body. I was first aware of her voice in the 1998 International Workshop Festival when the theme for the workshops and discussions was Rhythm. Dymphna was in the audience for every discussion and demonstration and became an invaluable contributor to our proceedings. One evening I needed to know the source for E.M.Forster's phrase 'Only connect' – *Howard's End* came the reply from Dymphna. It is appropriate that it was she who proffered this information since Forster's injunction is most apposite when thinking about the contents and argument of *Through the Body*. One of the problems the book addresses is precisely the need to connect body and mind and its extension into practice and theory.

While it is true there is no canonical body of physical theatre performance, there is a certain body of knowledge that has been slowly built up over the last century. There is – thankfully – no universal system for creating or teaching physical theatre, however what does exist is a wealth of practical know-how, an oral tradition whose sources are often undiscoverable. This wisdom is passed between practitioners and from teacher to pupil in the form of exercises and games – they are often introduced with the phrase 'I first came across this exercise when I was working with x', because very often no-one knows who first created it. Peter Brook tells the story of a friend who met him and was full of praise for his exercise. 'Which one is that?' Brook asked. His friend demonstrated it and Brook smiled. 'It's a great exercise, and I'll use it now, but I didn't create it.' This is why I say the tradition is Oral – passed on from practitioner to practitioner. However the exercises themselves aren't as important as what one does with them. Very often a teacher will begin a description of an exercise by saying 'You probably know this exercise already, but please pay attention because I have put it to rather a different use.' As he closes his book *Theatre Games,* Clive Barker hands on the responsibility for the games he has described to the reader:

> The work set out is my work and no-one else's. It does not 'belong' even to those actors who have worked for long periods with me. Whoever takes the work from me immediately makes it his own and from that moment accepts the responsibility for whatever he does. He is also entitled to the full credit for whatever use he can make of it.
>
> *Theatre Games,* Methuen, p 217

With exercises you don't have creators but carriers.

This gets to the heart of the problem of the exchange of knowledge in the field of physical theatre – can it be conveyed through the written word, that is, in a book? I think if Dymphna had simply offered us a series of recipes for making good theatre the attempt would have failed: what she has very wisely done is to mix the exercises and games with comment, anecdote and theoretical reflection. Apart from this commentary she has grouped them thematically and progressively – another sensible idea. In this way she provides a context for the exercises, demonstrating what they mean for the actor and teacher, and what other fields they touch on.

Let me now develop the distinction between a book of theatre exercises and a recipe book. Firstly, the instructions in a recipe can be easily followed as long as you have the right ingredients and equipment and, secondly, whoever makes it, the recipe will taste much the same if followed to the letter – which is not the case with a theatre exercise. There are three stages in understanding an exercise – firstly grasping the instruction at the level of language, secondly translating it into a physical movement and thirdly being sensitive to the emotional effect this has upon you. Even in that bible of theatre practice, Grotowski's *Towards a Poor Theatre,* I find some of the exercises impossible to understand even at the level of language. I can't figure out what's going on. Dymphna has been wise in keeping her exercises simple. But even if we do understand them we then must ask ourselves what are they for? Exercises aren't a *recipe* for success, rather they are open structures by means of which we can make psycho-physical connections within ourselves. They are possible pathways through our mental and physical structure which can lead toward a mental and emotional experience. So learning the exercise as some kind of routine that must be repeated until mastered is totally redundant: you will simply be involved in a dogged and deadly repetition. I remember being taught an incredibly complex exercise by Romanian director and teacher Andrei Serban (who worked with Peter Brook's International Centre for Theatre Research in 1971). One participant assured him that he would practise it assiduously until it could be performed on stage: Andrei laughed and replied 'But this exercise is completely stupid! Its only function is to get you co-ordinated.' The exercise is there to make contact, within yourself and between you and others – you have to be mentally present, alert and available at and to every moment. That is the only way they will be able to make something happen.

All this goes to say that I am glad that Dymphna has not written a handbook. This is not a do-it-yourself guide to physical theatre practice – it is a fantastic sounding of the collective wisdom in this field as seen from a British perspective. And it is now our responsibility to use these ideas and exercises wisely.

DICK McCAW

Acknowledgements

I would like to thank the following for their unerring support during the writing of this book: colleagues and students at the Drama Department, Liverpool John Moores University, Peter Ward of Hope Street Ltd., Graeme Phillips of The Unity Theatre, Liverpool, and particular thanks to Jane Hartley (Kaos Theatre) for reading and commenting on it. I would also like to thank Liverpool John Moores University for the award af a Research Grant which enabled me to research and write this book.

In addition I would like to extend my thanks to those whose workshops and shared thoughts have inspired and challenged me, including: Annabel Arden and Mick Barnfather (Theatre de Complicité), Lee Beagley (Kaboodle Theatre Company), Gennadi Bogdanov, Brouhaha, Nigel Charnock, Michael Chase (The Mask Studio), Guy Dartnell, Andrew Dawson, Antje Diedrich (Rose Bruford), Ann Farrar (Rejects Revenge), Hayley Carmichael and Paul Hunter (Told By An Idiot), Geese Theatre Company, Gooseberry Fools, Kate Hale and Naomi Cooke (Foursight Theatre Company), Jen Heyes (Cut to the Chase), Hoipolloi, Jos Houben, Ninian Kinier-Wilson, Xavier Leret and company members of Kaos Theatre, Dick McCaw (International Workshop Festival), Bim Mason (Circomedia), Garet Newell (Feldenkrais Guild, UK), Lucy O'Rorke and Aurelian Koch (Bouge-de-la), Nola Rae, Kenneth Rea (Guildhall School of Speech and Drama), John and David (Ridiculusmus), Trestle Theatre Company, Volcano Theatre Company, Henning von Vangerrow, and John Wright.

Special thanks to John Daniel and Annabel Arndt (Total Theatre) for their support and the use of Total Theatre archive, and Emma Callery for lending me her iMac. Also Nick Hern and Caroline Downing for their meticulous editing, and to Nick for his encouragement.

Not forgetting Sean Cubitt, without whom . . . and Alison Ripley.

Through the Body

Ideal acting is the expression
of the metaphysical through physical acts:
ideal theatre is the creation of an invisible world
through visual presentation.

Yoshi Oida

Introduction

This book offers a series of workshop exercises designed to activate a physical approach to acting. It is based on personal experience, both as a participant in a wide range of workshops run by contemporary practitioners and in my own teaching. It is rooted in conversations with a host of physical theatre companies and practitioners which have been an invaluable source of inspiration and information, and in my work with student actors.

The characteristics of physical theatre are many and varied. Indeed the term is virtually impossible to define. Yet the emergence of physical theatre at the turn of the millennium seems to represent a change in the nature of acting in response to a shift away from text-based theatre and the Stanislavskian notion of interpreting a role. This is exemplified not only in the increasing number of companies devising their own work, but in the way they train and work in the process of making theatre. And the way they train and work is summed up in the title of this book: *through the body*.

Ultimately good acting is about liberating the imagination. And my fundamental guiding principle is that working through the body can achieve this. My investigations into the ideas and practices of twentieth-century practitioners seem to support this theory and throughout the book I introduce the key principles behind their work, and offer suggestions for exploring these principles in action, through games and exercises.

Each section of the book embraces a coherent area of practical work, contextualised by material exploring its significance to twentieth-century theatre practice. Within each section the exercises demonstrate concepts and provide a skills base which can be utilised in generating a common physical vocabulary for performers. Exercises for individual actors are incorporated alongside group activities.

The rest of this introduction gives a brief overview of the history and origins of physical theatre, placing current practice in the heritage of twentieth-century experimentation in theatre. SECTION ONE concerns preparatory body work, incorporating Awareness, Articulation, Energy and Neutrality, laying foundations on which later work can be developed. SECTION TWO explores the basics of Mask-work, which I have found invariably effective as a catalyst for releasing the physical actor. This is followed by an investigation of the Body in Space, Presence, Complicité, Play and Audience in THE PLAYFUL BODY before moving on to more detailed work on Rhythm, Sound and Emotion in THE SENTIENT BODY. The book culminates in sections on DEVISING, including how to structure materials as well as generating ideas, and on applying work to text in THE PHYSICAL TEXT.

The importance of training in physical theatre cannot be over-emphasised. Control of the body and somatic interaction are keystones of physical acting. Yet as the first section points out, working through the body is not purely a matter of enhancing your physical responses. Regular work with the body also improves both your mental and emotional reflexes. Many of the exercises in this book work indirectly, via a ricochet effect, in the same way as training operates in sports like football, or as musicians practise scales and arpeggios. Mask work, for example, clarifies gesture, whilst work on rhythm has a whole host of applications. Ultimately, the aim is to develop understanding of acting as a combination of imagination and technique. The experience of doing the exercises lays down 'circuits' in the body which are reactivated at a later date. In other words, the body remembers.

WHAT IS PHYSICAL THEATRE?

At its best, all theatre is physical.[1]

At its simplest, physical-theatre is theatre where the primary means of creation occurs through the body rather than through the mind. In other words, the somatic impulse is privileged over the cerebral in the making process. This is true whether the product is an original devised piece or an interpretation of a scripted text. This does not mean that the intellectual demands of the idea or script are jettisoned. The intellectual is grasped through the physical engagement of the body because, as Lecoq puts it, 'the body knows things about which the mind is ignorant'.[2]

From the spectators' point of view, physical theatre accentuates the audience's imaginative involvement and engagement with what is taking place on stage. There is a greater emphasis on exploiting the power of suggestion; environments and worlds are created onstage by actors and design elements provoke the imaginations of the spectators, rather than furnishing the stage with literal replications of life. This is related to a pronounced emphasis on the alive-ness of the theatre event and the body-consciousness of the performers.

Understanding and preferencing the living quality of a theatre event lies at the heart of physical theatre. In a sense all the other features emanate from this. Physical theatre acknowledges the relationship between the stage and spectator in a way that, for example, film does not – and cannot even though film can represent reality – and that fourth-wall naturalistic theatre does not because its very nature is to pretend that the audience is not there. In essence, the idea behind naturalism is that the audience is watching a film, that they are the eye of the camera in a fixed position; a literal translation of events is placed on stage. In physical theatre the two-way current between stage and spectator does not operate merely at the level of suspense and empathy, but embraces the visual and visceral. Watching becomes a sensory experience, the magical and illusory qualities of the experience are paramount.

Physical theatre is not codifiable. The term is applied to such a diverse range of work that it has become virtually undefinable. Yet some significant parallels emerge from any investigation of those working in this field, and these features serve as a broad paradigm:

- the emphasis is on the actor-as-creator rather than the actor-as-interpreter
- the working process is collaborative
- the working practice is somatic
- the stage-spectator relationship is open
- the live-ness of the theatre medium is paramount.

The method of working is based on the idea that theatre is about craft, celebration and play, rooted in collaboration, and made by an ensemble dedicated to discovering a collective imagination.

CONTEMPORARY PHYSICAL THEATRE

Over the last three decades, a whole raft of companies have emerged who fall into the category of physical theatre. The most influential to date is probably Theatre de Complicité whose work twenty years on is grounded in beautifully choreographed stage movement and continues to surprise and challenge audiences. Their newest piece, *The Noise of Time* (2001), is a collaboration between the company and The Emerson String Quartet. This meditation on the life of Shostakovich, in which actors move but do not speak and which culminates in the Emerson's playing of the last quartet, represents a further innovative dimension of much physical theatre: the cross-fertilisation between theatre and other art forms. Examples of cross-art collaborations, such as Improbable Theatre's vibrant retelling of ghoulish nursery tales *Shockheaded Peter* (1999) which incorporated music from the self-styled 'junk opera' group Tiger Lilies, are increasingly prevalent.

Many current practitioners resent the way their work is categorised as 'physical theatre' when they maintain that they are simply making 'theatre', and their work should be viewed as innovative rather than marginalised by bracketing. Lloyd Newson complains the phrase 'physical theatre' is attached to anything which doesn't fit the staid conventions of commercial theatre. And as the examples above show, physical theatre tends to defy conventional views of what constitutes 'theatre'.

The term 'physical theatre' has evolved as a catch-all phrase to describe touring theatre companies whose work has a strong visual dimension, companies who have developed a theatrical style which focuses attention on the physicality of the performers, and those defining themselves as 'new mime'.[3] However, it was the dance company, DV8 Physical Theatre, who first used the term consciously in their name and whose impact meant it became more widely used.

DV8 was founded in 1986 by Australian Lloyd Newson who maintains that 'physical theatre' 'is a Grotowski-based term'.[4] The company quickly became renowned for their high level of physical (and emotional) risk in performance, and the fact that for the first time in contemporary dance, dancers spoke. Their focus on issues of identity, on matters of genuine concern to the dancers on stage, meant the content was also seen as radical. It was as though issue-based theatre had infiltrated the dance world.

Unlike many choreographers, Newson encouraged his dancers to create rather than simply interpret. Work was devised by the company through shared research and praxis. For Newson, language is a tool on a par with any other performance dimension, such as film, video, music.[5] The way dance has been reinvented in DV8's work is a challenge to preconceptions about divisions in the performing arts.

The arrival of this 'new dance' occurred at the same time as a host of theatre makers began reclaiming the language of the body, questioning the hierarchy of the word in traditional theatre. They were creating new work (frequently, as in the case of DV8, devised by the performers) with a deliberate focus on the physicality of performance. Examples of such companies include: Moving Picture Mime Show, Trestle Theatre, The Right Size, Kaos Theatre, Foursight Theatre, Bouge-de-la, Reject's Revenge, David Glass Ensemble, Volcano Theatre, Improbable Theatre and Theatre de Complicité. Having begun life on the fringe, many of these companies are now making inroads into mainstream theatre, notably Theatre de Complicité, The Right Size and Kaos Theatre.

DV8 have been cited as the first British exponents of German tanztheater, best known through the work of Pina Bausch. And this European connection is important, for the growth of physical theatre in Britain owes much to cross-channel influences, not least the schools of Jacques Lecoq and Etienne Decroux in Paris, where many young actors have gone to train since the 1960s. Steven Berkoff, for example, burst onto the London theatre scene in the 1970s with a distinctive high-octane performance style rooted in his training with Lecoq, and inspired a new generation of performers keen to explore mime and movement techniques.

The impetus of what has become known as 'new mime', promoted primarily by the ideas of Lecoq and Decroux, has carried the physical theatre movement in Britain forward and their theories feature significantly in this book. But contemporary physical theatre is not limited to the influence of these two practitioners. It draws on the whole gamut of theatrical experimentation in Europe from the beginnings of the 20th century, from Meyerhold through to Grotowski and Barba. Whilst the founder members of Theatre de Complicité trained with Lecoq, the members of Foursight Theatre met at Exeter University where they were inspired by their work on Grotowski, and Told By An Idiot met at Middlesex University working with John Wright. Other companies have mixed influences, for example, Kaos Theatre, Frantic Assembly, Volcano.

What they share is a commitment to the concept of the creative actor, to a physical approach to performance where language is only one of the performance elements, to the notion that within every actor lies creative potential which can be accessed through imaginative play.

When Newson writes that 'the visceral power of dance precedes thought, that's its power', he is reiterating Eugenio Barba's belief that true creativity resides in the 'pre-expressive' realm. As its name suggests, the pre-expressive is the pre-verbal, that hinterland of creative potential which is the source of artistic expression. Accessing this through provoking imaginative, somatic responses of performers in the making process is the aim. The paradigm of progressing from impulse to movement to action to gesture to sound to word, is one to which all the practitioners mentioned in this book subscribe, Newton included, and is articulated by Peter Brook in *The Empty Space*, when he states that 'a word does not begin as a word, . . . it begins as an impulse'.[6]

In physical theatre, whether the performers are dancers or actors, the process is still the same: ideas are scored in rehearsal through the body. Everyone starts by searching for the somatic impulse.

ORIGINS

Although the term 'physical theatre' is a recent coinage, its heritage is considerably older. The impetus of French 'new mime' espoused by Etienne Decroux and Jean Dorcy, for example, was inspired by Jacques Copeau, and Copeau himself was inspired by circus artists and the traditions of commedia dell'arte and Japanese Noh theatre.

The origins of physical theatre are complex, and any investigation of its roots leads backwards through the developments in experimental theatre which represent challenges to naturalism. For at the centre of physical theatre lies a desire to make theatre that reaches beyond realism, theatre which challenges the idea that a singly-authored text is primarily what constitutes a 'play', theatre which resists naturalistic approaches to performance, theatre where the spoken word is regarded as just one element of the performance idiom.

The legacy of theatrical experimentation in the twentieth century has far outreached the boundaries of the naturalism with which it began. At the beginning of the century theatre-makers were forced to re-assess the medium of theatre with the arrival of film. Realism had not yet been fully

explored, yet cinema's consummate ability to render credible represen-
tations of reality challenged the newly-minted concept of naturalism. Was
theatre necessary any more if film could fulfil the demands of realism
more effectively? Shouldn't theatre relinquish naturalistic copying of
nature in the same way that painters had given up copying with the onset
of photography?

At the same time as cinema burst on the scene, painting and sculpture
were catapulted into unfamiliar territory by the arrival of Cubism.
Received ideas about how we see and interpret the visual were suddenly
questionable. The focus shifted from *what* we see to *how* we see. This
seismic revolt against verisimilitude had its echoes in literature, as the
Russian Formalists suggested the purpose of the writer was to make the
familiar unfamiliar, and in music, where atonalism challenged the sup-
remacy of melody.

This radical reassessment of realism prompted a revival of interest in
commedia dell'arte. Artists found in commedia a new inspiration; commedia's underlying sense of parody and irony, its fragmentation and
framing devices became tools for the modernists, and its themes and
images permeated popular entertainment. In the early decades of the twentieth century, the commedia influence was evident across the spectrum of
the arts: in ballet, with the stunningly sensual new ballets of Diaghalev; in
music, with Erik Satie and Schoenberg, Debussy, Prokofiev and Stravinsky
all making significant use of it; specifically in painting with Picasso's
preference for Harlequin in his early career; and on screen too with the
character creations of Charlie Chaplin and Buster Keaton.

There was a distinct move away from the notion of art as a reflection of
reality. Instead artists began to claim a deeper re-presentation of life in
distorted and increasingly abstract images which refracted life, as though
through a broken mirror or prism, to reveal a darker truth. They found in
commedia an artifice which privileged the secular, sometimes the vulgar,
but was never cheaply escapist. For the comedic calls up the tragicomic;
and in its excessive laughter lie both the seeds of the absurd and the pathos
of humanity.

In theatre, Craig, Meyerhold and Copeau turned to commedia for its
inherent theatricality, its emphasis on the visual and on the actor as a
highly sophisticated physical improviser. For these three, naturalism, with
its emphasis on literal replication of reality, had become a dead weight
which stifled the imagination: the stage had become the province of scenic

painters and technicians, and actors succumbed to either rhetorical or emotionally indulgent delivery.

Craig railed against the creeping influence of Stanislavsky, with actors imitating everyday human behaviour which he saw as artless copying, merely 'kinship with the ventriloquist'.[7] But whilst he condemned Stanislavsky's 'system', along with any other systemised approach to acting, he maintained that movement and voice production should and could be taught. His ideal would be a 'school of experiment' because 'when you experiment, you find out for yourself'.[8]

As the Moscow Art Theatre continued its explorations of pictorial realism under Stanislavsky, his former pupil Meyerhold dismantled the proscenium arch and trained his actors to sculpt themselves in three-dimensional space through Biomechanics (which is dealt with in detail later in this book). His highly dynamic stage compositions utilised the relationship between actors' bodies to convey meaning rather than relying on words and behavioural gesture.

At around the same time in Paris, Copeau replaced the footlights and curtains with a thrust stage decorated only by platform levels, which focused attention on the actor's body. We owe the modern idea of scenic simplicity largely to Copeau; his principles of scenic design championed a lack of inanimate decoration, movable props, and the active role of light.[9] As the practitioner who introduced the idea of physical training, games and free improvisation into the rehearsal room, he has also been called the 'father of modern theatre'.[10]

The visual impetus which these three practitioners brought to the art of theatre has been sustained and reinforced by theatre-makers whose concern has been to reinstate theatre as an art which fuses image and sound, gesture and word, rather than one dominated by the literary text.[11]

The prophetic Antonin Artaud went further than his predecessors and dispensed with the architecture of theatre altogether, proposing a large unadorned space where the audience would be engulfed by the action, affected on a physiological level by the intensity of action and sound. The spoken word had become merely utilitarian for him, and thereby impotent. His vision was of a 'language half-way between gesture and thought' where words took on 'something of the significance they have in dreams'.[12] His ideal performance was the antithesis of realism: a polyphony of unpredictable sounds and movement serving a metaphysics-in-action, confrontational and disturbing. And, although he never achieved his ideal theatre, Artaud's vision of theatre's visual and visceral nature has influenced many post-war practitioners.

It was Copeau who recognised the concept of the 'total actor' rooted in corporeal awareness and expression, and his particular passion for mask work inspired his pupil, Etienne Decroux, to rescue the art of mime from naturalism and develop it into a strongly sculptural form.[13] Decroux was a purist who kept mime silent, but he also championed the ideal of performers creating their own work. His collaborator, Jean-Louis Barrault, was influenced by Artaud and recognised the possibilities of speech in mime, thereby realising the concept of 'total theatre' through the individual.[14] It is this idea of mime as a 'tool for the actor' which underpins much of the work of Jacques Lecoq, who is central to the development of physical theatre.

The legacy of Copeau is pivotal to developments in physical theatre. His ideas on actor training have filtered through British theatre via his nephew Michel Saint-Denis, who founded the Old Vic Theatre School in London. More significantly, Lecoq falls into his lineage, as Lecoq first learned about theatre and acting from Copeau's daughter Marie-Therese and her husband Jean Dasté in prewar France.

Jacques Lecoq is a key figure in post-war physical theatre because so many contemporary exponents have trained with him and continue to pass on his training methods through their education work.[15] Distinguished graduates include Steven Berkoff, Ariane Mnouchkine, Philippe Gaulier (who now runs his own school in and from London),[16] and the founder members of Theatre de Complicité. Lecoq's ideas have permeated physical theatre in direct and indirect ways, through the work of his graduates in both Europe and the rest of the world. But he is not the only major figure in the development of physical theatre. He is one of a second wave of theatre reformers who continue to exert strong influences, notably Joan Littlewood, Peter Brook, Jerzy Grotowski and Eugenio Barba, whose ideas and practice all feature in this book.

Like their predecessors, this second wave of theatre reformers have turned to the pre-Enlightenment idea of the actor-as-creator, the popular commedia ideal of the actor as improviser/dancer/acrobat, and to the corporeal techniques of mime artists to fuel their experiments. They have looked eastwards too, following Copeau, Meyerhold and Artaud in investigating Asian theatre forms, with their highly disciplined and stylised performance modes. The work of these reformers has yet to be fully digested and their impact assessed, but their collective emphasis on working through the body lies at the heart of their influence.

The liberated sixties ushered in a new emphasis on theatre as a live event, theatre as a vibrant encounter between stage and spectator. This was partly a reaction to the passivity of the film medium, but also to the conservatism of commercial theatre, with its reactionary content and conventional forms. The forerunner of this was Joan Littlewood's Theatre Workshop, where actors were trained physically through Laban, and developed a highly visual ensemble style. Grotowski paved the way for further investigation of the craft of the actor and the actor-spectator relationship with his Laboratory Theatre in Poland. And Eugenio Barba, a one-time apprentice of Grotowski's, who did much to publicise his work in the West, set up his own experimental company, Odin Teatret, in Denmark.

It was in 1968 Peter Brook published *The Empty Space* in which he suggests that for language to re-emerge, theatre may need to go through a period of 'image-saturation', and his work at that time (the seminal productions of *Marat/Sade* and *A Midsummer Night's Dream*) demons-trated an intense awareness of the visual potential of theatre. At the same time, Jacques Lecoq was suggesting that when theatre loses its way it resorts to mime to renew itself, and so began schooling his students in new mime techniques.

In the following decade two directors in particular made an impact on London stages with new vibrant image-based theatre: Mike Alfreds and his company Shared Experience with *Arabian Nights* and *Bleak House* and Steven Berkoff with *Metamorphosis, The Trial* and *East*.[17] Neither employed technological solutions to place and props. The spectacle was created by the actors alone – on an empty stage.

The vitality of Shared Experience, who 'slipped in and out of stories created . . . on a bare stage'[18] without costume, set and with only the simplest lighting, rested on the fact that Alfreds believed the actor was the one essential in theatre. Moreover, he believed in the power of the actor's imagination to transform herself and to transport the audience. Although untrained in mime, Alfreds began to develop the mime skills of his com-pany through trial and error, gradually building a common language and a close-knit ensemble where they could be open and daring, able to take risks and play in the moment. His particular emphasis on the actor-as-storyteller has influenced many since.

Berkoff had studied mime with Claude Chagrin and Lecoq in Paris. Lecoq's techniques 'gave me the opportunity to invent ways of presenting works whereby all elements of the human being are brought into motion. Some call it 'total theatre' and nowadays 'physical theatre.'[19]

THERE IS NO THEORY

If the origins and breadth of physical theatre are difficult to disentangle, the notion of a theory is equally problematic.

Stanislavsky believed that the techniques of a single universal system of actor training could be applied to the creation of any form of theatre, yet many practitioners have found his emphasis on building a text-based role has limitations.[20] Whereas Stanislavsky attempted to construct a system based on acting techniques for texts, others have searched for principles which govern acting *per se*. In so doing, they have rejected the notion of a system. Peter Brook sums this up in his statement: 'We have a theory which is an anti-theory: that no method exists.'[21] What does exist, however, is a belief in the idea of the actor-as-creator, as opposed to the actor-as-interpreter.

The idea of the actor-as-creator underpins this book. And the philosophies and experiments of a range of key directors and practitioners who have championed actor-centred theatre will be evident: Vsevelod Meyerhold (1874-1938), Jacques Copeau (1879-1949), Antonin Artaud (1896-1948), Joan Littlewood (1914-), Jerzy Grotowski (1933-1999), Eugenio Barba (1934-), Peter Brook (1925-)and Jacques Lecoq (1921-1999). All have worked as directors, exploring their ideas through the process of making theatre. And all have, in various ways, removed the text from the actor in training to focus on improvisation. None of them, however, subscribes to the notion that actor-training can be systemised.

The writings of theatre practitioners are letters from the chalk face rather than 'theories'. Practitioners practise first, and make their discoveries on the studio or rehearsal-room floor in much the same way as the scientist conducts experiments in a laboratory. However, these are not as readily codifiable as a scientific experiment, where a mathematical equation may offer a solution to the problem. In theatre, experiments constitute a constant search which will never reach a quantifiable conclusion. Experiments may, however, reach a qualitative conclusion: 'it works or it doesn't' is the maxim, where the measuring stick is an informed artistic sensibility.

Much of this book is about cultivating that artistic sensibility. It is only through 'doing' that you will understand. And that 'doing' has to be a commitment to discovery rather than merely to acquiring technique.

The rejection of theory does not mean the rejection of training. Quite the reverse, in fact, as all the practitioners who feature in this book maintain that training is fundamental. There might be no single method or route; the many pathways are not necessarily mutually exclusive, although they may differ considerably in their emphasis. What unites them is the belief that training for the creative actor means working through the body.

Whilst dancers and musicians are expected to train and practise, the actor somehow is not. There has been resistance in the West to the notion of physical training in the misplaced belief that somehow it limits an actor and denies spontaneity. Yet we see in music highly-trained and practised jazz musicians like John Coltrane and Keith Jarret producing complex improvisations and interpretations, both as individuals and as part of an ensemble, precisely because of their mastery of technique.

Decroux held an unswerving belief that mastering technique liberated the artist. And the notion that technique arms the artist underpins the disciplined approach of post-war practitioners. Barba claims that 'performers who work within a network of codified rules have a greater freedom than those who – like [Western] performers – are prisoners of arbitrariness and an absence of rules'.[22] And for Grotowski, 'Spontaneity and discipline, far from weakening each other, mutually reinforce themselves . . . to become the real source of acting that glows. This lesson was neither understood by Stanislavsky, who let natural impulses dominate, nor by Brecht, who gave too much emphasis to the construction of a role'.[23]

In searching for a grammar of acting, practitioners have found different solutions. Copeau and Lecoq have espoused the virtues of mask work, finding in the alchemy of actor and mask a potent catalyst for actor-training, whilst Littlewood found in Laban the physical impetus for training her actors. Meyerhold gives us an extremely precise physical language for the actor in Biomechanics. Barba's actors have developed their own individual training programmes from gymnastics and acrobatics.

Highly disciplined training is fundamental to Eastern theatre, and Eastern performers continue to fascinate Western practitioners with their presence, their physical stamina and control, their ability to command the space and the spectator's attention. Meyerhold became intrigued by Mei Lang, Artaud by the Balinese performers. Barba's interest in Asian performers was sparked by his observation of their ability to project a powerful presence seemingly beyond the reach of European actors. Brook has adopted some of the Japanese Noh master Zeami's concepts in his practise, the use of 'Jo–Ha–Kyu' for example, which is investigated in detail later in the section on RHYTHM.

Examples of exercises and methods used by key practitioners appear regularly in this book, and I frequently draw parallels between them, and with Eastern practises where appropriate, in order to demonstrate the correspondences between them. One can detect similarities between practitioners even if they were not necessarily influenced by each other. Meyerhold's notion of the actor in space strongly resembles Lecoq's, for example, although Meyerhold's emphasis on the distortion of the body is more apparent in Barba's anthropological interrogations of performance energies, and similar observations to those of Meyerhold on the fundamental properties of rhythm in performance surface in Brook's meditations on theatre.

The suggestions for practical work in this book represent an eclectic mix of games and exercises drawn from a pool of practitioners – past and current – and from my own experience. You may have encountered them before in different versions. And you may also find you can reinvent or modify them to suit your specific requirements. Games and exercises are passed on via practitioners and workshops, and sometimes through books like this one. Often no-one knows who invented them. Where I am able to cite a source, I have done so. But be aware that what is on offer here is my version of someone else's game. Feel free to reinvent them. They are intended to serve as inspiration rather than a regimented programme.

The structure of this book does, however, offer a logical progression so that newcomers to the area can follow a developmental journey. This is not to imply a rigid method. But the basic pattern of moving from impulse to gesture to image to word, upon which the progression here is predicated, is inscribed in the work of so many practitioners that it is worthwhile regarding this as a principle.

My focus is on the essential principles that govern working through the body. Initially, these are basic considerations concerning awareness of the body before moving on to more complex concepts. In 1960 Brook wrote that if he had a drama school, 'the work would begin very far from

Preparing the Body

Preparing the Body

An untrained body is like an untuned musical instrument – its sounding box is filled with a confusing and ugly jangle of useless noises that prevent the true melody from being heard.[25]

Ideally preparatory training should be a process of self-discovery as well as an opportunity to master skills. For the individual, it is time dedicated to developing and exploring performance potential. For a company, training is time spent working to a common purpose, a way of enriching the ensemble and accessing a common physical vocabulary, a route towards collective creative energy.

Physical training is a process leading to creative freedom rather than a prescriptive set of techniques. Its purpose is to enable actors to become more transformable and more expressive. It is not body fascism. It does not mean 'gym-fever'. Suppleness, flexibility and sensitivity are the key aims for actors. Peter Brook points out that it is easy to be sensitive in the fingers and the face, but the actor needs to be sensitive throughout the body, constantly in contact with every inch of it. Sensitivity begets precision. And stage movement requires definition and clarity.

Acting does not require athletic training. Rigid gym training tames the body, making it obedient, but in so doing the body becomes a muscular entity commanded by the mind. Used exclusively, it can exaggerate the separation of mind and body which is antithetical to acting where the idea is that the whole person, mind, body and spirit, enters into the process. It can also block the current of spontaneity because the body learns a 'right' way of doing things, rather than being flexible and open to stimuli. Learning control of movement before breaking down movement inhibitions can restrict rather than liberate the actor. This is why work with apprentice actors needs to focus on breaking down ingrained patterns of movement before acquiring new ones.

Eugenio Barba distinguishes between two movement categories: daily and extra-daily. In daily behaviour we operate in everyday mode where we 'move-without-even-thinking-about-it'. Extra-daily behaviour refers to

ways of moving acquired specifically in order to perform. Barba's thesis is
that when performing extra-daily activities, the actor deconstructs, or
breaks down, the automatic daily code of movement and replaces it, or
reconstructs it, with skills specifically acquired for performance. This is
evident in many Oriental forms of theatre, for example, where actors learn
to create a fixed axis with their hips, thereby creating tension between the
upper and lower parts of the body which 'distorts' the daily, or normal
balance positions. Trained in this way, the actor's muscle tonus is changed,
and he has to use a great deal more energy and effort to move, hence the
highly measured Noh actor's walk. The energy is so concentrated and the
effort so masked by practise, that the actor acquires a mesmerising onstage
presence.

Whilst not advocating the punishing life-long training required by
traditional Eastern forms, Western practitioners have placed a definite
emphasis on preparing the actor's body by deconstructing the 'daily'
before working on the 'extra-daily'.

'Undoing' muscular structures in order to study and analyse them
raises the level of consciousness, or awareness, of how the body works.
And incorporating exercises designed to distort your own muscular structures leads you on to assembling new ones, to physically create or interpret
characters different from yourself. This brings me to another reason why
systematic athletic and gymnastic training regimes can be inappropriate:
they are designed to serve a preconceived muscular structure, to create, in
other words, a characteristic body. Preparatory training for actors is about
attaining a more neutral body.

For all the practitioners under discussion, physical preparation is
central to actor training. In seeking ways of refining and developing stage
movement, they all found different pathways to the same outcome: actors
with highly plastic bodies capable of responding to imaginative stimuli.

Finding your own pathway, adapting other systems to your own
purposes rather than simply importing them is the key. Practitioners
frequently drop one system in favour of another. When Jacques Copeau,
for example, adopted Dalcroze's Eurhythmics he found that it cramped
the creativity of his actors; instead he opted for a combination of gymnastics and acrobatics to support his own improvisation games. Copeau
distinguished his use of gymnastics from 'aesthetic gymnastics'; his aim
was corporeal flexibility: 'control and balance of movements, and of
breath control'.[26] And to this end his actors would begin their day with

two hours of gymnastics and acrobatics, 'even making perilous jumps above a straw-filled mattress . . . to give the young actors a sense of reliance in gesture, agility and the mastery of nerves and muscles'.[27]

Precision is the watchword of Lecoq's analytical approach to movement. For him, 'Physical preparation does not aim to emulate a particular model, nor to impose established dramatic forms. It should assist everyone towards the fullest realisation of accurate movement'.[28] Lecoq rejects both generic relaxation techniques and purely athletic exercise in favour of the 'physical education of the body of an actor who lives in the world of illusion'.[29] Even strenuous acrobatic work has to be accompanied by dramatic justification in Lecoq's book. Technical mastery of acrobatic movements, such as jumps and catches, is useful because it will give the actors greater freedom to invent. Actors learn juggling, for example, so that they can incorporate it into a dramatic sequence, such as juggling plates in a restaurant setting.

Most physical-based theatre companies have their own chosen method of training. Some use T'ai Chi, some use aerobics, some incorporate Feldenkrais, for example. Others continue to practise methods they have encountered through their own training. Many change their training mode when they feel they are becoming mechanical. More often than not they develop an eclectic mix which serves their performance style.

Taking time out to refresh skills or retrain in a new field is essential to the committed performer. You can't learn Biomechanics or Butoh techniques in a week, but a workshop with an experienced practitioner feeds your development and opens your eyes to different approaches. Actors are increasingly invited to lead workshops with their colleagues to introduce new techniques. This concept of skills-sharing is growing as companies invite practitioners and directors to contribute to their research and development processes. The 'interchange model',[30] where different companies share their working methods through structured workshops, is another example of this.

You won't attain a highly plastic or neutral body on the basis that 'anything goes'. Observation and analysis of movement lie at the heart of actor training. At Lecoq's school all classes begin with movement work related to the content of the session that follows. The relationship between preparation and exploration is a cornerstone of Lecoq, Grotowski, Littlewood, Brook and Barba. And, whatever their methodology, all of them begin with the idea that, as Barba puts it, training is a process of 'creating a bridge between energy and consciousness, between states of intensity and states of consciousness'.[31] In other words, between energy and awareness.

This section is devoted primarily to these two fundamental concepts which preface an examination of the principle of neutrality.

AWARENESS

Awareness means the consciousness which is not linked to language (the machine for thinking) but to presence.[32]

We are surprisingly unfamiliar with our bodies and many actors are inhibited about using them. Yet the body is the actor's primary instrument. To be brave and open requires a sentient and responsive body free from the limitations imposed by self-consciousness or fear. The first base is to make contact with your own skeleton and muscles.

Activating and sharpening the physical nature of perception is fundamental; it develops a consciousness linked to theatrical presence: being awake, alert, attentive, constantly being 'in the moment'. To borrow Barba's term, actors need 'extra-daily' awareness, having a kind of 'third eye' which monitors what is happening within the self. Imagine this as a compass needle working like a seismograph to register the internal vibrations of the nervous system. The information feeds your 'inner computer' and eventually becomes second nature. You have to be constantly curious about what is going on within.

Increasing awareness improves physical sensibility. Observing the sensations of different movements, noticing how the body responds to each articulation and how these responses affect the inner being, promotes an understanding of fundamental basic sensations used in acting. It also promotes a focus on the act of *doing*, a concentration on the exact task in hand, which is crucial for performance.

Lift the arm

Try lifting one arm from hanging by your side to shoulder height – without juddering. Notice what happens in order to enable you to do this. Return the arm. Now lift it again at a different speed. Try accelerating and decelerating at the start and finish of the movement. See if you can begin quickly and slow to a halt, and vice versa.

Notice all the time what your body has to do to achieve this. What happens when you fail? Now try the other arm. Is it easier or more difficult to achieve the same movement on this side? Let the arm rise as though pulled by a string. And fall as though the string has been cut. Imagine the arm is balancing a cushion as you lift it. As it returns it pushes something to the ground.

If you try the same exercise with your eyes closed you'll notice the way concentration turns inwards whilst your sensory awareness turns outwards. And how a kind of internal dialogue goes on where you pick up signals and interpret them. Our self-image consists of four components: movement, sensation, feeling and thought;[33] working continuously in a reciprocal manner these sustain the 'body-mind' link.

Exploring one simple movement with total concentration propels you into a new relationship with your body. You begin to acquire a dispassionate perspective on what you can and can't do. You can also explore how imaginary forces impact on movement. Now lift one arm palm upwards. What feeling does this provoke in you? How might an audience interpret this gesture? Lift the arm palm downwards and compare the result. Does this provoke a different feeling?

Monitoring physical sensations during training creates a current of exchange between the reflective inner and the observable outer, and back again. Doing an exercise, we can experience internal muscular activity whilst simultaneously cultivating an 'outside eye', i.e. working out how our body image appears to an observer.

Meyerhold used this concept of visualisation in Biomechanics to train his actors to sculpt their movement in three-dimensional space. Developing this 'outer eye' expands the concentration, counterpointing the focus on the inner self. Yoshi Oida suggests that 'imagining you are being watched by an audience produces a kind of split awareness, but in addition the body learns something when it thinks it is being observed'.[34] Practising like this prepares actors for working in front of an audience.

An added benefit gained by doing exercises with the sense that they are being done for an audience is a greater desire to avoid sloppiness, and so the quality of work improves. A simple way of establishing this initially is to set up training sessions so that the company stop occasionally to watch two or three participants. Observing others executing the same movement increases awareness of what we look like to an outside eye. This way we learn from others, and the idea of ensemble practice is reinforced since everyone realises that the whole troupe is in the same boat, that the work is a collective endeavour.

It is *never* a question of 'just doing the exercise'. The purely mechanical work-out will lead to mechanical articulation of the body. Doing something half-heartedly is inherently destructive. And all the training in the world is of no use if you can't engage in the imaginative world on stage.

The imaginative impulse which provokes movement in the actor is not the same as the physical impulse from which a dancer works, for example, so actors need more than a purely technical understanding of the body. Embracing the imaginative realm can be guided by a workshop leader through suggestion. However, encouraging participants to find their own imaginative connection with exercises is far more valuable, so that rather than everyone attempting to become a 'sinuous snake' when undulating the spine, each finds their own imaginative justification for the movement.

Involving the imagination also reduces exhaustion: 'If you do a simple exercise such as knee bends and think only about the muscles involved,' says Yoshi Oida, 'your legs will quickly become heavy and painful, and the movement becomes hard labour. But if you use the image of puppet strings holding you between sky and earth, the action becomes easier, and you have a focus for your inner concentration'.[35] Try it.

Awareness has to be a constant. It is through awareness that we learn essential things about the body, its resistances, points of balance, its potential plasticity. The aim is to learn organically not cerebrally. Eventually the kinaesthetic sense takes over and you 'know' when a movement 'feels right'.

To start with it's useful to have a set of questions that help you reflect on how your body organises itself to accomplish any exercise:

- *which* part of the body moves first?
- *where* is the movement projected?
- *what* speed does the movement utilise?
- *how* much muscular energy is expended?

It is clear that 'extra-daily' awareness is about the engagement of the whole person – body, mind and spirit. It is also a kind of 'invisible' dimension of actor training, and difficult to quantify. Yet it is crucial in leading to awareness in *action*.

ARTICULATION [36]

The body must be disciplined in the service of play, constrained in order to attain freedom. [37]

One of the most valuable routes to promoting awareness is articulation, breaking down movement into component parts. Frequently termed 'isolation exercises', these are fundamental to the physical performer because they encourage muscular awareness and control, and increase the range of expressive possibilities. Think of the body as an orchestra with individual parts that can act as 'soloist' as well as playing to accompany.

Most actors are familiar with the relaxation exercise where you lie on the floor and contract and release muscles in your body, isolating them from the feet to the face. This is a great exercise, not least because lying on the floor takes away the need to defy gravity, and the body instantly loses tensions. Closing your eyes makes you more aware as you turn your attention inwards. And the more you break down the sections into smaller units, the clearer your understanding of the geography of the body.

Differentiating the separate parts of the body and clarifying the relationship between those parts, develops economy of movement which frees the performer to control the space around them. Try doing a somersault in slow motion. It forces you to find connections between each part of the body and your centre of gravity. The Odin performers see slow motion as a 'principle of training' [38] because it focuses attention on the process of the movement rather than the result.

Analysis of the process of movement is a principle concern at Lecoq's school. For example, the simple actions of punting are broken down into component parts and then presented in a sequence of nine 'attitudes' which are neutral and non-psychological. Pupils do not present 'characters' pretending to punt or a situation built around punting. Rather they present, as transparently as possible, the action of punting.

Choose simple actions which, like punting, have a very clear movement cycle. Break the complete cycle of movement down into essentials, separating each unit of action so that you can 'perform' it on its own. Then put them back together in sequence.

The next stage is learning to 'punctuate' action by interrupting the sequence at any moment. Stopping at any moment, reversing the action, as though rewinding a video, then going forward again, not only makes you more aware and more controlled, but you find more detail in the movement.

Thomas Richards, who worked with Grotowski in the later stages of his painstaking analysis of the craft of acting, found that the more often an actor repeats a line of physical actions, the more likely the sequence will degenerate into mechanical rendering. As the actor divides them into ever smaller and smaller units, segmenting each individual unit, movement becomes more fluent and economic whilst actions become more complex. Ultimately, the more detailed the line of physical actions the more interesting it is to do – and to watch.

It's as though the casing of a clock is removed so that we see the springs and ratchets operating within. This does not mean robotic movements like those of the white-faced street performer. But rather it is as though a strobe light catches a living painting. A simple turn of the head, for example, if meticulously controlled and precise, can speak volumes.[39]

The following game puts the 'theory' of body-awareness, articulation and precision into practice.

Slow motion race[40]

Several actors line up as runners for a 100m sprint. Define the race-track and stadium areas. Spare actors become spectators at the race, reacting and responding to what occurs on the track. All this happens in 'real time' with vocalisation. As the referee calls the start of the race, everything goes into 'slow-motion' (like a TV action replay) and silence. The aim of each runner is to lose the race by being the slowest.

There are a few rules:
- *runners must keep in motion all the time*
- *they must lift their foot to knee height with each step*
- *they must take the longest step possible*
- *they must not fall over*

When the first runner reaches the 'tape', everything breaks into 'real time' and sound levels with the spectators applauding the result. At the end of the race, runners and spectators swap and play the game once more.

I have yet to find a better game for testing concentration, focus and body-awareness. The effort involved in balancing the body and moving forward incrementally is intense. And when actors remember to look at the 'tape' they discover the necessary focus. Converting a normally fast action into a slow one necessitates a different quality of energy.

ENERGY

One does not work on the body or the voice, one works on energy.[41]

Theatre deals not only in the compression of time but in the intensification of energy, and physical theatre exploits the intensified energy of action on stage to forge a strong link with the spectator. When a performer takes a physical risk on stage, tension increases in the spectator, as for example in the circus high-wire act. Not all physical theatre involves this degree of physical danger, but the principle is the same.

Actual physical risk is one sign of intensified energy and is apparent in the slick choreography of 'near misses' that companies such as Kaos and Frantic Assembly execute. But more crucially, in physical theatre the performer reinforces the visceral nature of the medium, showing the physiological impact of events. Empathy in physical theatre is more sensual than sentimental. Performance is body-conscious. The physical performer has an enhanced awareness of their own body as a conduit of meaning and expression. The high-level risk of catapulting bodies in DV8 or Volcano is one aspect of the intensified energy of physical theatre, but a certain quality of stillness is another. Both rely on a highly developed performance energy.

Physical exercise nourishes our internal energy; it is not just the idea of 'fitness' that drives people to exercise their bodies. Exercise promotes a sense of well-being, of being in tune with ourselves because it releases endorphines into the body which are necessary for a healthy, balanced life.

Different forms of exercise, however, generate different types of energy. Some can block energy, others can give energy back. Two hours of yoga will generate a different kind of energy to half an hour of aerobics, for example.

Yoga certainly promotes suppleness and flexibility, but if done exclusively can inhibit rather than release actors. When Grotowski's troupe began using yoga, they found it very fruitful in creating a supple spinal column, endowing confidence and enhancing spatial awareness. But eventually they found the kind of concentration produced was introverted and destroyed expression; Grotowski called it 'an internal sleep, an inexpressive equilibrium, a great rest which ends all actions'.[42]

They then tried using acrobatic and gymnastic exercises, working themselves to beyond the point of fatigue, and found they could break through the mind's resistance to physical exhaustion. As a result the actors made fresh discoveries and were able to explore previously unforeseen capabilities.

There is considerable mileage in the idea of energising the body through strenuous exercise on the principle that expenditure = investment, i.e. that energy begets energy. A valuable by-product of such work in the long term is physical stamina.

Playing 'Tag', or any other high-octane physical game, at the start of a workshop is a familiar strategy for generating energy. What concerns me is not the generalised energy we get from such activities, but the particular way in which energy informs presence and movement on stage. The few simple exercises suggested here focus on increasing awareness of how energy can be accessed, understood and exploited.

The striking presence of Oriental performers fascinated Barba. They exuded a 'kernel of radiating energy' not associated with any premeditated interpretation or expression of meaning. This was partly, he concluded, due to extra-daily body techniques, but also to the way in which they used energy in performance. Developing human energy was important, he realised, but the actor also needs to be aware of the origins of that energy, where and how the body generates it, so that rather than simply taking the energy, s/he starts to unify with it.

Energy is neuromuscular power, or force. Performers have to tap into the surplus or latent energy present in all of us but not utilised in everyday activities. Let loose it can be destructive. To give energy expression it has to be moulded. Energy, if you like, is available in a 'pre-expressive' realm and is channelled by technique.

In daily life we perform actions so as to conserve energy. Extra-daily techniques consume greater amounts of energy and are often characterised by strenuous effort in order to produce distortions. This allows the actor to 'discover a different quality of energy', which 'induces a dynamic state in the performer'.[43] When shifting the centre of gravity or creating oppositional tensions, for example, weight is transformed into energy. One can see this demonstrably in the stance adopted by the All Blacks when performing the *haka* before a rugby match, where lowering the centre of gravity creates a powerful dynamic stance.

Haka-walk

Imitate the stance used by the All Blacks, with your legs wide apart, your knees bent and the weight equally distributed over both feet. Keep your back long so that you could stretch forward or to either side whilst your feet remain firmly planted on the floor.

Now try shifting all your weight onto one side, and then from one side to the other. Use your arms outstretched to balance you. The more slowly you do this, the more you become aware of how your body shifts the weight, what muscles are involved and where tension is created.

As you get better at doing this, start to punctuate the action by stopping and reversing: you'll find you are withholding your energy and using it to hold the 'dead' weight back. You are establishing opposing tensions, mostly in your legs.

Really dynamic quality in movement on stage comes from establishing opposing tensions in different parts of body. From the Haka position, come to standing, but maintain the level of tension you have established in your legs. This means contracting the muscles in the outer thigh and calf, and pushing the weight towards the outsides of your feet. You will not look odd, but more powerful. You will certainly feel more energised and 'present'.

Keeping that opposing tension in the legs, shift your weight onto the left foot. Then lift your right foot and shift the weight back over to the right as you place this foot forward on the ground. Continue this walk for a few steps. You might feel you are walking like someone in Star Wars, but notice how shifting the weight prepares you for the next step. Play around with this walk and find out what happens when you speed up or slow down.

Dramatic tension at this physical level, changing between different qualities of energy in movement: fast/slow, holding/releasing, open/closed, keeps actions alive. Playing around with them is a fertile source of physical characterisation. Charlie Chaplin's 'Little Tramp' is an illustration of how opposing tensions between the upper and lower body create something distinctive. But the key point is that changing the direction and speed of the energy, especially just before it 'dies', keeps it alive. Actions which follow only one speed and direction are never as fascinating as actions which contain such in-built oppositions.[44]

The All Blacks stance is similar to that of many martial arts. Martial arts techniques place the source of energy low in the centre of gravity, nearer the earth. In Japan the centre of gravity in the solar-plexus is the source of the creative energy called *hara*. This is similar to *taksu*, the creative energy which 'sleeps' at the bottom of the spine according to Hindu philosophy,[45] and the *chi* of T'ai Chi.[46]

The pelvic area is in fact the engine room of human movement, our most powerful actions emanate from here. It also houses sexual energy. One sees how Eastern philosophies marry the physiological and the spiritual. Whether or not exercises that are focussed on this area generate creative energy, they undoubtedly tap a vigorous physical source. Whilst exercising the spine (see SECTION THREE) is excellent for sensitising the body, exercising the pelvis energises the body in a more concentrated and earthy manner.

Pelvic graffiti

Imagine a paint-brush attached to the base of your spine. On an imaginary wall behind you, paint your name in letters as large as possible. The more you involve the whole body, the larger the pelvic movement and the larger the letters will be. This necessitates placing the feet firm and wide and bending the knees so that your body is organised to swing the pelvis back and forth and from side to side.

Now imagine you are standing on an enormous stick of sea-side rock. Without moving your feet trace the letters of your name – or Blackpool, Margate etc., if you prefer. Again the bigger the letters the better.

This exercise loosens up the pelvic area and increases awareness of it because we have to think *inside* the movement. Apply the principle of articulation mentioned earlier to separate each letter. See how precise you can be with each one.

Throw the object

Stand with your legs about a metre apart and knees bent. Imagine a heavy object in one hand. Take this hand as far behind you as you can and, using your pelvis to swivel you round like a discus athlete, throw the object into the space. Try to sense the precise moment at which you let go of the imaginary object. In this action you are shifting the weight in the same manner as in the 'Haka' exercise. Then the energy was directed towards the floor to maintain a low centre of gravity. But now you feel a cumulative energy build from the pelvis which almost lifts you off the floor.

Next, try using both hands to throw the object. You will feel a continuous wave of energy flow through the body. You can increase and reduce the intensity of energy to create varying dynamics in the movement. 'Modelling' the energy, according to whether your object is a rock or a cotton sheet, gives you a sense of contrasting qualities of energy – strong and soft.

Energy is related to performance rhythm. Actors need to be sensitive to each other's energy and able to maintain the collective energy on stage. Whilst a game of 'Tag' will release energy it also dissipates it. Played so that the idea is to pass the tag through a soft tap, rather than a hit, aiming for only the slightest pause between its transference, sends a current of energy through the group and generates a much more focussed collective energy.

A collection of broom handles is invaluable in training workshops. As we shall see later they can be used for a variety of purposes. In the following exercise, they serve as a kind of metaphorical vessel for moving energy between players.

Pass the stick

Standing in a circle, everyone holds a stick in their right hand. On the signal they pass the sticks clockwise round the circle, so that each person takes a new stick in their right hand and passes it into their left before sending it on its way. The idea is to establish a seamless flow of sticks round the circle.

On a signal, change direction and send the sticks anti-clockwise.

This exercise creates a concentrated energy. It's quite difficult to sustain the same level of energy and focus. Inevitably sticks clatter to the floor. But it's a useful demonstration of how energy operates between partners in exercises – and ideally onstage. A less serious game which illustrates a similar principle is Lecoq's *Gamme de rire* exercises adapted below.

Pass the laugh

Four or five is an optimum number for this game. You can play it sitting or standing in a line.

Someone enters with the laugh merely a glint in their eye. As they make eye contact with the next person they 'pass the laugh' and it becomes a slight twitch of the mouth. As it is passed along the line of players, each raises the level of 'laugh-energy' so that they move from smile to giggle to belly-laugh – and to tears eventually.

Thinking of energy being infectious is really helpful. Any actor who has been involved in a production where they are on stage all the time, even when not 'performing', as in a chorus or narrative role, knows this demands a concentration which focuses energy towards what is happening on stage. The constant presence of actors recharges the energy onstage.

Being 'alive' on stage when not directly engaged in the action demands an energised stillness. An audience is often drawn to an actor who seems to be 'doing nothing'. For, as Brook says, 'The body doesn't have to be expressive all the time. But it has to be so alert in its stillness, that at any given moment it can become part of the total utterance.'[47] This is a sort of distilled energy, the energy of animals, whose bodies are devoid of tension yet ready to move in any direction at any moment – to defend themselves or attack. They appear quite still, yet their attention is focused and aware.

This brings us to the notion of neutrality.

NEUTRALITY

The empty space of theatre exists inside the actor.[48]

Neutrality is a crucial principle in actor training. It is a state of 'being' untrammelled by personal idiosyncrasies, a state where the actor attains an *energised stillness* . Copeau called it a 'state of readiness', with the idea that any movement or action could begin from this.

The neutral state is not a passive state but a potent one; it is para-doxically a place of calm and a place brimming with vitality, where the actor has a kind of 'presence in absence'. (There is a correlation between neutrality and presence, although the two should not be conflated.) This state is of paramount importance in preparing the actor for somatic improvisation in order to allow the free flow of creative impulses through the body: 'The result of understanding neutral is far-reaching; one learns to react to the thing itself, without past experience or future projection intruding upon it.'[49]

In terms of movement, neutrality is like a car with its engine running, but without being in gear.

In Meyerhold's Biomechanics, standing in neutral always prefaces the execution of a movement, even the preparatory *dactyl* performed before each of the études. In Biomechanics the neutral position is quite specific:

- feet are parallel
- hands are by the hips
- fingers point towards the floor
- eyes look towards a point in the distance
- the weight is slightly forward with the knees very slightly bent.

Try this and you will find that you are poised for action as opposed to standing in a pose. You might also find that the stance gives you a feeling of anticipation, similar to that of waiting to run a race, and your attention tends to turn outward. It also gives you the idea of your body in a state of alert stillness.

However, the neutral state is more than just this alert stillness. It embodies the notion of the empty actor, uncluttered by any attitude or personality trait, open (in the sense of being 'available') to creative stimuli. In improvisational terms the state of neutrality offers the actor a blank page on which to create; in text-based interpretative acting there is the necessity of dropping the personal body 'in order to incarnate the character's body [and] in order to make this process easier, it is helpful to start from a "neutral body".'[50]

The ideal of neutrality is fundamental to Peter Brook's thinking. He speaks of the need for actors to 'strip away their outward personalities, mannerisms, habits, vanities, neuroses, tricks . . . until a higher state of perception is found . . . [the actor] must shed useless skins . . . he must transform his own being'.[51]

The notion of neutrality is not new in theatre. For Copeau it was a state to which the actor should aspire, a silence of a body with a sense of preparedness and openness, in which the actor is alert but resting, poised to respond to the next stimulus. Having stripped the stage bare and created a stage with a 'neutral atmosphere', he became painfully aware that his actors were full of ingrained habits and mannerisms which detracted from the simplicity he sought. He realised that simplicity in the mise-en-scene required a similar simplicity in the actor, that 'the actor would have to be stripped as bare as the stage, only then could he express himself clearly and simply'.[52]

It was in mask-work that he found 'a certain physical and mental neutrality' which enabled his actors to 'exteriorise the interior conflicts inherent in drama'.[53] Now the term neutrality is most commonly associated with Lecoq's development of the *masque neutre*, an expressionless mask made of leather which he uses as a training tool in order to cultivate students' awareness of the neutral state.

Lecoq's neutral mask is extremely difficult to make because it is so precise. You are advised to buy one from a recognised mask-maker who has attained the necessary mastery of woodcarving and leather work. Interestingly, you will need to buy two: one for females and one for males as our skeletal and facial architecture is determined by our biological gender. Good quality leather neutral masks are expensive, but the impact of working with them is enormous, and as beneficial for the observer as the wearer in promoting understanding of how even the slightest nuance of physical movement affects the transmission of information.[54]

At the heart of Lecoq's philosophy lies the idea of recognising the world through the body. In order to achieve this, the student must first 'forget'. Forgetting, for Lecoq, is the prerequisite for learning. He wants actors to acquire a state of pre-expressivity, the equivalent of the precognitive state of being before language, to find a simply 'human' body, one which does not reflect the individual's personal or cultural history.

The neutral mask is the essential ingredient in Lecoq's process of 'forgetting', but 'neutral does not mean absent; it means without a past, open, ready'.[55] It is never used in performance, for it is not a way of performing but offers rather 'a way of understanding performing'.[56]

It is a tool for developing a physical language and approach to character as opposed to a psychological and intellectual one. Lecoq uses it to lead actors away from the familiar, and from habitual habits and intentions which colour gesture, towards a state of 'unknowing' or 'non knowing' where they are completely open to creative impulses or stimuli. It is, if you like, a way of paring away the actor from the acting, of finding the physical embodiment of the existential within us all. It is in this sense that the neutral mask is more of a 'collective' person representing the universal rather than an individual, a generic human being.

Jos Houben, himself a graduate of Lecoq's school, refers to the neutral mask as 'a human without an emotional past, without personality' who represents the universal in us, a kind of 'unnamed person' that everyone carries in them, someone 'with no history and no future . . . it is a kind of place where everybody is and nobody is'.[57]

Lecoq states that 'the neutral mask opens up the actor to the space around him. It puts him in a state of discovery, of openness, of freedom to receive'.[58] Once the actor has experienced the 'equilibrium' of the neutral mask, Lecoq finds that s/he is better able to express the imbalances and conflicts of characters. He also suggest that 'for those who, in life, are always in conflict with themselves, with their own bodies, the neutral mask helps them find a stable position where they can breathe freely'.[59]

Looking at an actor wearing the neutral mask, you look at the whole body. In effect the body becomes the face, and every movement is revealed as powerfully expressive. Once worn, the neutral mask becomes the 'reference point' for the actor because s/he has experienced, momentarily, being without artifice.

Suggestions for working the neutral mask are contained in the next section, which deals in more depth with masks. However, it is not the only route used by practitioners to train actors to achieve the neutral state. How else can we find the 'silence within' that Brook associates with powerful presence?

Working with objects is a strategy which takes attention away from the self. Sticks, boxes and bottles are suitably neutral themselves and are useful to have around. In addition to the broom handles mentioned earlier, I use a set of bamboo canes about 2 metres long. The following exercise is done with these canes.

Stick on the head

Each actor takes a cane and balances it on their head in line with their nose, one end pointing forwards and the other backwards. The cane will sit happily in the middle of the scalp, rocking slightly. Find a point where it rocks least, so that approximately half the cane points out in front, and the other half behind. Once you feel it is reasonably stable, advance up the room as slowly as possible, trying to keep the cane as still as possible. Keep your eyes focused on the cane end in front of you.

As individuals get the hang of balancing the cane as they walk, try a group walking across the space together. See if they can find a mean pace. Notice whether they are more interesting as a group if they maintain the same pace, or when individual variances occur.

Student actors report a heightened sense of awareness, especially of the process of walking, feeling every inch of the foot, transferring the weight as smoothly as possible. And breathing changes, becomes deep and steady.

A palpable calm descends on the group as they move. They talk afterwards of feeling 'hollow' inside yet with an enhanced perception of the space around them and their partners.

We used this exercise in rehearsal to try and achieve the slowness of famine victims for a production of *Pericles*. There was no sense in which the performers 'played' famine victims. They simply moved across the space as slowly as possible (stick-less of course in performance), and, within the context of the play, produced an extraordinarily powerful moment. The audience was visibly moved. Somehow the more unclut- tered and uncomplicated an action or gesture the more full of meaning it becomes for the spectator.

The concept of neutrality embraces both the idea of stripping away our habitual ways of moving and discovering an inner calm where we are relaxed and open to possibilities. The act of balancing the stick, like the neutral mask, offers a way of experiencing this. The Feldenkrais Method offers another: 'Both neutral mask and Feldenkrais work, by differing means, to enable a person to bring awareness to limiting habits and in so doing let go of them'.[60]

Feldenkrais is the most significant movement system to be recently adopted and adapted by physical theatre practitioners. Like the neutral mask, Feldenkrais enables you to feel more 'present': you become less attached to past habits and seem to fill the space around you. It promotes economy of movement, since it is based on discovering the least effort and maximum ease demanded by any action. The concept of moving in any direction is also embedded in the Feldenkrais Method.

It is largely through Monika Pagneux, a movement teacher at the Lecoq school in the 1970s, that the ideas of Moshe Feldenkrais have become known to theatre practitioners in Britain.[61] She introduced Moshe Felden- krais to Peter Brook in 1972, and together they taught his actors exercises which they practised daily on their trek through North Africa during the *Conference of Birds* project. The founder members of Theatre de Com- plicité, who met at Lecoq's school, worked with Pagneux and introduced her to many of their British colleagues. Since then, her workshops have drawn many key practitioners from the world of 'physical theatre' includ- ing John Wright.[62] Although she is not trained as a registered Feldenkrais practitioner, John Wright says of her: 'Feldenkrais runs through Monika like Blackpool through rock'.[63]

Unlike Alexander, Feldenkrais does not propose a 'correct' posture, although the work serves to correct flaws in posture. The only goal is improving the quality of movement. The Feldenkrais Method bears strong resemblances to Laban in terms of its philosophy, that movement is life and, like Laban, adopts a holistic approach which does not differentiate between body, mind and spirit.

After a Feldenkrais lesson you look at the world with different eyes. It has a similar effect to that described by Joan Littlewood after working through Laban: the world seems clearer and you notice how people's movement behaviour signals their inner state.[64] But whereas Laban's system was specifically aimed at dancers and actors, Feldenkrais developed his system to promote improvement in the quality of human movement *per se*. It is, however, increasingly being used by actors, dancers and musicians.

Some detail is necessary here on the Feldenkrais Method[65] to give some insight into why it is a valuable preparatory tool for actors and how it works in developing that seemingly elusive ideal of neutrality.

Moshe Feldenkrais (1904-1984) was a Russian Jew who emigrated to Israel and became a respected nuclear engineer as well as an accomplished Judo expert. He worked in France and Britain during the war and eventually ended up in America. It was a soccer injury which prompted him to apply his scientific and technical training to the study of neurophysiology, after he'd been informed by a surgeon that an operation on his knee would have only a fifty percent chance of success. He developed a series of hundreds of movement exercises which eventually evolved into the Feldenkrais Method.

The Method has two implementations: Functional Integration offers hands-on one-to-one manipulation and is used with people suffering motor disability or impairment, Awareness Through Movement offers group workshops where sequenced combinations of movements, called lessons, are communicated orally. The aim is to improve the range and quality of movement.

We normally distinguish two states of existence: waking and sleeping. Feldenkrais defines a third state: awareness. Activating this inner awareness enables the individual to unlearn bad or inefficient habits and re-learn more efficient and effective ways of moving. I say 're-learn' because Feldenkrais's system is founded on the fact that the most drastic test of movement is self-preservation, that human movement is fundamentally initiated by this principle which enables movement to be direct, efficient and harmonious. However, social and cultural pressures have intervened in the civilisation process, causing us to lose touch with our instinctual mobility.

Observation of the animal world tells us that all beasts conserve energy, moving in the most efficient way either to escape predators or attack their prey, known as the flight or fight reaction. As animals grow older they may get slower whilst remaining graceful, in other words they avoid the stiffness that we associate with old age. Feldenkrais maintains that the question of good movement is essentially whether it assures survival: 'Our nervous system is constructed to make self-preservation possible, and continuous movement easy, but if you don't have this fundamental thing right, then whatever you learn afterwards is just piling up mistake on mistake, until you . . . say my posture is bad'.[66]

Good posture for Feldenkrais is one which is dependent on being able to move in any direction. Feldenkrais does not teach a correct posture, nor does his method insist on a right way to accomplish movements. The emphasis is on the individual finding the most comfortable, least strenuous route for themselves. The fact that under the guidance of a trained practitioner this invariably turns out to be similar is because our heredity is common, we are constructed in the same way. The essential ingredient is the skeleton.

Feldenkrais particularly emphasises the role of the skeleton in human movement, and practitioners are trained in anatomy and physiology. Imagine a skeleton held from above by a string. The arms and legs will dance freely around a pivoting spine with a mobile head while the pelvis maintains a more solid and stable relationship with space. The pelvis is the powerful part, around which the strongest muscles are located. This is the power base, and 'hands and legs only transmit that power to the place where you need it'.[67] Although the head gives the direction of a movement, the pelvis initiates the movement.

One principle dominates Feldenkrais's teaching: every movement has to be reversible. In an interview with Richard Schechner, Feldenkrais states that awareness is implicit in reversibility, because 'when you are fully aware of a movement you can change its intensity, speed, rhythm and intonation'.[68] We can see how this is applicable to understanding and executing movement on stage.

Another crucial point in the application of Feldenkrais to actor training is that he draws no distinction between mind and body. He dismisses the received notion of a duality between mind and body as a relationship; rather he maintains there is a *functional unity* between the mental and the motor process so that feeling and thought are inseparable, changes in the nervous system and their concomitant muscular configuration are 'two aspects of the same state'.[69] Action cannot be divorced from feeling, sensing, thinking; they are, for Feldenkrais, one and the same thing.

The way his Method actually works is not dissimilar to the way a piano is tuned, gradually, note by note, distinguishing infinitesimal gradations and tightening or loosening the internal machinery of strings, until the harmonics are balanced. The pace is slow, the movements gradual, the emphasis on awareness through observation and experience of what is happening within your own body.

In Awareness Through Movement (ATM) lessons you become a spectator of your own body – from the inside – as the learning seems to happen almost inadvertently. Perhaps this is because the sensory stimuli activated lie closer to our unconscious or subconscious functioning than to our conscious understanding. The effect is palpable, however, and the body retains the lesson.

Because of its emphasis on gentle, non-strenuous activity, the Method contradicts received wisdom that exercise has to operate at high-energy levels in order to improve our motor efficiency and effectiveness. Feldenkrais distinguished between exercising, where we do the thing we already know which becomes familiar and better through repetition, and his method, which turns exercise into self-observation, enabling people to learn different ways of doing things. His Method works 'the way the mind actually functions and sees things in another light. By comparison exercising is an idiotic habit'.[70] It is designed to eliminate habits that impede efficiency of movement – to promote the minimum effort for the maximum result. New choices in movement are learned, and eventually made unconsciously, by the nervous system rather than by force of will.

In ATM lessons the teacher never demonstrates: pupils initiate movements in response to verbal instructions. You spend most of an ATM lesson lying on the floor, released from the muscular tensions of resisting gravity. Yet this is not a state of complete relaxation: 'What we want,' says Feldenkrais, 'is *eutony*, which doesn't mean lack of tension, but directed and controlled tension with excessive strain eliminated'.[71]

The instructions provoke sensory cues so that each movement, however small, generates sensation, i.e. a perception of physical change, which is then received and used by the nervous system as information. It is the *awareness* generated by this sensation which is used by the nervous system to reorganise itself.

One of the most extraordinary discoveries Feldenkrais made was that once the body has reaped the benefits of a lesson, the individual can undertake the sequence of movements *in their imagination* and the nervous system will respond and absorb the information as if the lesson had actually been conducted actively.

At the heart of the Feldenkrais Method is the notion of 'the learning that enables you to do the thing you *know* in another way, and one more way, and then three more ways' for 'learning means having at least another way of doing the same thing'.[72] His philosophy is rooted in the idea that human dignity is dependent on freedom of choice. We rarely think of choice in relation to movement, assuming that our movements are automatic. Most of us accept the habitual ways in which we move without a second thought, until they go wrong or start to malfunction. But even in a healthy well-balanced individual, it is likely that some parts respond more easily than others.

For the actor, increased awareness of each nuance of the body and discovering new potentialities opens up a realm of possibilities, the most obvious being increasing the ability to control movement, maximising the power of gesture, and even creating physical character.

There are hundreds of ATM lessons, focusing on different aspects of functioning but always based on the premise that improving one will promote improvement in the general dynamic. You might discover how to move from lying to sitting to standing in one complete fluent movement, or find yourself learning to crawl like a baby, or even how the repeated movements of the eyes in a certain sequence can enhance your spatial awareness. Every lesson will generate learning that is generalised to other activities, so that you may not only begin to eradicate specific harmful habits and find an improvement in the general dynamics, range and control of your physical movements but also be able to connect more reliably with the expressive realm.

Where Feldenkrais has been used in the performing arts there are reports of increased creative sensitivity in addition to physical and emotional well-being and healing of injuries. The San Francisco Ballet Orchestra have regular Feldenkrais lessons, for example. The British Association of Musicians and Performing Arts Medicine refer people to

practitioners because musicians and dancers find it can enhance performance and help recovery from injury.

When Monika Pagneux introduced Feldenkrais-based movement lessons to the Lecoq school and to Philippe Gaulier, she influenced a whole
generation of performers. Several contemporary practitioners in Britain
are now qualified Feldenkrais teachers, notably Andrew Dawson, Jos
Houben, Andy Paget, and Scott Clark.

The Feldenkrais Method promotes somatic awareness, which can be
harnessed in actors. This is related to clarity in articulation and the
development of economy of movement. And since the kind of awareness
provoked through Feldenkrais promotes choice, the Method can facilitate
an ability to experiment with different ways of moving. For John Wright,
working through Feldenkrais 'takes us right to the root of being creative,
which is why I use it, and why I think it's brilliant for actors'.[73]

Like the neutral mask, the Feldenkrais Method is a training tool which
doesn't have a direct application to stage work as Laban does, for example.
It can, however, have a direct influence on the actor's ability to understand
the concept of neutrality. In addition it promotes economy of movement,
choice in movement and, through the self-discovery inherent in the
Method, an increased sense of potential. Above all, it teaches how to be
truly aware.

SECTION 2

(Un)masking the Actor

(Un)masking the Actor

Give a hypocrite a mask to wear, and he will be rendered incapable of further lying.[74]

The study of past European mask-forms from Ancient Greece and *commedia dell'arte*, together with Eastern forms like Noh theatre, has fuelled the twentieth-century search for alternatives to naturalism. Edward Gordon Craig referred to masks as the paramount means of dramatic expression. Craig, who even called the influential journal he published *The Mask*, was convinced that masks would find their way back into theatre in the twentieth century. However, he warned against collecting masks from the past or from the East in order to copy them. That was playing with antiquity. What he envisaged was a rediscovery of the power of the mask which would enable theatre to reach beyond reality, to restore expression to the stage, what he called the 'visible expression of the mind'.

Craig's words were remarkably prophetic, for although there might be relatively few examples of contemporary masked theatre, masks are increasingly used in training actors, and there are several highly skilled mask makers in the UK who are developing new masks for theatrical and therapeutic use.

For Craig the mask presented a highly symbolic idealised human being which offered the actor control and clarity of statement: 'Craig recognised that the control offered by the mask could be deeply moving, certainly more so than the unplanned and fleeting expression of the actor's face'.[75] Similarly Etiennne Decroux, whose career as a mime artist developed out of his encounter with mask work through Copeau, believed the face to be the least essential source of physical expression because it represents 'the self the actor must leave behind'.[76]

It was Copeau who discovered the potency of the mask in actor training. After visiting Craig in Florence in 1915, he became inspired by the notion of commedia and the possibilities of mask work. Legend has it that Copeau became frustrated with an actress who was so obsessed by her appearance and fear of the audience that her movements became wooden, and in desperation he made her repeat the scene with a handkerchief over her face. Immediately she relaxed and her body became expressive. Somehow erasing her personality liberated her.

That might be how legend has it. Copeau himself writes more profoundly in his *Registres*, the unpublished documentation of his work, that 'even the most assiduous gymnastic training could not overcome the actors' "excessive awkwardness"'.[77] He recognised the reason for their 'corporeal impotence' was 'modesty', and in attempting to release them from this he looked back into theatre history and realised that from behind the mask, the Romans, Egyptians and Greeks had 'ventured gestures and postures they would never have dared with bare faces'.[78]

The face, wrote Copeau, is 'tormenting', the mask 'saves our dignity, our freedom' and the wearer 'acutely feels his possibilities of corporeal expression'.[79] Covering the face enables actors to hide their individual persona, and temporarily separated from their own identity they can access new realms of inspiration. Having something to hide behind means, paradoxically, that they no longer need to hide and can therefore take greater risks. Instead of imitating life in behavioural terms, they begin to find dramatic expression.

Together with Suzanne Bing, his teaching associate, Copeau developed a series of exercises using what he called the 'noble mask', a forerunner of Lecoq's *masque neutre*. They found the mask both simplifies and amplifies the action of the body, forcing the actor away from habits and clichés. Their actors worked virtually naked, thus emphasising the contours and expressiveness of the body, how the line of the body, the stance, and the way the body moved 'beneath' the mask contributed to expression.

Mask work took them towards an acting style where words become more emphatic and less naturalistic, the face more neutral and the body more versatile. Their actors mimed basic actions, a man being bothered by a fly for example, fear, anguish, or despair, in scenarios, and these were executed frame-by-frame rather like a slow-motion replay, except the masked actor produced not a slowing down of fragments of reality but the slow flowering of gesture.

Michel Saint-Denis, (Copeau's nephew who established the Old Vic School in London) refers to the way in which wearing a mask creates an awareness of 'inner feelings' which accumulate behind the mask and seek expression through the body: 'It enables the actor to experience, in its most virulent form, the chemistry of acting: at the very moment when the actor's feelings are at their height, beneath the mask, the urgent necessity of controlling his physical actions compels him to detachment and lucidity'.[80]

The discipline inherent in working a mask trains the actor in creating a calm and balanced body and executing simple yet powerful gestures, for masks can only be animated by controlled, strong, and utterly simple actions which depend upon the richness of the inner life.

The mechanics of mask work operate on unconscious auto-suggestion. This is what Brook calls the 'two-way traffic' of the mask, for even though the actor cannot tell what the mask looks like on, s/he can produce the most extraordinary impressions. It is as though the mask sends a message in and projects one out through the wearer. The identity of the mask and wearer are completely separate. Yet as the body discovers a stance and movement, a kind of feedback between the physical response and the creative impulse is established and 'character' emerges spontaneously. And whilst the mask gives the wearer freedom to play, to be open to intuition, it also imposes its own rigour.

In addition to training in control and precision, masks can give actors essential character types. Western actors cannot of course deploy the traditional techniques used with culturally specific masks. They approach a mask as they would a role – as an encounter between themselves and the character embodied in the mask. The mask therefore acts as a catalyst, releasing potentialities in the actor. This is why each actor will create something slightly different even when working with the same mask.

Getting involved with the design and construction of masks gives actors a tactile contact which begets familiarity with the evolving psyche of a mask character. Copeau insisted that his pupils learn to model their own mask, and their attempts served as research, sharpening their knowledge of facial expression, deepening their understanding of how the face works. Jean Dasté recalls: 'We had to find this instrument, the mask. In the beginning we fumbled about. We first covered our faces with a handkerchief. Then, from cloth, we moved on to cardboard, raffia, etc . . . Without Albert Marque [a sculptor] we should have continued to make masks 'small and pretty'. A good mask must always be neutral: its expression depends on your movements'.[81]

Masks create a degree of abstraction. Ko-omote, a young woman's mask of Noh theatre, is barely a personality, she is all grace, with a curious smile reminiscent of the Mona Lisa's, playing around her lips. Yet this

mask can release an enormous range of emotions depending on the angle
it is 'held' in relation to the stance of the body. What seems mono-
dimensional hanging on the wall becomes multi-dimensional when worn.

Decroux favoured a veiled face, pulling translucent fabric over his face
like a stocking, to retain the merest outline of his features. The expressionless qualities of his 'veil' allowed both the portrayal of the deepest feelings
without being ridiculous, as well as the potential to project contradiction.
Decroux's veil served to minimalise the impact of the face, focusing
attention on the sculptural properties of the body.

Some of Copeau's masks were made of cardboard and the inherent
rigidity of the material itself placed constraints on the flexibility of the
actor. Giorgio Strehler, too, found that home-made masks created problems for the actors when working on Piccolo's first production of Goldoni's
The Servant of Two Masters.[82] The original masks of commedia were made
of leather, a material more akin to the properties of human skin and
therefore more 'natural'.

The most significant training mask currently used in actor training is
Lecoq's *masque neutre*, the neutral mask. It was Copeau's son-in-law, Jean
Dasté, who introduced Jacques Lecoq to mask work and made him aware
that the simpler the design of a mask the more powerful its effect. Later,
working in Italy at the Piccolo Theatre, Lecoq pursued the idea of
developing a neutral leather mask with Amleto Sartori, who had begun
reconstructing the techniques of making the half-masks of commedia in
leather at Strehler's instigation.

Lecoq's idea was to develop a full leather mask that would have no
character, no sense of past or future, no ambition, no desire, above all no
inherent conflict, a mask close to the purity embodied in the Japanese Noh
mask of calm. This was to be a mask that would enable actors to find that
innocent 'human' body which does not 'reflect . . . individual history',[83] a
teaching mask which forces the wearer to act and think with the body. It
took Sartori ten years of experimentation to find it.

The mask is made by sculpting a wooden block and stretching the
leather over the shape. Unlike commedia masks, the neutral mask is full-
face and devoid of any hint of expression. The features are there – eyes,
nose, mouth – but there is no sense of a person, merely smoothly chiselled
serenity.

A good neutral mask is strangely beautiful. When worn, it highlights the
idiosyncrasies of the wearer's posture and accentuates any mannerisms,

until they discover a neutral way of standing that allows the mask just to 'be' and erases any evidence of their personality.

Neutral mask work occurs in the first year of Lecoq's two-year programme and lays a foundation for all that follows. Then students work with Expressive and Larval masks, where they discover how their bodies 'correspond with or complete the attitudes and behaviour of the masks they are wearing'[84] and go on to work on the concept of the 'counter-mask', portraying the opposite of what the mask displays.

Counter-mask work cultivates the actor's understanding of, and ability to project contradictions, how the proud woman may be sad, how the lonely man feels joy. A simple example of a general principle here is that lifting the mask from the chin lightens it, and lowering it from the forehead darkens it.

Lecoq's programme moves from full-face non-speaking masks through to the speaking half-masks of commedia. Whilst it retains the alienating properties of the full mask, a half-mask merges into your own face, freeing the mouth and voice. Pupils move on towards the end of their second year to what he calls 'the smallest mask in the world' – the clown's red nose, and the search for one's own clown. The neutral mask is fundamental to this search because it exposes the personal idiosyncrasies and faults (gestural and psychological) that each individual first learns to erase and eventually to capitalise on when they discover who they are as a clown.

Lecoq's neutral mask empties the actor: 'The minute you put on a mask that covers your whole head you are transformed. Your own person ceases in that instant and you are what happens'.[85] Like Shakespeare's Bottom, clad in an ass's head, the actor is then ready to enter into an imaginative world where anything can happen.

Steven Berkoff suggests that the dehumanisation, or *unmasking*, of the actor via the donning of a mask releases 'bundles of . . . animalistic energy that have no need to conform to civilising behaviour patterns'.[86] Putting on a mask paradoxically unmasks the actor. Maybe because it provides an anonymity by erasing the facial self. Masks bring a freedom from rational thought which enables the actor to rise above realistic illusion, to reach beyond reality. It is as though being alienated from one's own body frees the actor to become 'possessed'.

In cultures where masks are integral to ritual, they are regarded as mediators between the supernatural and the human. Masks give access to the spirit world, not as a means of escape but as a means of participating in the invisible forces of the universe. As such, the mask wearer is seen as the custodian of spiritual power. In some cultures only designated people are permitted to wear them.

Traditional masks in this context are assumed to have spiritual significance, sometimes potency, and can be described as 'soul portraits' which embody a complete and sensitive résumé of either an ancestor or a god. When they are regarded as the gateway to the spirit world, the wearer is someone singled out for the task rather like a shaman or priest. The principle is that masking is an act of transformation in which both concealment and revelation reside: the wearer is hidden, but, once worn, the mask takes life and reveals itself.

By their very metaphysical nature, masks can possess the wearer. Peter Hall found that although masks provoke honesty in expression they also unleash an 'alarming energy' which can be both nightmarish and hilarious. In comedy such anarchy is valuable. But two actors working on his *Oresteia* had to withdraw with nervous breakdowns.[87] Keith Johnstone points out the dangers of working with masks with inexperienced performers, who can lose control in the mask and may be at risk of harming themselves or others. And Dario Fo warns that the mask can fall over the face like an encumbrance and 'easily transform itself into a torture chamber'.[88]

It is worth noting these warnings. Respect for masks is a necessary adjunct to working with them. Brook found that when his actors fooled around with Balinese masks as though they were from a dressing-up box, the masks were no better than toys. Approached later with respect, they released their magical properties.

If neutral masks are about a state of being, character masks move towards the individual and idiosyncratic. Naive, or Larval, masks represent the first stage. These are larger-than-the-human full-face white masks with small pinhole eyes and simple features punctuated by well-defined noses. As a consequence they tend to look quite stupid. The restricted vision forces the wearer to move the whole head in order to see, and consequently exaggerates the movement of the rest of the body. The idea for them originated during the Fachnacht Carnival in Basel, Switzerland and they are sometimes called 'Basel Masks'. Michael Chase of the Mask Studio makes and works them in the UK. They are extremely effective in encouraging a hugely enjoyable child-like creative anarchy, and offer a highly inspirational route to play which escapes the strictures of realism.

Archetypes are the next stage. They can represent personality traits such as the 'bully' or the 'victim' as well as folklore types such as the 'ogre', the 'trickster', the 'wise woman'. Working on archetypes is an excellent way of extending the range of character acting: they generate the idea of character traits and personality types as physical and gestural. The distinction between archetypal and stereotypical behaviour also becomes apparent. And since archetypes so often project us into the world of myth, they are great catalysts for imaginative devised work. Again, the better quality the mask the better the work. Michael Chase and Ninian Kinier-Wilson currently make a large range of mythic archetypes, ancient and modern. (See Appendix.)

The idea of behavioural archetypes has been developed to a sophisticated level by Geese Theatre. The company has an international reputation for innovative work with offenders and has developed a wide range of masks which are used predominantly to mirror and reveal aberrant behaviour. In 1998 Sally Brookes, their resident mask maker, developed a set of 'fragment' masks which illustrate ways we 'blag' to avoid difficult emotional situations. Although designed for use with offenders and youths at risk, these have resonances beyond that world, as a few of the mask names demonstrate: 'Motor Mouth', 'Cool', 'Joker'.

A resurgence of interest in mask-work has been fed in Britain by the work of John Wright, as well as graduates of the Lecoq school. A new interest in making masks that reflect contemporary concerns is evident in the work of Trestle Theatre, who established themselves as a major presence through both their touring theatre productions and their education work. An early production *Ties That Bind* (1989), directed by John Wright, was one of the first pieces of theatre to address the subject of child abuse. The flesh-coloured fibre-glass masks exuded an emotional depth which defied the unmoving lines of their fixed expressions.

Trestle's highly legible, visual style forces the audience to 'read' the thoughts of the character in movement, as the masks do not speak. Their work has developed along more whimsical lines in the intervening years, until their most recent foray into scripted theatre, a production of Besier's *The Barretts of Wimpole Street* (2000). The father is the only masked, and therefore non-speaking, character, which serves to highlight the fearsome control this patriarchal figure exerts over his family.

Trestle's genius has been to see the connection between the emotional charge of mask work and naturalism. Many of their productions exploit the mask as a catalyst in revealing the subtext through the actor's body. Their educational packs of masks range from basic cartoon-style designs to more naturalistic replicas from their productions. With the highly accessible notes and exercises that accompany them, they provide a stimulating resource for developing performance skills in younger actors. In particular, they aid an experiential understanding of physicalising subtext.

Trading Faces also have series of masks drawn from their own productions. These are closer to caricatures and include a set of modern stereotypes, such as 'Dippy Typist', 'Mad Doctor', which are reminiscent of Copeau's notion of a new commedia. They provide a useful introduction to comic improvisation, although they do not have the inherent anarchy of true commedia half-masks.

Half-masks demand all the physical skills of full masks, but the actor also has to discover the voice of the mask. A half-mask fits with the upper lip of the wearer in such a way that the cut of the mask influences speech. Whereas full masks usually project a serious world, half-masks invariably operate in the comic realm. They seem to have a natural anarchy which is allied to a high level of energy, and provokes a crazy logic.

Several important pedagogical functions are served by mask work:

- it clarifies and refines the actor's movement
- it channels expression through the body
- it liberates the actor.

Through mask work actors experience transformation at a profoundly personal level. And it offers a kind of 'instant theatre' through non-verbal improvisation, accessible and vibrant.

The first logical step is to work with the neutral mask as a way of accessing a neutral state before moving on to work with masks inscribed with character.

WORKING WITH MASKS: NEUTRAL MASK

A neutral mask puts the actor in a state of perfect balance and economy of movement.[89]

Following on from the explanation of the concept of neutrality in the previous section, you can begin to explore accessing this state via neutral mask work. Neutral mask work enables actors to discover the power of economical movement and gesture; such experiential understanding promotes a more discriminating attitude to clarity on stage. It also usefully prefaces work with other types of mask.

Technically, work with the neutral mask offers opportunities for analysing the composition of movement, as well as providing each student with a chance to view themselves as a *tabula rasa* open to creative possibilities. The aim is to move with absolute economy, using the least amount of movement and energy, so it is essential to preface neutral mask exercises with work on the body.

If you watch video footage of Jos Houben taking a workshop on the neutral mask you will notice that he spends the majority of the time in preparing participants' awareness of the body before putting the mask on someone.[90] He is, in fact, using Feldenkrais Awareness Through Movement lessons to activate the actors' somatic awareness. Even if you have no access to Feldenkrais, attempting neutral mask work without some body preparation is counter-productive, because the mask itself depends on economical gesture to be effective. The exercises in SECTION THREE: BODY are a useful starting point.

The best method of learning about the neutral mask is to go and experience it by attending a workshop.[91] The video mentioned above was made primarily as an 'aide memoir' for the workshop participants rather than as a teaching aid; having said that it does offer an insight into how to approach the neutral mask, particularly how valuable the observer is to the wearer, and how much can be learned from watching. This is very important. Even if you could afford it, there would be no point in putting more than one person in the neutral mask at a time. It is a teaching tool. It is at its most effective when used by one person at a time in front of a group in a workshop context. And there is an enormous amount to be gained by watching others struggle with it, perhaps even more than wearing it.

If you or members of the group have never undertaken mask work before, or if you are unable to buy or borrow quality neutral masks, I suggest you start with the simple notion of covering the face. Seeing and experiencing how the absence of the face transfers attention to the rest of the body has a profound effect. We are used to focusing our attention on faces in communication – and in modern life television accentuates the face over the rest of the body. Theatre accentuates the body of the actor. This next exercise provides tangible evidence of the potential of the actor's body in communication.

Brown paper bag

Take a simple brown paper bag large enough to pull over a head without ripping. (These are quite difficult to come by nowadays – a traditional cobbler is a good starting place.)

Step 1

Ask a volunteer to sit in a chair facing the group.[92] They should sit with their back firmly against the back of the chair, their feet flat on the floor, their hands resting on their thighs and their head upright with the eyes looking ahead.

Once they are comfortable, place the bag over their head. Wait a moment or two, then ask them to raise one arm slowly and point in any direction and then return their hand to their knee. The power of this gesture will be observed by the group.

Ask the volunteer to raise their arm and point in the direction of the group and hold the gesture. When the finger ends up pointing at a person in the group, the gesture appears quite threatening. Remove the bag before attempting to discuss and analyse what has happened.

Step 2

Next cut two holes in the paper bag the size of a fifty-pence piece, and repeat the exercise with another volunteer. This time you will notice how we tend to focus on the eyes of the mask-wearer – and how they seem to look so much more directly at us. The paper bag can also be usefully employed to demonstrate the notion of the mask's 'gaze' by exploring the technique of moving the head slowly from left to right as though they eye of the 'mask' is located at the end of the nose. This also helps to keep the chin lifted.

Step 3

As individuals volunteer to try the paper bag you can move on to making simple suggestions of states that they present gesturally from the comfort of their chair, such as 'anger', 'hunger', 'despair', 'elation'. This forces the wearer to channel their response to each suggestion through the body, to think with the body. The idea is to project the idea of anger, hunger, despair, elation rather than to express it.

Observe the degree to which each gesture is successful and how, in many cases, clichéd gestures appear, for example 'despair' frequently produces the wringing of hands. The extraordinary thing is that a consensus emerges as to what 'works' and what doesn't in the majority of cases. And sometimes it is hard to put your finger on exactly what makes one gesture more effective than another; sometimes the cliché contains an essential grain of truth which resonates with the spectators. What is noticeable is the way precise, measured gestures are more effective than quick flourishes.

It is important not to stress the idea of being innovative. Rather, each volunteer should merely respond to a suggestion as honestly as they can in their own time.

Notice how if hands stray too close to the 'mask' the effect is diminished; similarly how sudden or florid movements detract from the power of a gesture. Simplicity begets clarity.

Often wearers will say that their face is working behind the bag; this is normal, for as our bodies move our faces work in tandem to express ourselves, but the danger is that the state or feeling is being channelled through the face rather than through the body. Try asking the mask-wearer to repeat and exaggerate the gesture; this usually makes them aware of where they are channelling the response.

Experimenting with this simple paper-bag mask demonstrates some basic rules of mask work:

- keep the mask facing the audience
- slow gestures/movements are more effective
- keep the hands away from the mask.

There are several 'do's and don'ts' to bear in mind before embarking on work with a leather neutral mask, not least that it is extremely challenging. The most difficult thing to do in front of an audience is nothing, because the pressure is felt to 'perform'. Yet the neutral mask requires that the wearer does nothing except 'be'.

The work is slow, so you need to allow plenty of time. The energy level needs to be concentrated rather than high. It is also essential that participants have undertaken preparation in body awareness, otherwise you are wasting everyone's time and will achieve very little.

The neutral mask, like all other masks, has a 'gaze' and it is the gaze which will 'do the work'. The wearer has to resist expressing anything in order to allow this to happen. The neutral mask differs from character masks in that the whole head becomes the eye, and the body becomes the head, resulting in a magnification of presence. The eye must stay in the middle, so that the wearer has to turn the whole head in order to show the mask looking in a new direction, with the rest of the body following in a sympathetic movement.

Slowness is crucial. Full masks rarely move as quickly as half-masks and their effect is seriously diminished by rushed movement. Measured, deliberate articulation of the body is far more effective.

The previous exercise, with the paper bag, uses the idea of expressing an internal state through the body. When working with Lecoq's neutral mask, attention shifts from the internal world of feeling to the external world of seeing. The goal is to transmit perception through action.

Neutral mask

Step 1

A volunteer takes the mask. S/he faces away from the group and shoes (i.e. puts on) the mask. When s/he feels comfortable she turns 180° and stands facing us. The spectators observe the stance of the body beneath the mask and how symmetrical it is. Adjustments may need to be made to bring the body into line, eg straightening the shoulders, or bringing the feet to parallel. When the body appears balanced beneath the mask, you will find that the wearer appears less themselves, but with a degree of presence that holds attention. Discuss the effect. The volunteer turns back 180° and removes the mask.

Step 2

The next volunteer repeats the exercise, but this time is asked to let the head lead the turn towards the group. And then to turn back leading from the knee, leaving the head till last. The effect is of the mask announcing itself and then saying 'goodbye'. We feel we have met someone about whom we know nothing.

Once all the participants have experienced presenting the mask to the group, you can move on to the following exercise in which the mask-wearer learns to project their imagination.

Step 3

The volunteer shoes the mask and turns exactly as before but now ask them to walk through a mist, and, coming out of the mist, to stand and see the sea.

You may find there is a tendency to want to 'show' the sea by painting imaginary waves in the air, or to present a reaction in terms of 'this is what the sea makes me feel'. Neither of these will be successful. 'If the Neutral mask looks at the sea, it becomes the sea,' says Lecoq.[93] The task is to present the content of the gaze, content which is imagined by the wearer at that moment, not as a recollection of a particular ocean view, but as an identification with the idea of 'sea'. (NB: This can be done by using a simple gesture involving both hands which stretch first towards the horizon and then move slowly outwards as if encompassing the volume of the sea and its nether distance, before almost halting and returning to the sides.)

Training in identification with the natural world is a major theme of Lecoq's training, and the neutral mask is fundamental to this because 'the natural world speaks directly to the neutral state. When I walk through the forest I *am* the forest'.[94] Corporeal impression is more important to Lecoq than corporeal expression.

The question in neutral mask work is not 'who am I?' or 'what do I feel?', but 'what do I see?', and the task is then to convey that to the spectator. Houben suggests that the student should breathe in the rhythm of the sea. The successful execution of the exercise results in the spectators being able to 'see' the sea, to be convinced by the actor that it is there. This is the essence of the actor's art – to present illusion: 'We make what is not there seem to be: that is our art'.[95]

Neutral offers up the delights of the absurd. Therefore if you attempt to 'play' in neutral you invariably end up in a Beckettian world! There's no psychology and no reason for things happening – a world simply exists. Clowns in this world exist in their relationship to each other and that world. There's no reason or psychology behind their behaviour – it rests purely on the interactive relationship. Improvising like this, of course, can be very valuable when tackling texts from the absurd such as Beckett. But don't try to use the neutral mask to do this. Use the mask to locate the state of neutrality. Neutral masks cannot interact face-to-face with another mask. For interactive mask work, you need to move on to expressive or character masks.

WORKING WITH MASKS: CHARACTER MASKS

The mask . . . forces you to go to the limit of a feeling being expressed.[96]

A character mask is like an incomplete sculpture which implies an entire physical entity. The shape, colour and dominant features will guide the actor's body. It is through physical skills and dexterity that the wearer imbues the mask, an inanimate object, with life and expression and so 'completes' the mask. Few teachers recommend using mirrors. I have found it far more productive to replicate the stage/spectator relationship by working masks in front of an audience. Their response guides the wearer towards what 'works'.

The instant you put a masked actor before an audience you realise there is no fourth wall. Masks 'speak' directly to the spectator, and an audience will 'hear' what the mask is thinking although there is no speech. This is what keeps them engaged with the action. Mask work is undoubtedly an effective way to generate understanding of how theatre works through the imaginative response of the audience.

The following exercises will work with any full character masks, from simple home-made ones to more sophisticated types such as the Trestle masks mentioned earlier. If you are mixing types of mask, be aware that masks made of different materials and design are sometimes unable to work effectively together because they seem to come from different worlds. In the absence of any professionally made masks, a simple white cardboard or plastic mask is an acceptable substitute. I get groups to design their own by outlining key features like eyebrows, eyes and mouth in black. The simpler the markings, the more effective they are to work with. Initially, it is better to work with a mask another person has made. You then keep a certain distance from your own creation, and are also able to watch yours working from a spectator perspective.

The following exercise replicates the actor/spectator relationship, but allows the spectator 'directorial' rights, so that s/he can provoke the mask to extremes.

More please!

Step 1

Working in pairs, X closes his/her eyes and Y chooses a mask. Y puts the mask on X.

X stands and opens his/her eyes. S/he 'performs' for Y – this can be literally anything, the only rule being to respond to Y's encouragement and enthusiasm. Y enthuses and encourages using phrases such as 'Yes!' and 'More please' in response to how the mask is 'working'. Swap roles and repeat. Feedback on the process.

Step 2

Try the same process again with a different mask, but this time actors may feel the contours of the mask before shoeing it – no peeking! Swap roles and repeat. Compare the results.

[NB: Leave this step out if using cardboard or unmoulded plastic masks. Cardboard is too angular, and cheap plastic masks are machine moulded, i.e. they are all the same.]

Step 3

Repeat the exercise but this time choose a mask with your eyes open. Swap roles and repeat. Discuss the process.

What you notice as the spectator/director in this exercise is as crucial as what you experience behind the mask. It is in observation that you see what makes a mask effective, and what detracts from its power. And you can then apply this to your own work as a mask-wearer.

Now move on to presenting a mask to a group. Most full masks do not work 'side-on'. So the wearer has to maintain the idea of always keeping three-quarters of the mask facing the audience. You need to use that 'outside eye' mentioned earlier in the section on awareness and cultivated in the previous exercise.

The nose is the key aspect of a mask as it tells you where the mask is looking – that's why mask noses tend to be so prominent. They are the 'eyes' of the mask. John Rudlin makes the point that facial expression is replaced by the gaze of the mask, and the wearer should imagine the single eye of the mask is located in the nose.[97] He is referring primarily to the

half masks of commedia which have very pronounced features; nevertheless the principle applies to all masks.

Presenting a mask

*Now explore what happens when an individual chooses a mask and
presents it to the group acting as audience.*

Step 1

*Use the same process as with the neutral mask, so that one volunteer shoes
the mask before turning and presenting it to the audience. Audience reaction
will encourage the actor to find a stance that 'fits' the mask.*

*As the actor moves you will be able to detect when the impulse is working in
tandem with the mask, and when the actor tries to impose something. Mask
work becomes an exercise in honesty. It is always apparent when movement
is false – you 'see' the actor beneath the mask. When it is honest, mask and
actor seem fused into utterly convincing character.*

Step 2

*Characters do not exist in a vacuum and we find out about them through
reaction and interaction. So the next stage is to put two masks together.
Allow one to enter first and establish a rapport with the audience before a
second one arrives. Again it's an exercise in honesty. What happens between
two masks cannot be imposed by the actors. Allowing the masks to 'lead'
provokes wonderfully spontaneous and inventive improvisations.*

*If you put three masks together like this, triangular relationships evolve which
mimic life, with alliances between two against one and changes in allegiance
occurring.*

Step 3

*Masks love to play. Set out a table with a motley assortment of objects and
clothes. (Avoid things with sharp points. The point made earlier about
anarchy is relevant here: masks are often like disobedient children and an
umbrella can unwittingly become a lethal weapon.) Encourage the actors to
avoid squabbling over items. Following another mask's 'lead' with an object
generates more subtle improvisations where conflict is less overt.*

From free improvisations like these, narratives begin to emerge. Watching, you see possibilities for scenarios and stories. This is where you become aware of how critical the director is as an outside eye, someone who can see the whole and take the audience's position.

Masks can generate intense emotional heat, so it is likely that you will find passions running high in these improvisations. Interestingly, the simpler the mask, the more ambiguous and contradictory the 'character'. Masks allow you to explore a range of feelings and extremes of passion that are far less accessible with the naked face. Full masks do not speak, so you are, in effect, delegating expression to the body. Masks demand the involvement of the whole body in order to work effectively, so the emotional and expressive intensity you experience in mask work will become a reference point when acting without masks.

Although the benefits of the mask work suggested here are related more to training performers than devising theatre, such improvisations can be used as a basis for developing short pieces of masked theatre. Alternatively you can use them as a foundation for devising character-based pieces by removing the masks once the actors have a strong understanding of who they are and what is happening. You may find that once you take the masks away actors revert to channelling thought and feeling through the face, and when allowed to use their voice they begin to concentrate on what they are saying and forget what they are doing. The characters seem less bold. Playing MORE PLEASE! with the characters you have created, but without their masks, may help actors rediscover their original creations.

Silent mask work often fails to transpose successfully into unmasked speaking theatre. It is therefore advisable to gain experience with the speaking half-masks of commedia first.

COMMEDIA DELL'ARTE

I would prefer to tag this kind of theatre not commedia dell'arte but 'actor's theatre'.[98]

The leather half-masks of commedia dell'arte represent a raft of fixed character types which were instantly recognisable to sixteenth-century audiences. The Italian commedia players were masters of improvisation rooted in physical training, highly regarded for their skills and profes-sionalism. Actors specialised in one stock character and improvised around scenarios, embellishing the basic plot outline with polished physical routines known as *lazzi*, (similar to circus or Music Hall routines), and virtuoso linguistic digressions (equivalent to the verbal riffs of modern stand-up comedians).

The study of commedia as an exercise in recreating the original characters and scenarios lies outside the confines of this book and is dealt with extremely well elsewhere [see John Rudlin, 1994 and Barry Grantham, 2000]. What is interesting is how practical exploration of commedia has re-invigorated modern theatre, and what it can offer modern actors.

Within commedia lies more than the essence of comic acting. Commedia was seen 'as a model for improvisatory and movement-orientated performance' at the beginning of the twentieth century,[99] and its energetic spontaneity revealed the centrality of the actor. Craig, Copeau and Meyerhold recognised the richness commedia offered: acrobatics and bodily training, improvisation and ensemble practice, clarity in staging techniques. All three recognised that the revolt against the psycho-realism of the naturalistic stage necessitated a shift in emphasis from text-centred to actor-centred theatre. And in commedia they found the perfect antidote.

Craig saw in commedia 'a timeless universality which offered a model for the theatre of today'.[100] Copeau was influenced by the simple trestle platforms on which the action was played when he reconfigured the stage at the Vieux Columbier in 1913. He later removed his Paris troupe to rural Burgundy to explore masked improvisation as a preface to developing a 'new commedia' with characters more relevant to modern society than their original counterparts. For Meyerhold commedia was a passion. He saw it as an essential foundation for his experiments with the 'grotesque' and the study of commedia was a key element in his training programme.

A kind of 'street psychology' can be seen in the commedia characters and in this respect they are fertile sources of inspiration for improvisers. Fisher suggests that 'in the character of Arlecchino, the leading *zanni* of commedia, modern theatre found a model in which to embody an absurdly lyrical vision of contemporary humanity, leading to such creations as Chaplin's 'Little Tramp' and Beckett's and Ionesco's existential clowns'.[101]

Charlie Chaplin exemplifies the discipline inherent in the word *dell' arte*: a mastery of the body and precision in execution which is the basis of comic improvisation. His mask-like make-up and characteristic walk are as fixed as those of a stock commedia character, although the tricks and situations change. Chaplin started out as a professional in Fred Karno's troupe, which, like the original commedia troupes, 'trained as an ensemble and developed a repertoire of pantomime bits and – as it were – *lazzi*, all serving as the basic grid upon which improvisation was built'.[102] Through improvisation, Chaplin created the quintessential clown of the twentieth century, who has the power to intensify and distil the essence of individual existence. Similar clowns surface in the work of Beckett and Fellini, clowns who stress the monstrous cruelty of the world they unmask. Through comedy they enable us to glimpse tragedy.

Silent movies are an excellent resource for physical acting. And you can fish them for visual gags. Many contemporary practitioners are keen collectors of Chaplin, Keaton, Laurel and Hardy, and the Marx Brothers. The familiar characters of Groucho, Harpo and Chico bear more than a passing resemblance to commedia's *Il Dottore*, the old pedantic peda-gogue, and *zanni* such as *Arlecchino*.

Current revival of interest in commedia has been stimulated by speci-alist courses which have flourished over the last thirty years. Commedia is a particular concern at the schools of Jacques Lecoq and his one-time associate Philippe Gaulier. When Lecoq first witnessed commedia on the streets of Italy in the fifties, he recognised it as a form close to the people that had a warmth and humanity he could relate to. This inspired his concept of *le jeu,* or 'play', which underpins his philosophy of actor-training.

One could argue that Lecoq took on Copeau's project of a new commedia, especially given the dominance of mask work and play in his pedagogy. Like Copeau, he was not interested in the stylisation of old forms but the creation of new ones. In his book, *The Moving Body*, Lecoq complains that the 'so-called 'Italian' style of performance', i.e. replication of the old style, 'is nothing but clichés. Young actors have done short courses in commedia and the playing has becomes lifeless'.[103] This led him to examine the principles underpinning commedia dell'arte in terms of what he calls *la comédie humaine,* i.e.'the human comedy'. He found a characteristic pattern emerged: '*How to lay a trap* for whatever reason: to get the girl, the money, food and drink. The characters are rapidly betrayed by their own stupidity and find themselves ensnared in their own plots'.[104] Moreover, characters and situations operate at an intense level, and 'the driving force is not *what* to play, but *how* it should be played'.[105]

The latent cruelty of commedia is what fascinates Lecoq. It has the power to reveal the basest of human motivations, but it also shifts quickly from one state to the next, making it a fertile source for learning the art of transitional acting: 'Harlequin is capable of passing in an instant from tears at the death of Pantalone to delight that his soup is ready'.[106] In studying commedia, Lecoq realised that in addition to physical agility, it requires a basic quality of naiveté in the actor, a quality which he believes essential for the modern clown in particular. He sees it as a key foundation for the creative actor.

WORKING WITH MASKS: COMMEDIA

The character is a collaboration between the actor and the mask.[107]

To really get a sense of how commedia masks operate, nothing beats attending a workshop run by an experienced teacher. The suggested format for exploring commedia here is intended as a basic introduction. For more detailed instructions see Grantham's excellent training guide, *Playing Commedia, A Training Guide to Commedia Techniques* (2000). This and John Rudlin's *Commedia dell'Arte, A Handbook for Actors* (1994), offer ways of working with commedia masks and characters, as well as giving information on the background and history of the form.

As with the neutral mask, there is no real substitute for the professionally-made leather mask, if you are exploring commedia in any depth. In Britain, Michael Chase and Ninian Kinier-Wilson are mask-makers who have also trained in commedia, with Carlo Mezzoni-Clementi and Carlo Boso respectively, and their masks are imbued with their practical understanding of the style. For those of you with craft skills, John Rudlin offers an excellent introduction to making leather masks in his handbook, and Barry Grantham gives patterns and instructions for a highly effective cardboard practice mask, and for making papier-maché masks. It is worthwhile beginning by constructing your own half-masks, without reference to commedia characters, before working with the traditional masks, as it encourages you to think about how essential characteristics are embodied in the moulding of a mask.

The style of commedia is extreme. Because commedia demands high levels of energy, warm-up preparation should take account of this. On a scale of 1 to 10, commedia operates at ten and beyond. Simple acrobatics and gymnastics are great energisers. With a somersault or cartwheel you can feel and see the energy travelling across the space. Commedia masks travel across the stage with similar focus.

Almost all commedia masks refer to animals: 'They are taken from courtyard, domestic and tamed animals; Harlequin is a mixture of cat and monkey, the Captain is a cross between bloodhound and mastiff, while Pantalone is born from the turkey and the cockerel . . . Brighella is half-dog and half-cat and the Doctor is pure pig'.[108] Prefacing mask work with animal improvisations is therefore useful. Putting a mask on an actor during such an improvisation suddenly reveals the relationship between beast and mask.

Animal pairs

Step 1

Prepare a selection of animal names on pieces of paper, ensuring that there are two of each. Animals with contrasting movements work best for this, for example dogs, snakes, monkeys, hens, lizards. Distribute the names, which the players keep secret.

Everyone now moves round the room according to their animal name. Exaggerate the movement features of the animal as much as you can – and more. Try to let the movement generate any sound, rather than simply imitating the noise you know your animal makes. You are aiming for a stylised imitation, not an exact replica!

Step 2

Now invite the animals to interact and see what happens. More often than not simulated fights and copulation occur at this stage.

Step 3

When the room appears like a cross between a zoo and an asylum, invite everyone to pair up with their partner, i.e. the other actor playing the same animal. Now each takes it in turn to tell his/her partner about the 'adventure' they have just had with another animal in Step 2. Keep the action and verbalisation (which should be animalesque gibberish, rather than language) high in the exaggeration stakes. The more ridiculous you look and sound the better.

Lecoq points out that in commedia 'you die of everything: of desire, of hunger, of love, of jealousy'.[109] Working on animals, as above, encourages actors to work at the outer limits of expression, finding extremes which they tend to contain when working from a behavioural perspective.

Commedia, like other mask work, demands discipline. Grantham articulates four principles which actors working commedia masks should cultivate: stillness (including the ability to maintain an emotion or intention in a pose), awareness of your partners on stage (including listening), communication with the audience as individuals, the ability to express feelings and thoughts through the body.[110] You may find it useful to raid SECTIONS THREE and FOUR for games and exercises which nurture these before returning to commedia work.

The following is a basic outline structure for exploring commedia masks (whether your own practice masks or professional leather ones). Feel free to reinvent it. But note that the rules governing space and direction are important and give a spatial organisation which enhances the movement of the masks. They also usefully establish the principle that comedy works best on horizontals (ie: stage right to left); the vertical (ie: downstage to upstage) being reserved for tragedy. The assumption is that actors have undertaken the previous work on neutral and character masks before embarking on this work.

Commedia play [111]

Step 1

The best way to use commedia masks is to replicate the original trestle stage arrangement by setting a screen or flat upstage to use like a back-curtain for entrances and exits. Define an oblong, preferably wider than it is long in front of the screen which is to be the stage or playing area. Spectators sit in the traditional end-on position. (In the sixteenth century, of course, the platform would have been raised, so the audience would have been looking up at the performers.)

Lay out a range of masks on a table behind the screen.

Step 2

Commedia characters are motivated by basic human instincts. These masks do not suppress their desires. They are driven by them. More often than not they revolve around greed, and three common examples are sex, money and food. Most masks will respond well to these, and they give actors something straightforward to deal with.

A volunteer waits behind the screen. They choose a mask and shoe it. The only choice they make about the mask is what it wants: sex, money, or food. As they enter they cross diagonally downstage and 'talk' to the audience about what they want. Improvising in 'made-up' language takes away the need to worry about what you are saying initially. This also allows the actor to discover the voice of the mask in tone and range. As with the previous exercises, spectator response is the best guide to what works.

Meanwhile a second volunteer waiting behind the screen, chooses a mask, decides what it wants, waits and listens.

Step 3

When the first mask begins to 'flag', the second one appears from behind the screen from the same side as the first mask, and shouts 'Aha'. The two masks make eye contact. As the second mask crosses diagonally downstage, the first one moves across the front of the stage horizontally.

Spontaneous interaction governs what happens next in the improvisation, though dependent to a large extent on what the masks want. It is not necessary for them to be in conflict. A mask that wants food may use sex as a bargaining counter, for instance. Or both may end up with their desires gratified.

The masks work most effectively in the space when the actors circle each other and use diagonal and horizontal trajectories for movement.

Step 4

As the improvisation draws to a close (actors will sense when it begins to flag), the first mask finds a reason to leave. As they exit they shout 'Farewell!' leaving the energy on stage for the remaining actor. S/he then 'talks' to the audience about what's happened, or the weather, until another mask enters. And so on.

NB: Make sure the energy level remains high. When it drops comic moments get lost. You may need to 're-charge' the actors by playing a high-energy game if this happens. Alternatively, take time out to play the exercise 'Changing Gears' in section four: play, and the games suggested there.

This exercise is such fun to watch that sometimes actors are reluctant to leave the audience and become the next volunteer. Played many times over, as actors gradually develop their skills in working the masks, the improvisations advance in depth and complexity. Eventually, introduce ordinary language. Once actors have got the hang of the characters, they can construct scenarios to be played out through improvisation, and rehearse gags and routines to insert into storylines. This replicates the method of original commedia actors, and develops ensemble skills.

The important thing to remember is that although commedia dell'arte is associated with improvisation, it was, in fact, a highly disciplined form into which rehearsed variations and prepared visual gags were slotted. The improvisatory aspect of the performances arose from the provisional nature of the scenarios. Actors specialised in one mask, or role, and worked out speeches and acrobatic routines as individuals, and in pairs/ trios, which were used on a given signal. For example, Arlecchino rubs his nose and the next minute dives through the legs of Brighella, who has parted his legs on seeing the nose business, to make a comic exit.[112]

Lecoq also suggests that commedia is difficult for young actors who have not enough life experience to tackle what he sees as its tragic underbelly. However, he incorporates commedia work because he believes students will 'retain a memory, both physical and mental, of this level of acting' which they can use later.[113] And Grantham identifies 'three essential qualities' necessary to working commedia: 'The willingness to work as a team, the gift of being able to seize the 'moment of opportunity in improvisation', and the ability to act with truth and sincerity'.[114] These are generic qualities which every actor should cultivate. The following sections are devoted to developing them.

The Playful Body

The Playful Body

Strive to get pleasure from carrying out acting instructions. That's axiom number one![115]

From the foundations of the previous two sections we move on to developing somatic responses, related to key concepts, through games and exercises for the physical actor. Although not fiercely prescriptive, the order in which this material is presented has a progressional logic. The obvious place to start is with attaining flexibility in the body. And you cannot have true play without a shared belief between performers (termed complicité), for example. The work culminates in an exploration of what is probably the most important dimension of all: the audience.

It is essential to respect the need for a conducive working atmosphere. You cannot achieve good work in the midst of mess or piles of chairs. Always clear the space before working. And, if high-energy work is going on, ensure the environment is safe. It is important that players take responsibility for their own actions and be aware of when they might endanger others. This is often why workshop leaders use 'trust' exercises. The games and exercises in this section will build trust as a by-product.

'An actor can improvise only when he feels internal joy. Without an atmosphere of creative joy, of artistic *élan*, an actor never completely opens up,' wrote Meyerhold.[116] Grotowski used the same word, 'élan', to describe the kind of upsurge of energy and spiritual drive with which actors should enter their 'line of physical actions'.[117] Lecoq and Gaulier use it too, again with the idea of entering into the spirit of any game or exercise, but also to describe the thing which keeps it alive.

To some extent this relates to energy and concentration, keeping absolute focus on the task in hand. It is also about the joy or pleasure of doing whatever you're doing. Enjoyment does not merely come from playing, however, it is reaped in relation to the attitude with which you approach the work. An actor without élan in performance is as unwatchable as one who can't act. And an actor without élan in workshop or rehearsal is hard work for everyone else.

This applies to individual work as well as group exercises. Meyerhold believed that actors should have a 'symphony' playing inside them during training. In a workshop on Biomechanics, Gennadi Bogdanov invited actors to 'hear' their favourite tune playing in their heads as they stretched and somersaulted, balanced sticks or constructed movement phrases. This really helped concentration as well as making the more difficult or strenuous tasks more pleasurable.

Meyerhold had another strategy for cultivating joy in the work, which was to shout 'good!' to the actors even when they were playing badly because he noticed that 'when an actor hears your 'Good!' . . . lo, he will in fact play well. One must work happily and joyfully'.[118]

THE BODY

A good actor is comfortably stable; not rigid like a tree, but soft like water.[119]

As we discovered in SECTION ONE, raising awareness of the basic organic principles on which the body operates enables actors to discover fundamental rules. To go from one characteristic walk to another, for example, requires a general grammar of movement. When actors are aware of their own habitual ways of moving, and have a grasp of general phenomena, such as the image created by transferring weight, or pushing the pelvis forward or backwards, they can depart from their own characteristic movement and embody others.

Flexibility is the key. Actors' bodies, said Meyerhold, should be malleable as wax. Whatever body preparation methods you employ, the further suggestions here are directed at becoming even more flexible.

Most body-work systems begin with stretching the spine. The old adage of 'standing tall' contains more than a grain of truth. The spine is designed to be flexible and stable, enabling free movement of the torso and limbs. Correct alignment is fundamental. Muscular activity on top of poor alignment will only compound problems.[120]

The spine is a conduit for internal energy as well as being the main support of the upright human form. It is the route through which the nervous system passes information into the musculature. So exercising the spine is a key to stimulating nervous reactions: 'If the spine is active, and each vertebra can move freely, then the nerves can function better. And so you become more sensitive and aware. In a way, spinal movements act as a kind of massage for the entire nervous system'.[121]

The following exercises offer different ways of flexing this central coordinating mechanism.

Spine roll

Most actors are familiar with the exercise of rolling the body down to the floor and up again to flex the spine. Execute this slowly, making sure the top of the head leads on the way down, and comes up last on the return. If you allow your head to fall gently backwards before rolling down you give the neck an extra stretch on the front. Rocking your head back and forth before rolling down also reminds you how the head sits on top of the spine almost precariously.

Most importantly, don't forget to breathe! Holding the breath is a physical expression of effort (and defensiveness). Breathing has to accompany every action/movement. Play around with exhaling as you go down and inhaling on the way up, and vice versa. Explore which makes the movement easier.

Exercises in which you lie on your back on the floor for a period will help elongate the spine. Here is a simple massage with the floor as masseur.

Back massage

Lie on the floor. Notice how your back engages with the surface. There is a gap in the lumbar region where the lower back arches away from the floor. And the top of your spine at the neck will make another arch. Put your feet to standing, so that your knees point towards the ceiling. The lower arch of your back will flatten towards the floor.

Place your hands behind your head and link your fingers. Try and keep your elbows as near to the floor as possible, but don't strain. Feel the weight of your head in your hands.

Now lift your head very gently with your hands so that your forehead travels closer to your raised knees. Let your eyes look at your chest.

As you roll your head back and replace it, let your eyes linger on your body, so that they arrive back last. When you repeat the movement let your eyes come last until your neck is fully curled, and then look at your chest again before rolling your head back to lie on the floor. Repeat this several times.

Now replace your arms and legs so you are lying straight. Notice any difference in the way your back engages with the floor.

Slowly lift your legs up and, as you bend your knees, wrap your arms around them so that you are curled loosely. Now let the floor surface massage your back as you rock from side to side and backwards and forwards – a comforting way of loosening the back muscles around the spine.

Lie down straight again and close your eyes. Mentally travel up and down your spine, noticing where it contacts the floor after the massage in relation to where contact was before.

To get up, roll over on your side first, and find a way of getting up as smoothly as possible, leaving your head until last.

The next exercise provides each actor with an excellent spine-stretch. It comes from Clive Barker's book *Theatre Games.*[122]

The raft

Two actors stand back to back. X links their arms through Y's at the elbows. X places their feet very firmly about a metre apart. They need to be able to bend their knees so as to distribute the weight evenly on both feet (rather like the All Blacks haka stance referred to in section one) as they lift their partner onto their back. X positions themselves against Y so that Y's buttocks fit snugly into the hollow of X's back.

When you are sure that this is happening, X bends forward and, gradually straightening the knees, lifts Y into a prone position on their back so that their legs dangle loosely. Only when both parties feel stable do they unlink arms. Y drops their arms to the sides, closes their eyes and lets their head fall backwards to rest on the top of X's spine. If X sways slightly from side to side, this gives Y a delicious feeling of floating.

Make sure you reverse the process carefully as you replace your partner to standing. And of course swap roles.

The spine is the centre of the nervous system, and the following exercise serves to wake it up.

Spine-tapping [123]

Tap two middle fingers gently down the spine of your partner who stands with their back to you and their eyes closed. When you get to the coccyx start again from the top. You may sense places where your partner's spine seems to need more tapping; linger at points if you do. As you continue tapping, your partner will respond as follows.

As the person being tapped begins to gain a clearer sense of all the vertebrae, they gradually allow their spine to move in response to the tapping. Let yourself sway and undulate. And let your breathing accompany the movement to maximise the ease and enjoyment. As breath passes through the larynx, allow a sound to come with it. It is easy to become inhibited at this point, as the sounds that emerge can be quite strange. However, the more you let the voice through the more liberating the sensation both bodily and vocally. This is an excellent preparatory exercise for voice work.

After a few minutes, swap over and repeat the exercise, so that both of you have experiences being tapped.

Whilst lengthening the spine is important, because the vertebral column is central to expression, the 'driving impulse' for movement 'stems from the loins . . . even if it is invisible from the outside'.[124] Whilst the pelvic region generates powerful movement, it is necessary for the legs to remain soft and fluent, for, as the Noh master Zeami points out: 'If every part of the body is working equally strongly the acting can appear rough and crude . . . an element of control and contrast . . . creates a far more intriguing and polished performance.'[125]

The next sequence of exercises frees up bodily movement from the pelvis whilst developing 'soft knees'.

Ball on the wind

Use a large beach ball for this exercise. Players stand in a circle with about a metre or so between them. As they pass the ball from one person to the next, they must involve the whole body, in other words bend the knees and let the impulse from the pelvis direct throwing the ball to their neighbour. The aim is to create a sense of the ball bouncing softly around the circle as though wafted along by the wind.

This is more difficult than it sounds. What is required here is a delicate touch with the ball, with strong and controlled movement in the legs and torso. It won't work with a small or hard ball. Notice your breathing. It should work with the movement, not impede it.

Once everyone is working through the body to pass the ball, invite them to emit a sound as they exhale when throwing the ball as in the spine-tapping exercise. Players may laugh as the sounds can be amusing (and actors have to be able to laugh at themselves). When less inhibited, they may be able to invoke the sound of the wind blowing the ball along the beach as in the further development of this game in section four: rhythm.

Stick balancing will help you develop flexibility, and has the virtue of being something you can practise on your own. Broom handles, approximately one metre long, are required for this.

Stick balances [126]

Step 1

Place the round end of a broom handle on the palm of your hand. Keep your hand flat and the arm slightly bent at the elbow. It may take a while, but you should be able to balance the stick on your hand whilst walking. The trick is to keep your eyes on the top of the stick and move underneath it. Keep your legs soft and malleable. You'll find you can feel the movement emanating from your pelvic region.

Transfer the stick to your other palm by letting it 'hop' over. Repeat the balance on this hand. You may discover that you find it easier with one hand than the other. Be careful not to curl your palm around the stick – that's cheating!

Some people find this exercise easier than others. Beware the person who seems to do it effortlessly. There is a way of balancing the stick by controlling the movement from the elbow which isn't what it's about. This will become evident when the person tries to work with a partner in Step 3.

Step 2

Once everyone can balance their stick, gather them at one end of the room. Sticks balanced, they advance down the room in unison. This is an astonishing experience. At one with your own stick, you also feel instantly part of an ensemble. Visually, it is very striking.

Step 3

Work now in pairs. Keeping your own stick balanced, hold hands with another person. Try to move together. Although this is extremely difficult initially, you start to see how you have to accommodate another person's rhythms. And there's an enormous sense of achievement when you eventually balance your sticks and walk together.

Step 4

Some people find they can balance the stick on their elbow, shoulder, chin, forehead etc. Have fun exploring where it can go and what possibilities there are. The principle of moving underneath the stick is fundamental wherever it is balanced. As you become more experienced you stop needing to look at the top of the stick, it is there in your peripheral vision. And in time you may be able to transfer it to different parts of the body with considerable fluency. The more you practise the less you need to move to maintain the stick, although the body is always soft beneath it.

For those who have difficulty in getting through Step 1, it is worth noting that if you come back to the exercise after a break, or the next day, you'll find you can do it with considerably more ease. It's as though the body needs time to absorb the requirements of this new skill.

Because the focus of this exercise is on an object, it shifts attention from the self to a task, a valuable lesson for actors. It is also useful preparation for controlling props onstage. More importantly, it demonstrates the necessity of involving the whole body. This is the fundamental law which Meyerhold observed in the great Sicilian Grasso's acting, that the whole body has to be engaged in whatever you do on stage, however small the gesture, and which Grotowski maintained was Meyerhold's greatest discovery.[127]

Generally speaking, movements which originate in the torso appear more free than those which begin in the limbs and leave the torso static or passive. Understanding the way movement begins from impulses in different parts of the body is essential to controlling the body on stage.

Whilst Decroux's early technique designated the spinal column as the point from which all movement emanates, his colleague Barrault shifted this focal point to the navel, a point where not only movement but breathing begins. Placing the centre in the navel coordinates action and respiration. (This is closer to the *hara*, that point just below the navel which in Japan is believed to be the major source of energy.) This will give you a sense of power and control. Shifting the centre of gravity allows you to play with different states.

Shifting gravity

Stand with your feet parallel and shift the centre of gravity forwards. Explore moving, walking, sitting etc. whilst you maintain this. Then shift the centre backwards and explore that. What emotional states do these shifts provoke? You might find shifting forwards makes you feel anxious or curious, and backwards more relaxed or haughty. Note where you 'normally' carry your centre.

If all this sounds very serious, you can lighten up proceedings with the following exercise.

Ministry of silly walks

Keeping your face as neutral as you can, let the pelvis 'point' in one direction whilst the chest points in another. Where does your head want to look? Experiment. Let your stomach lead, or your feet, as though your centre resided there. Think about your eyes too: they can lift the head, or pull it in different directions. You will find people look as though they are in a Monty Python sketch.

Try greeting a partner with any of these stances – it is very important to keep everything else in neutral, otherwise the stance becomes 'justified' with psychology or character and the walk ceases to be comic.

You'll find that looking outwards influences the size of your actions. You work in relation to a larger space if you focus outwards rather than the floor, and consequently enlarge your presence.

However much the pelvis drives the movement, the point of command (rather like the operation centre) is the chest. Explore the idea that it is your chest that 'looks'. What does this feel like? Do you see more or less than merely looking with the eyes?

Allow each part of the body to be the eyes. Always observe the effect on the control of the flow of energy in the body and its intensity. How much is required? How economically can you achieve a 'look'.

Try using the palms of your hands to 'look'. Or the soles of your feet.

This work is great for comedy. But it is also a seriously useful way of experimenting with the physical potential of transforming the body to create characters. And an actor should always know where every limb or finger is and what it is doing.

THE BODY IN SPACE

The ability to position one's body in space is a fundamental law of acting.[128]

The actor's working area is the space around them. Space is not a vacuum. Any movement in space displaces air. A simple demonstration that we move *through the air* in space is to line up a group on one side of a room and run in unison to the other side, stop and turn: everyone will feel a breeze flow past them. This breeze is the air displaced by the movement of the group. This usually causes a ripple of wonder to pass through the group with a request to repeat the exercise.

You can move on to explore the space by imagining the air has various densities, from cloud to mist to thick fog. The sense of *pushing* through space is a useful starting point for mime work, where using the body's tensile opposition creates resistance to space.

Commanding the stage demands a control of the space. An actor who looks at the floor is uninteresting. Like a rally driver navigating the road ahead, the actor has to 'read' the space. But in order to do this s/he has first to really 'see' it, to create parallels of attention so that the whole space becomes their field of vision.

Controlling the space

The following sequence expands your spatial awareness and ability to control the space. Don't rush any of these steps. Allow enough time to really absorb each surface, several minutes for each at least.

The notion of the chest as the 'command point' is extremely valuable here.

Be careful to ensure that even when using the centre of the chest in this way, the eyes still lead the head.

Step 1

Stand and observe the room. How much of the space can you see? Find the limit of your vision. Then, very slowly, survey the space with roving eyes, dividing it into sections and looking at it segment by segment. Now re-assess the limit of your vision. Has it increased? Is more of the peripheral space included in your gaze?

Step 2

As you move around the space, notice the floor. Really scrutinise its surface, taking note of its texture, any blemishes or patterns until you feel you know every inch of it. Gradually increase your range of interest so that you include more and more of the floor space in your gaze. Move in different directions in order to take in more.

Step 3

Continue the exercise in relation to the walls, again noticing their composition, texture, lights, any notices or scratches etc. and increasing your range of interest to encompass every section of every wall. Do this without losing your knowledge of the floor area just acquired.

Step 4

Finally turn your attention to the ceiling, investigating each section of it – without forgetting the presence of the floor and walls.

At the end of this exercise stand and consider the room as a whole. It will seem larger as well as very familiar, even if you have never worked in it before. Your spatial awareness will have increased, and you may feel 'bigger' yourself.

Lecoq has defined seven 'laws of motion' based on the 'ceaseless play between forces in equilibrium and disequilibrium'.[129] These are abstract notions which become concrete once you apply them on stage, incorporating, for example, the idea that standing upright necessitates opposing gravity, that holding a suitcase in one hand means you must compensate by lifting the empty arm. Their value lies in the actor's ability to place him/her self in relation to others on stage and to the surroundings, in other words, realising the importance of spatial relationships. Fundamental to this is the concept of a 'fixed point'.[130] This is explored in very simple terms in the next exercise.

The actor needs to know where s/he is going every time s/he comes on stage and every time s/he moves. Definite moves are far less distracting for an audience than aimless wandering or unmotivated hesitancy. During the following exercise, try to cultivate your own 'outside eye'(as mentioned in SECTION ONE), in effect becoming your own audience. Don't at this stage construct a reason for moving other than knowing where you are going. Ask yourself simply: Where am I moving to? How am I moving? What kind of image am I constructing? Paying detailed attention to what you are doing in this way helps you to maintain your focus.

Fixed points

Step 1

Since the head naturally follows the eyes it is crucial to learn to place the eyes. Place your eyes on a specific point, something you noticed during the previous exercise whether on the floor, wall or ceiling. Keeping your eyes on this point, walk towards it and when you arrive stop, let your eyes lead your head and torso in a turn until something else arrests your attention, then walk towards this new point.

Keep moving across the space, making sure you have a fixed point to go to, defining each turn clearly and establishing your trajectory across the room before each move in a new direction. Remember that you are moving through air. Feel it brush your skin.

[NB: It is rare for players to bump into each other during this exercise provided they are concentrating on the task in hand.]

Split the group so they have an opportunity to observe each other. When you watch you'll notice how everyone seems very purposeful, and thereby interesting to watch. You start to realise how clarity of direction holds the spectator's attention. Now start playing with the space.

Step 2

Play at cheating the space: the space thinks you're going to look in one direction but at the last moment you look somewhere else. Try changing direction unexpectedly. Then change speed. Then the level at which you move. [You may need to reduce the numbers before doing this exercise with a large group to avoid the danger of collision.]

Always 'mark' the spot at which you change direction, initially with a precise turn of the head. As you progress in the exercise, begin to reduce the outward emphasis you place on this 'marking', and allow it to become an internal decision. You are still moving according to fixed points, but they will become less apparent to an onlooker. Don't allow this to dilute the energy or spontaneity of your work.

Step 3

You can change the command point by placing the eyes in different parts of the body, for example the right knee, the left thumb, the back of the neck, as though that is the place from which you are looking.

Step 4

Let small groups of individuals play at creating different trajectories across the space based on the preceding steps. Each actor selects three or four from this series to string together as a short montage, making sure the transitions between each movement are smooth. Then show these and discuss them.

As you observe, notice how some individuals appear to have specific intention or purpose in their actions. In other words, you can't help 'reading' the movement and constructing 'meanings', or see moments at which potential 'stories' begin to emerge. This demonstrates how, as spectators, we constantly search for meaning, even in abstract composition. Of course, we can enjoy the movement in purely aesthetic terms. That is, after all, how much modern dance works. But it is fascinating how an uninflected, or 'empty' movement seems to allow the spectator in.

Games which encourage actors to apply this spatial awareness are vital. You need to know where everyone is on stage and use the space in correspondence with others. No actor should block another actor, even when they are standing behind them.

If you have been discussing the previous exercise, a quick game of tag will quickly re-energise the actors and the space. The following versions of tag will activate an enhanced spatial awareness. (While you are watching, notice points at which you see evidence of 'fixed points'. These will, of course, be unintentional.)

Pass the tag

Actors should use a soft tap rather than a 'hit' to pass the tag in this game. Whereas in the traditional form of tag each person plays competitively as an individual and the space is constantly fragmented, the rule in this version is to pass the tag as fast as possible between the players so that there is only the slightest pause between its transference. The result is a more harmonious use of space.

Name tag[131]

Define a square approx 10 x 10 metres in which to play this game. When people are 'out' they stand round this area to watch. In this version, if you shout someone else's name just before being tagged you escape being 'it' and the named person becomes 'it' instead. If you are unable to say a name and you are tagged you are 'out' and have to stand and watch until the last two players remain to claim victory.

This is more difficult than it appears. Players frequently become tongue-tied just when they need to shout a name. And if the names aren't articulated clearly, confusion arises as no-one knows who is 'it'.

As the number of players decreases, notice how those left begin using the space more effectively and keep eye contact with the remainder of the group.

Sock tag[132]

Each player tucks a sock in their trouser waistband – like a tail it must be visible. The objective of the game is to collect as many socks from others whilst retaining your own. Once you lose your sock you are 'out'. The trick is, of course, to face opponents whilst ensuring there's no-one behind you.

Putting this into practice in the following improvisation emphasises the importance of relating to others *in the space*, rather than merely as talking heads.

Long lost relatives

Two volunteers wear a sock in their waistband as in 'Sock Tag'. One is waiting at the station, the other is a relative returning home after a long time. They play the situation whilst simultaneously trying to take the other actor's sock.

The game forces the actors into a relationship with the space whilst trying to establish one with each other. The way they create distance between each other feeds the improvisation. It can take a while for actors to realise the necessary balance between playing the game and sustaining the improvisation.

In our daily lives we work with real distances. On stage the dimensions change. Just as stage-time is highly condensed with events moving far more quickly than in real time, stage-space expands and contracts. An actor can use space to represent emotional distance, as in the previous improvisation; but given a different context s/he can use it to cover vast distances in a few strides.

The trick here is to imagine the stage space bigger than it is and focus the eyes accordingly. Practise walking across the space as though you are travelling to a distant horizon rather than towards the door. This does not necessarily mean taking larger strides. You have to 'see' beyond the walls of the room. Involving the imagination in terms of distance in this way gives even the smallest gesture immense power.

This brings us to the question of presence. For imagining the space larger than it is and focusing your attention outwards will give the impression of enhanced presence.

PRESENCE

Why, when I see two actors doing the same thing, do I get fascinated by one and not the other? [133]

Presence is often thought of as some kind of god-given talent to mesmerise an audience. And when an actor has this 'presence' it can make us feel that we're standing very close to them, wherever in the theatre we're sitting. What do we mean by it? Can we acquire it?

To some extent it is manifest when an actor seems insolubly connected to the space they occupy, which is why the actor needs to learn to control the space. But that's not the only thing. Some actors simply appear bigger than their physical reality when performing. Kathryn Hunter is a performer who illustrates this: in real life she is tiny, little more than five feet tall, but she has a magnetism on stage which belies her size.

Actors who possess such presence may show nothing of this offstage. In fact they can often appear reassuringly real and human. It is not the same as 'charisma', which relates more to an individual's personality. Yet, just like charisma, there is no reliable system by which it can be acquired.

It is, I believe, a great deal to do with awareness, energy, and controlling the space. And combining these in training goes some way towards increasing an actor's presence. Crucially, actors need to recognise that when training they are working towards the idea of a body which is *more resonant*, if not 'larger-than-in-life'. It is, in Jos Houben's words 'being magnificent'.

The following exercise gives actors a taste of this.

Magnificence [134]

You need a large space for this exercise, preferably one with a depth of at least 20 metres .

Step 1

Line up half a dozen actors opposite a blank wall or curtain, with their backs to any spectators. As they advance at a measured pace up the room, they gradually lift their arms from their sides to the furthest extent of their reach. The aim is to calculate the distance to the opposite wall so that on arrival the body is stretched to its full extent, feet on tip-toe and hands reaching heavenwards.

When actors reach the opposite side they turn slowly and face the audience, lowering their heels to the floor, letting their hands fall quietly to their sides and looking directly at the spectators. Try and keep the face neutral. The gaze should not be aggressive.

The feeling this generates is that of seeming bigger, and of 'filling' the space. It may not achieve this effect for all actors on first encounter. So repeat the exercise with the focus on judging the gradual raising of the arms (no juddering!) so the complete exercise happens very smoothly, with a seamless transition from starting point to the final position. It is also a good idea not

to tell actors what the outcome should be. Just conduct the exercise and see
what their response is.

Step 2
Take two bamboo canes, approx. 2 metres long. Invite a volunteer to repeat
the previous exercise on their own, holding a cane in each hand as though
they are extensions of the arms. Discuss the results.

Actors can get an extraordinary feeling from this exercise. Allow them to
keep the canes stretched outwards for about 15-20 seconds as they face the
spectators. Then take the canes gently from them. Ask for their response.
Often you find, for a short time afterwards, they can still 'feel' the canes in
their hands. And if you later have a sense of an actor losing some of their
'power' on stage, remind them of the canes and that can sometimes
reactivate this.

Energy is a critical element in presence. Peter Brook has said: 'When
great energy crosses space, it is quite fascinating',[135] yet for him presence
is also to be found in 'a certain silence within'.[136] Yoshi Oida, who has
worked extensively with Brook, refers us to how a spinning top operates,
how it remains upright and fixed even when it is spinning very fast. On
stage, he says, the body is the same: 'When you are required to be calm or
immobile, there is a huge inner dynamic. You 'spin' very fast inside. If this
inner powerhouse is absent, quiet actions or moments of stillness have no
impact'.[137] Conversely, strong or violent movements require the actor to
maintain an inner core of tranquillity: 'When you discover physical
dynamism, you must balance it with inner calm'.[138]

Undoubtedly there is a correspondence here with the concept of
neutrality and the idea of the 'empty actor'. But it is important to note that
neutrality is an ideal state from which the actor begins and to which s/he
can return for reference; presence is an ongoing inner dynamism.

Great presence often seems like a contained or distilled energy. The
actor has an intensity which is not necessarily allied to any emotional
expression. When Barba became fascinated with the concept of presence
through his observations of Eastern performers, he identified two fundamental elements which contributed to their ability to magnetise the
spectators: extra-daily technique and their use of energy. In addition, he
noted these had nothing to do with any premeditated interpretation or
expression of meaning. This is an example of how technical discipline

informs Asian performance forms. And we can learn a great deal from Barba's analysis of them, even if we cannot imitate them.

Barba prefers to use 'body-in-life' or 'bios' (Greek for 'life') rather than the term 'presence'. And in attempting to articulate the way this is sustained by Oriental performers he uncovers the principle of opposition and the concept of 'energy in time'.

We have already seen how establishing opposing tensions in the body relates to creating dynamic movement in SECTION ONE. The principle of opposition is evident in the way mime artists exploit counter tensions in the body, and it can be observed in the positions of commedia characters: Pantalone's vigorous stance of wide-spread legs and concave back, for example, creates a series of tensions throughout the body. Oriental performers deploy a similar but more pronounced mastery of oppositional tension which results in highly stylised movement. Altering the normal equilibrium of the body creates what Barba calls a 'dilated body'. Just as our pupils dilate in darkness, the technical demands of Oriental performance serve to dilate the body: onstage the actor appears larger, more defined and more present.

The concept of 'energy in time' is more alien to Western performers. A Noh actor, for example, uses far more energy to execute an action on stage than is required to execute the action in that space. It's as though he uses extra energy to resist the action whilst doing it, taming the energy without reducing it. Meyerhold used the idea of *tormos*, which means applying a kind of internal braking to the rhythmic pattern of movement and gesture, which is investigated in SECTION FOUR: RHYTHM. Again this is a way of 'organising' internal energy.

Although we cannot emulate Oriental performance, acquiring neutrality and learning to balance oppositions, working on our inner energies and awareness, will all help promote a sense of being 'in the moment'.

There is one further dimension of presence; that awkward word 'truth'. The aim of working on presence through the body is what Michael Ratcliffe calls 'the truthfulness of the actor in and with his/her own body – no mystery given or withheld at birth'.[139] The first step to this truthfulness is: whatever you do on stage, never be indifferent.

COMPLICITÉ

It is through collaboration that this knockabout art of theatre survives and kicks.[140]

The word complicité has crossed the channel via Jacques Lecoq and his one-time colleague Philippe Gaulier. The word has a deeper resonance than the English word 'ensemble', and for Theatre de Complicité the fact that it also means a shared belief between actor and spectator is of crucial importance.[141] Both Lecoq and Gaulier also use the phrase 'le jeu', or play. It is the essence of their work, the foundation of all their training.

There are two types of complicité: complicité between those performing on stage, and complicité between the performers on stage and the spectators.[142] The latter is investigated in detail in the final part of this section: audience. First we explore the concept of complicité between performers.

At its most fundamental level, acting is a living exchange between actors. Complicité amongst performers is the crux of ensemble practice, a shared belief which depends upon intense awareness and mutual understanding and produces on-stage rapport. Being fully open to other actors is not simply a matter of creating pleasant working relationships. You must be able to work as an ensemble to tell the story moment by moment.

Building true theatrical complicité needs more than playing team games, however enjoyable. Eye contact is a crucial ingredient, so is a heightened sensory awareness of others in the space. The series of exercises below is designed to foster group awareness and cultivate a collective sense of rhythm and timing, promoting an *open relationship* between players. They are followed by a further series of games and workshop exercises designed to develop a sense of play between participants. In the section on 'audience' we move on to establish a sound grasp of the potential in the current of exchange between stage and spectator, and the confidence to exploit that potential.

Firstly, players need to learn to respond to each other spontaneously, without verbalising. These games offer ways of achieving mutual understanding through mute means to develop collaborative somatic creativity. They also develop democratic working practice.

Ball in the air

Use a soft ball for this game, about football size. Players spread out around the room and hand-volley the ball to each other whilst counting out loud how many volleys before the ball crash lands. The idea is to break each successive record of volleys – and yesterday's record.

Try to avoid making a circle. The idea is to use the whole space. Twelve is more than enough for each group. Higher scores can be reached if you get underneath the ball (as in the stick balancing work) and tap the ball softly.

This is a good game to repeat at the start of a series of workshops or rehearsals, as groups enjoy beating their previous record.

Lifting the glass

Players stand in a circle, with equal spaces between them. They imagine a large circular plate of glass on the floor. They work together to lift the glass off the ground. Then they are asked to move it to a new position and replace it gently on the ground, without any potential breakage! The exercise takes place in silence. Only eye contact between players operates as communication.

This is a useful 'test' exercise. If you play this after a period of developing work on complicité, improvement in executing it can be tangible.

Stop and go

This is a group awareness and concentration exercise which enhances the use of peripheral vision, and builds a satisfying sense of unity. Once again, the action takes place in silence. The enjoyment comes from the sense of finding mutual agreement: no individual takes responsibility for leading but a silent consensus emerges. The assumption here is that the group know each other's names.

Step 1

Walk around the space at your own natural pace. Criss-cross the space, being careful not to bump into others. Notice the variety of pace amongst the group.

Step 2

As you pass each other, acknowledge your partners by eye contact and perhaps offer a smile. Keep on weaving around the whole space without clustering.

Step 3

Gradually moderate your pace to agree with the mean of the whole group, so you are all walking at the same speed.

Step 4

Leader calls: 'Freeze/ Close your eyes/ Point to Susan' and the group follow each instruction. Then they are asked to open their eyes and discover how accurate they are in pointing to the named individual.

Repeat this stage a number of times with different names and notice how the level of accuracy starts to increase.

Step 5

Continue walking around the space as before. When the Leader calls 'STOP' the whole group gradually slows and comes to a halt together. Try this several times until the group begins to slow in unison and comes to a halt at the same time.

Step 6

From everyone in the still position, the Leader asks for a group decision to start, and everyone begins walking again. The call is the prompt for the group decision, which is arrived at via mute consensus, so it may take some time before the 'moment' to move arrives. Be patient. If an individual 'leads', point this out and begin again from stillness. Groups will eventually learn to sense the moment, but it requires commitment and repetition.

Practise these two stages several times until the group can slow to a halt and restart in unison.

There is no communication between players other than eye contact. Eventually, the group will become more harmonised in slowing, stopping and starting, and more accurate in pointing.

This game lays the foundation for the next one, which is a sort of imaginative 'follow-my-leader' in which leadership is constantly changing. The word kaleidoscope means 'beautiful form' in Greek, and players will find as the game develops they are making patterns similar to those seen through a child's toy kaleidoscope.

Kaleidoscope [143]

This game can be played with 12-24 players, providing the space is large enough to take two parallel lines of equal numbers. Players create geometric shapes in the space between these two lines. The game operates in silence.

These are the rules of the game:

- *an individual's decision to enter the space is an invitation to others*

- *never refuse an invitation*

- *group decisions govern what happens*

- *group decisions govern the moment of leaving the space*

Other useful instructions are: always know which group you are in, always work as a group, and be aware of the whole space.

Step 1

Stand in two equal parallel lines opposite each other and using the convention of a 'group decision to move' established in the previous exercise, 'Stop and Go', attempt the following:

- *Whole group re-form into a circle*

- *Whole group re-form into a square*

- *Whole group re-form into a triangle*

- *Whole group return to two parallel lines*

Step 2

- *Any player can move into the space: Person X;*

- *Another player positions themselves in relation to X with the idea of creating a circle or square or triangle;*

- *A third person joins them and takes a position with the idea of continuing the creation of the shape;*

- *One by one, more players enter the space with the idea of continuing/completing it;*

- *When the shape appears complete, the group take a decision to leave and melt back into the parallel lines.*

- *The game then starts over as another individual enters the space.*

Always allow a point of stillness as each new person positions themselves. Never allow the space to remain empty.

You'll find you cannot predetermine what the shape will eventually be early in the game. The second or third person may, for example, find that whoever follows them is 'seeing' a different shape to the one they had in their head.

Step 3

Once the basic rules are understood and the group can realise clear shapes, more complex developments can be brought in, such as making two shapes/patterns, experimenting with the size of each shape and the levels of the bodies within it. These make the patterns more interesting, and players soon begin to take pleasure in becoming more inventive.

Step 4

Work develops through playing the game of making shapes and patterns in three-dimensional space, always bearing in mind the rules, and adding variants, such as when a pattern is established, one person can simply cross from one line to join the other. This can be further developed by varying the speed and types of movement used to cross the space.

Soon the space is filled with a variety of shapes and punctuated by people hopping, running, or snaking across the space, even through the shapes.

Step 5

Work continues to becomes more complex as players exploit the possibilities of creating more abstract shapes, or images related to a theme. As ideas and sequences emerge they can be used as the basis for constructing improvised performance.

The concept of a group-decision-to-move established through playing this game and the awareness generated in responding to others, develop a common vocabulary which can be applied in choric work. It provides a useful foundation for the orchestration of crowd scenes, for example. In more advanced choral work, where there can be a tendency for the majority to fall into passive mode and move and/or speak just behind the beat and/or leader, it promotes the idea that everyone has an equal responsibility to take the initiative. So they can 'find' the moment to move and/or speak together. When this happens it's as though any sense of leadership or repetition vanishes and a collective sense of being 'in the moment' is reached.

If those on stage are not aware of each other it can look as though two or more different stories are being told, whether in improvisation or in text work. There is only one story being told, so actors need to be in tune with each other and tell the same story to the audience.

Frogs in a pool

This is an energetic way of finding complicité in smaller groups of, say, four upwards. Each group defines their 'pool'. One player is the stone, the others are frogs. The 'stone' jumps and the frogs jump in relation to the ripple created by the strength of the jump and the distance they are from the stone. If, for example, you are standing close to the 'stone' and the 'stone' jumps high, you need to respond very quickly and move a distance away. The further from the stone, the later and more subdued your response. Where frogs jump is determined by the strength and trajectory of each of the 'stone's jumps. Eventually, you find the frogs have moved to the perimeter of their pool.

A development of this game which gets rid of the idea of a leader is to dispense with the stone. All players become frogs, and any frog can jump at any moment. The others must jump according to where they are in relation to the most recently jumping frog. This can get quite hectic. Make sure you wait until all the frogs have finished one response before beginning another to start with. When players have exhausted themselves, they find that moments of stillness between bouts of jumping make the game more effective.

The notion of keeping something going as a group whilst varying the rhythm and pace is integral to collaborative ensemble work. The following game was played extensively by Theatre de Complicité during rehearsals for *Street of Crocodiles*.[144] It is a challenging exercise in complicité.

Shoal of fish

This is a deceptively simple exercise. A group of players move around the room in the same way as a shoal of fish. Feet should travel over the floor with minimal sound. Shifts in pace should occur in much the same way as underwater. Leader(s) change with each turn. And occasionally fish dart off at a quicker rate and in a new direction, or lag behind the general formation. Individuals have to be aware of their relationship to the whole shoal and respond to every other person's movements in addition to suggesting a single fish.

PLAY

Play: to occupy oneself in, amuse oneself in a game.[145]

Play, of course, deepens complicité as much as it relies on it. Companies such as Theatre de Complicité and Peter Brook's troupe (and in the 1950s Joan Littlewood's Theatre Workshop, in the 1920s and '30s Copeau's Les Copiaux) who play together in their training and rehearsals are renowned for the high calibre of their ensemble skills as well as the quality of their acting.

Clive Barker frequently refers to the way in which Theatre Workshop worked like a jazz ensemble, able to 'read' each other through the improvisational avenues laid down during Littlewood's rehearsal process. The analogy is a useful one. Anyone who has ever played in a musical band knows that improvisation can be 'free' in the sense of a 'jam session', and structured when it fits into an overall schema. Theatre is similar. You can simply 'play', or use improvisation in a more structured way.

Improvisation and play are often conflated, yet there is a distinction to be drawn between them semantically: although 'improvise' can be equated with 'play' in terms of definition, play has a much more expansive range of meanings. The aim of improvisation is to 'make something up'; improvisation uses play to achieve an unforeseen result, whether to create something or explore parallel situations in relation to a text. Play is a much looser concept, just like a jam session. And just as a jam session is never completely anarchic because individuals observe the 'rules' of musical keys and rhythms, so in play rules apply, sometimes in relation to games, sometimes in relation to structures.

You can play with space (as suggested earlier in CONTROLLING THE SPACE), with objects, with energy, with each other, without necessarily creating any tangible product. And the exercises below suggest ways of doing so. Play is about process. It also has delightful connotations with childhood. And this is integral to the way the word is used by practitioners. To be childlike, in the sense of being perpetually open to discovery, is the aim of play.

Jacques Copeau was the first practitioner to introduce the notion of play to theatre.[146] Copeau searched for a broader, freer, more audacious dramatic imagination. His genius was the rediscovery of the art of play: 'In a practical way, the teaching of dramatic feeling in the actor-pupil is conceived by analogy to the child's instinct for play.'[147]

Observing his own children at play alerted Copeau to the powerful freedom of the child's imagination. His co-director, Suzanne Bing, had been teaching in a Montessori school in New York during the First World War and returned to France armed with a host of games.

Much of Copeau's play was allied to mask work. And Jean Dasté writes that through 'daily exercises with masks . . . Copeau wanted us to return to the spontaneity and talent for inventiveness and disguise that children have'.[148]

Mask work travelled from Copeau through Dasté to Lecoq, as previously noted. Copeau's legacy also resides in the countless games and their derivatives which formed the core of his and Bing's work at the Vieux Columbier School.[149] Through the dissemination of these games via his nephew Michel Saint-Denis (The London Studio and The Old Vic School in Britain), and son-in-law Jean Dasté (Commedie de St Etienne in France) and from him to Lecoq, the concept of learning to act through play has fed into drama training.

Children playing are utterly absorbed and focused in what they do and the world they create. They have a quality of naiveté. Watching five-year-olds, one observes how serious the process of play is, how '*sans* attitude'. To play we do not have to pretend to be five-year-olds, rather we have to find the child within us. Joan Littlewood's masterly use of games to feed the rehearsal process led her actors to 'the kind of concentration . . . that you had as a child, making something out of plasticine'.[150]

The *ad hoc* introduction of any old game, however, will not automatically guarantee such naiveté or high quality ensemble work. The key is in finding or creating games and exercises which have a direct relationship with the text or theme being explored, or a tangible impact upon principles of acting and theatre praxis. The game SHOAL OF FISH, for example, fosters complicité because individuals have to respond to each other and cooperate whilst also, at times, following an internal impulse. And BALL IN THE AIR can be seen as a metaphor for sustaining energy in performance and keeping the story alive. Neither of these games is competitive. The atmosphere generated by competitive games is very different to that of co-operative games, and it is worth giving this some thought when deciding which games you use. An alternative is to re-invent familiar games to serve your purpose.

Playing games remembered from childhood is an obvious route to rediscovering the child within, something Littlewood realised. Her rehearsals for *Macbeth*, for example, began with the actors playing cowboys and indians and moved on to a large-scale improvised battle before the text was introduced. Grandmother's Footsteps is a good example of a game we remember and love to (re)play. It's also a wonderful game for practising balances and lightness in footwork. The following versions are more complex re-inventions.

Grandmother's footsteps plus a jumper

The same rules apply as for the original game. However, a baggy jumper, or jacket, is deposited a few metres behind 'Grandma'. (The jumper needs to be roomy to make it easy to get on or off). The objective of the game is not merely to reach Grandma without her seeing you move, but to don the jumper too before you get to her. If Grandma sees you move whilst you're wearing the jumper, you not only go back to the beginning again, but replace the jumper on the floor. But you can be partially dressed in the jumper and remain in the game provided that you are not moving when Grandma turns round.

There are two further developments you can play. Players can compete for the jumper even when someone is wearing it. Or players can work together to get the jumper on one player and 'protect' this player until s/he reaches Grandma.

In yet another version players work in pairs, so if Grandma spots one of them moving, both have to return to base. You can play this with or without the jumper.

Simon McBurney talks of how, in the early days of Theatre de Complicité, they would 'construct a playground in the rehearsal room, and then out of the playground things would start to emerge'.[151] At that stage the company were producing work that was closer to the comedy circuit than mainstream theatre. Yet they still use the idea of the rehearsal room as a playground, sometimes incorporating costumes and props which the actors raid like a dressing-up box, whether they are interpreting texts or devising their own material.

Brook not only uses play as a starting point, as a basis for personal growth and self-development in his actors, but his company also regularly show their work-in-progress to an audience of children. After a show based on *The Bee Man of Orm* by Frank Stockton, nearly a hundred children joined in a free improvisation using all the props, sticks, balloons and ropes used in the play, and for two hours: 'there was a free releasing of energy, kids doing the most incredible things together. They used the sticks to invent games, create corridors and gates, become animals, make up instruments or relationships or rhythmical exercises. It went beyond anyone's imagination'.[152]

One of the things that emerges from this is the way children use objects to create worlds. Play is very much about creating worlds, whether individually or collaboratively. We have all built dens in the garden or the living room from blankets, or used sticks as weapons. Objects act as catalysts in the world of play. Playing with objects in a 'silent universe' is a fruitful avenue to explore. Without words we are often less inhibited, more able to enter into imaginative realms. Some companies (eg Kaos Theatre, Bouge-de-la) use background music; as long as it is non-invasive this can work.

I mentioned earlier the usefulness of having a collection of objects such as sticks, plastic bottles, and boxes, balls of string, ropes etc. For the next exercise, you can use broom handles but more preferable, if you can get them, are cardboard tubes from carpet or lino rolls or plastic piping of the type used by builders for drainage (5cm diameter), cut to size (2-3 metres lengths). These are less harmful than broom handles if you accidentally hit someone. They also have the virtue of being playable as musical instruments à la Rolf Harris. Ask at your local DIY store!

Tube sculptures [153]

First of all, conduct a thorough investigation of your tube. Feel its weight, what you can do with it, roll it, swing it, jump over it etc. Find a multitude of things to do with it. The possibilities are legion!

Then, with a partner, explore what you can do with your tubes – throw and catch, roll, create shapes, etc. Let the weight of the tube or stick lead the movement, and keep the space animated.

After a period of exploration, select several actions that please you both and construct these units into a sequence. Work in silence until you need to choose your favourite actions. The sequences you create can be shown to the rest of the group.

Follow on with groups of four or five playing with the tubes, finding rhythms, noises, shapes that please, again the possibilities are endless. And eventually create a sequence to show the other groups.

There is no need to make anything 'literal' or realistic with the tubes. It's the pleasure in playing with them that is important. Abstract sculptures are often far more satisfying to create.

Jumble play [154]

A simple movement can transform a banal object into something else. Animating objects such as you might find in a props cupboard or old jumble wardrobe items – even sheets of newspaper – can be huge fun. You need a large collection. And the more odd the assortment, the more surreal the play. Things such as corrugated ventilation tubes, suitcases, fur coats, feather dusters, a music stand, various handbags, and a sandcastle bucket featured in the Bouge-de-la workshop where I learnt this game, for example.

Step 1

To begin with, let the actors find an object to play with. Or rather, invite them to let the object 'choose' them, so whatever seems to draw their attention is what they end up with.

Each actor takes his/her object and, as with the tubes, conducts a thorough investigation of it, weight, smell, feel etc. What does it do? Does it open? Can I get in it? Will it sit on my head? And so on. Weight is important when you come to move with it. If you let the weight of the object lead the movement, you find more imaginative possibilities open up.

You may, as with the tubes, ask each actor to develop a sequence of movements with the object which they show. This is useful with more advanced actors who aim to improvise on stage, as it replicates spontaneous playing in front of an audience. It also gives other members of the group a chance to see what possibilities there are in the objects they did not choose first time around.

Step 2

The next thing to do is let actors play with the objects. If you invite everyone to join in together you are likely to create chaos. Just as games have rules, make up your own to regulate the anarchy. Setting the objects on either side of the space, and the actors as spectators in front, for example, is helpful. Then actors can enter the space one at a time, or in response to what's already happening.

Musical accompaniment works well in this instance; working in silence here can be unproductive, although the 'silent universe' still applies for the actors. Vary the sounds, so actors don't get locked into particular 'moods', for it is virtually impossible for the music not to affect what happens. Moving from techno to Oasis to opera and on to jazz followed by Mozart might seem an odd combination, but such variations provide contrasts which surprise the actors. Playing music they are unfamiliar with is a useful strategy.

You need to allow plenty of time for this. It is useful to preface it with the previous tube game, and the two together can take up a whole morning with ease.

I never tire of watching this game. Every individual will play with the objects in a different way. And this brings to light another aspect of play, that there is enormous pleasure to be gained from watching others play, and an enormous amount to be learnt about how theatre works.

True play comes from actors who see, hear, and react fully to each other. It is found in the partnership and chemistry between actors. The following games explore and harness this.

No-ball tennis [155]

This game operates like a game of tennis or ping-pong: impulses are tossed back and forth between two players. Like 'Frogs in a Pool' it's essentially a game which relies on reaction.

X and Y walk towards each other across the space. X pauses and Y reacts, then Y pauses and X reacts and so on, reaction and pause following alternately for up to a minute. There is no dialogue. Reactions are purely physical and should be a spontaneous response to the other person. There are no limits set on what these might be.

Each reaction can be any length but must have a clear beginning and end, like a phrase of movement on a tennis court. Just as in tennis, you can move closer to your partner or further away depending on how the moment takes you. The crucial thing is not to think about your response. The pause comes after you move, not before. Make sure this is happening. A pause before reacting means you're thinking. Don't think. Simply move, pause and watch your partner's response.

To some extent this is an exercise in clarity and definition. More importantly it is about the chemistry between actors, the 'alive-ness' of the moment. It is pure play.

The alchemy between different partners is evident when you play with new partners, as a different chemistry will operate. It affects your instincts, so you have to play 'off' the other person. In purely physical terms, someone slighter or faster or bigger than you forces you to change tactics. And then every person will have their own way of playing. Personalities shine through. Sometimes the way two people play, as in life, is 'more than the sum of two parts'.

You need to be open to playing with everyone in a group. The more you react to different partners the more you find out about yourself, and move into new territories. Play the following game with different partners and it will be different each time.

Cane dancing [156]

Use long bamboo canes (2 metres) for this. Lay one cane between two players. They should stand a couple of metres away from the cane and make eye contact, then walk towards it. Keeping eye contact, they pick up the cane at the same moment using only the tip of the middle (longest) finger. It is now balanced precariously between them. As they move around, the cane remains supported between them until one of them drops their end.

You can play this as a competitive game where the aim is to make your opponent drop the cane by forcing them into awkward positions. The 'dance' will be over quite quickly.

If you aim to keep the cane between you for as long as possible whilst still aiming to make your partner drop their end, the 'dance' becomes more intricate as you both try and find more subtle ways of outwitting each other. In soccer terminology, you are playing the ball not the man.

Both these games explore the chemistry between different partners, which to some extent will depend on the kind of energy each possesses. But establishing and sustaining the level of energy on stage is a collective responsibility. In both improvisation and text work, it is essential for actors to be able to assess and alter the levels of energy operating between two or more partners. This means working out what energy level others are playing at and learning to sustain the same level, as well as learning how to increase and decrease the level of tension.

The following exercise is play with a purpose, play designed to develop skills in modulating energy levels. It works on escalations of energy, moving up and down through the 'gears' of tension. In top gear we all know that as everything goes faster it becomes more difficult to control. The sequence here establishes an understanding of controlling tension in relation to partners on stage through physical play.

You may find it useful to reprise the STOP AND GO walking exercise described previously in COMPLICITÉ. Play this up until Step 3, but find a mean level of energy – which is different to pace. It is about the physical intensity with which you walk, not the speed. You might find as you go up the scale you still tend to go faster. So try to increase tension in the body. This might exaggerate the walk or action rather than speed it up.

Changing gears

Step 1

This builds on the game 'No-Ball Tennis'. Distribute letters X, Y, Z etc. so everyone knows their turn. X comes onstage and establishes a physical level of energy. Make the choice of energy clear: low or high, desperate or elated. Y enters with a new level of energy. X responds and they play at the new level for half a minute, then X goes. Y sustains the new energy level alone. Z enters with a new and different level of energy. Y responds and so on.

By all means use an imaginative situation to work on, but a simple body gesture with no context will work just as well. For example, if you jump up and down we don't need to know you've just passed your driving test. You're working in a 'silent universe' so it's the level of energy that's important. And whilst two players jumping up and down might work in the short term, it is more interesting if you find a different action at the same level of energy as your partner's.

Remember to leave the energy on stage when you exit. In other words you keep it until you're out of view, rather like a corps de ballet.

Step 2

Introduce the idea of a scale from 1-10. Establish a norm of 5, and variations in degree above and below. 10, for example, should be frenetic; 1 is fairly subdued.

Then run the previous Step 1 again but this time X starts at 1, Y enters at 2, Z comes on at 3 and no-one leaves. In other words, once the newcomer establishes the next level, all those on stage play at the new level until everyone is playing at 10.

These scales of tension demand that each person has to fit in with what's already established and modify their actions incrementally. And the more people on stage the more the degree of subtlety required.

We noted earlier that commedia operates at the scale of 10 and beyond, and it may be that you find this level promotes a grotesque style suitable for comedy. But remember too, that tension sometimes provokes slowness and silence rather than excessive noise and movement. Play the level of energy/tension, not a situation.

In all of these suggestions for play, with objects, with partners, with energy, it is the actor's body which expresses what is going on imaginatively. And ultimately, this is the medium through which the spectator will connect with the world on stage. Simon McBurney reports that after *Three Lives of Lucie Cabrol*, 'the excitement generated amongst the audience . . . was close to that of children'.[157] Inviting an audience into an imaginative collusion with what is happening on stage is the objective of the physical actor.

AUDIENCE

The art of theatre is to be able to communicate with the audience.[158]

Theatre is a transaction between actor and spectator. It operates through a reciprocal current of exchange, which Joan Littlewood calls a 'continuous loop'. And the true magic of theatre lies in this alchemy between actor and audience sharing the same air. 'When you act well,' wrote Meyerhold, 'the audience breathes along with you'.[159]

Enabling a truly open relationship to work takes a particular kind of energy and sensitivity. Actors cannot put up defences. A defensive attitude towards the audience, as though they have come to judge or, worse, assess any particular actor's performance, is counter-productive. Similarly, an attitude of 'selling' the show by using a kind of 'kick' energy will alienate rather than engage spectators.

The goal is a real exchange, a sharing in the event. The actor's task is to provoke the spectators' imaginative participation, not to show what s/he can do: 'The actor is like the driver of the car that transports the audience somewhere else, somewhere extraordinary'.[160]

The term complicité defines the relationship struck between actor and audience which operates when 'performer and audience create the piece *together*',[161] in addition to being used in the context of ensemble practice. Annabel Arden (of Theatre de Complicité) describes it as 'an excitement which works to bridge any sense of distance between audience and actor'.[162] Eye contact is often a factor, and physical-based theatre is predicated on an absence of any fourth wall, allowing a direct and open relationship to operate, a heightened imaginative collusion between spectators and the action on stage. It is about creating a 'sense of common understanding which exists in that room for the evening'.[163]

Simon McBurney believes this understanding can only be achieved when the performers have a 'more creative hand' in the process of making theatre, which is why he set out deliberately to work collaboratively with people. This is true of Littlewood, Grotowski, Brook, Barba and Berkoff, who work from an ethos of facilitating the actor's creativity. Their work is also rooted in exploiting the suggestive power of theatre, a power which distinguishes it from the arts of television and film.

Brook defines three kinds of 'fidelity' necessary for the actor: fidelity to oneself, one's partners and the audience.[164] His experiments in the stage-spectator relationship are illuminating, in particular those undertaken during his journey across Northern Africa with a troupe of actors. With no precedent of 'strolling players', the indigenous audience came unarmed with preconceptions. The actors learned that true spontaneity is tested under such circumstances. They found themselves relying on each other and a pair of the actor Bagayogo's shoes to create a piece of theatre on their travelling stage-carpet, a piece of theatre that could transcend language and cultural differences. Essentially what they discovered was the need to 'mirror the richness of the African crowds' in a way that led them to see the 'true meaning of the words "spontaneity", "danger", "events" and "relationship", "openness", "meeting".'[165]

Those who watch other people play transmit an energy which players must acknowledge and honour. Brook's search for the essence of the stage-spectator relationship has led him to the belief in the audience as a mutual partner in the creation of the theatre event: 'The audience is always "the other person": as vital as the other person in speech or love.'[166]

The fact that actors will learn more about their craft from working with an audience is reiterated by practitioners from Meyerhold to McBurney. Meyerhold maintained that he never saw a production ready by the premiere because performance 'ripens' in front of an audience. Feeling the pulse of working in public is a vital element in theatre-making. Presenting work during training is immensely valuable for actors as actors, and as spectators, of course, they will increase their awareness of what works on stage.

Addressing dialogue to an audience makes that audience more alert and responsive. The most familiar theatrical manifestation of this is in pantomime; it is also the very essence of the storyteller's craft. But you can speak openly to the audience whilst also speaking to your partner on stage and 'awareness of the presence of the audience enables actors to extend their range enormously'.[167] The way the following exercise uses spontane-ously improvised material means the experiment relies on the response of the audience and therefore involves an exciting sense of risk.

Stick stories [168]

Don't try this experiment 'cold': it is best placed at the end of a session exploring aspects of complicité and/or play.

In groups of three-to-five, actors have no more than five minutes to improvise a story. They speak only in gobbledygook, i.e. a made-up language; bodily expression is, of course, integral. Players use a stick to a) 'pass the story' between them and b) represent any object relevant to the story (an oar, rifle, parrot or whatever). The story is developed spontaneously in improvisation by this means, in much the same way as 'No-Ball Tennis' above. It should not be based on any existing myth or story, although the results may bear passing resemblances to stories we know!

One person begins and either when s/he runs out of steam, or feels the moment is right, passes the stick to another player who carries on the 'tale', and so on, each player using the stick to describe landscapes, people, animals, objects etc. When players are not 'telling', they react appropriately to whatever the actor with the stick does and says, and may join in as necessary.

Play the stories immediately in front of an audience (i.e. the rest of the group) or, with more inexperienced actors, allow them a short period to experiment with the idea before 'performing'. The objective is to create 'instant theatre', not present a preconceived or worked-out idea.

The following comments were made by a student actor after this exercise:

By removing the intellectualising process of converting ideas into words, the actor's experience of the story happens simultaneously with the audience. Consequently both actor and audience are able to live through the thought as it happens. It creates a spontaneous and dramatic experience for both audience and performer.

Brook's troupe regularly invite children to view their work-in-progress because they learn from them what works and what doesn't. Photographs of Lecoq teaching remind us he always replicated the stage-spectator relationship in his school. And I have pointed out the value of working in front of such a proto-audience in training, as well as an imaginary audience in the section on awareness. There are, however, certain key elements which promote an understanding of the kind of stage-spectator relationship discussed here that can be explored through practical work.

Firstly, the notion of the power of suggestion through creating 'incomplete' images on stage: an audience needs convincing impressions from the stage in order, imaginatively, to fill in the 'gaps'. The transformation of Gregor Samsa into an insect in Berkoff's *Metamorphosis* is an example of how this can work via the physical manifestation of an actor's body. The actor scrabbles about a steel cage-frame in imitation of a beetle. It is the *idea* of man as insect that is conveyed rather than any technically superimposed or costumed illusion. Similarly, as the Samsa family argue, 'the actors mouth further imprecations against each other while a drum rolls . . . as if you were watching a fight at a distance and could only imagine the terrible things said'.[169] Again the spectators are invited to fill in the gaps, imagining what is being said.

The integration of design and performer during the making process is one way in which practitioners frequently exploit the power of suggestion. The result in performance is a kind of visual innuendo through a sign language incorporating objects and mime, movement and gesture. The way Berkoff uses door frames in his version of Kafka's *The Trial*, the way an arrow is carried across the stage in Brook's *The Mahabharata*, the way the pages of books flutter like birds in the hands of the actors in Theatre de Complicité's *The Street of Crocodiles*, are all imagistic devices working metaphorically: the spectator completes the picture suggested by the action.

It is useful to be familiar with playing with tubes and sticks, such as the games in the previous section PLAY, before playing this next game as it builds on that work.

Change the object

Select any reasonably neutral (and unbreakable) object, such as a broom or large plastic water bottle (empty!). A volunteer uses the object in any manner other than its actual purpose in life. So a broom cannot be used to sweep but can be used as a horse, spade, canoe paddle etc. – the possibilities are endless. The rest of the group immediately construct a scene around this.

The most important thing is that the rest of the group react to the use of the object and develop appropriate scenic action in response. So, for example, if the broom is used like a gun everyone might play being in 'hold-up' situation, if used like a canoe paddle the scene shifts to white water rapids, and so on. Clarity in using the object is imperative, otherwise no-one else knows what is going on.

You can call out 'change the object' when a scene begins to 'die'. Or ask the group to sense when an idea is exhausted so another actor takes the object and transforms it into something new. This encourages them to 'feel' how long a theatrical moment can stay alive, and recognise the impulse to move on to the next moment.

This is a really good game to watch, as you can see instantly how necessary it is to convey a convincing impression on stage, not only for the object-user but everyone else, for the ability to connect with what is happening and construct convincing impressions does not just revolve around the person using the object.

I prefer to invoke a 'silent universe' in this game, although it is possible to incorporate speech. Wordless work tends to access more surreal dimensions. Language tends to direct actors towards the prosaic.

The second key element in developing the stage-spectator relationship is eye contact with the audience. Looking at the audience is something from which many actors recoil. Some look above them, or worse, at the floor. But eye contact is essential to creating an honest relationship with spectators. Real eye contact, not that pretend look out into the auditorium with glazed eyes.

In large auditoria the assumption is that it is more difficult to establish this. In smaller spaces a more intimate relationship seems easier to build. Yet the clown at the opening of Cirque du Soleil's *Allegria* succeeded in making a connection with everyone in the vastness of London's Albert Hall without a word. All he did was look at us directly with the belief that we wanted to 'play'. So much of acting is concerned with this 'belief'. You have to have faith in the audience as a partner, complicit in the event.

The clown can teach us a great deal, for clowns need complicité with the audience in order to function. This may be one reason why Lecoq's teaching programme culminates in the exploration of the clown. Certainly the way clowns 'clock' the audience is a key factor in comedy, especially in executing visual gags.

Classic comedy routines such as putting up a deck chair and getting it wrong are excellent for playing with the idea of 'clocking' the audience. Physical comedy teacher Davis Robinson advises you to 'seek complicity' through three points of focus: looking out at the start of an action, looking out in the middle of failure, and looking out when planning your next step.[170] This is not dissimilar to the CLOWN/CLOCK routine below. You are keeping the events on stage public by constantly referring to the audience through eye contact.

Clown/clock [171]

Imagine the stage area as a clock with the 12 upstage and the 6 downstage nearest the audience. A player runs around the stage and at 3 o'clock on the second circuit makes brief eye contact with the audience. S/he continues running but at 9 o'clock trips up and falls. Upright again, s/he runs around clockwise for a third time and trips in the same place. S/he continues running around again but looks back at 9 o'clock and then at the audience. As s/he approaches the 9 o'clock point once more, s/he jumps over the 'obstacle' and smiles. Then at 3 o'clock s/he trips, and falls – and looks at the audience in disbelief.

This simple sequence invariably elicits laughter. You can play around with the moments at which the clown trips and looks at the audience. Make sure each look is very definite and direct, as clear as the mask's 'gaze'.[172] Without the looks at the audience, of course, the laughter is reduced – if there is laughter at all.

The art of clowning is to realise that the vulnerability of the clown is what draws the audience. The clown wants to please, but rather than getting things right, gets them wrong. However, the clown actually tries very hard and very seriously to get things right, as Laurel and Hardy, and Charlie Chaplin demonstrate. It is the clown's failure, despite hard work, which seduces the audience into laughter.

A third key element is pulling the audience in, for as well as mastering the art of looking at the audience, there is the art of getting them to look at you. Silent characters often draw the attention of an audience. Jos Houben became fascinated by the mechanics of laughter when working with The Right Size. Initially they worked on creating material from themes with the express purpose of making people laugh. Jos was the 'straight man', which he says gave him the opportunity to observe a lot. Gradually he noticed that by doing nothing he attracted more of the audience's attention – and laughter.[173] By 'doing nothing' he means being a silent non-active partner on stage, but one who is completely engaged with what is going on.

In Biyi Bandele's *Happy Birthday Mister Deka D*, performed by Told By An Idiot (1999), Mister Deka D sits absolutely still on stage for over an hour, apart from one move offstage and back on again, and one speech. The actor playing him said that he felt he was under a microscope, that every time he swallowed the audience would see his Adam's apple going up and down.[174]

This kind of 'doing nothing' is probably the most difficult thing to achieve on stage. And is most usefully approached by exploring the concept of neutrality which is dealt with earlier in this book. Experiments in 'doing nothing' formed part of Brook's LAMDA Theatre of Cruelty season in 1965, and Brook refers to Robert Wilson's experiments in the 1970s which showed 'how lack of motion that is inhabited in a particular way, can become irresistibly interesting, without the spectator understanding why'.[175] I am not talking here about presence, but rather the idea of theatre as encounter, or event on a micro-scale, where the interest is in each moment as it unfolds, in tandem with the spectators' response.

The following exercise is designed to explore this encounter. I call it 4:33 after John Cage's piece of the same name.

4:33

Try seeing how long an actor can do nothing in front of an audience. Ask an actor to sit in a chair (where there is less likelihood of movement) in front of the rest of the group. See how long s/he can sustain immobility. Time this so you reach 4 minutes 33 seconds before breaking the spell.

What becomes fascinating is the audience response. On the several occasions I have run this experiment, the actor has been able to maintain a composure which comes close to doing nothing. But the audience find it really difficult. After considerable fidgeting and much re-aligning of bodies, they frequently end up in similar poses. In other words the audience becomes 'one'. They speak afterwards of how their interest deepens after a couple of minutes, when they stop waiting for the next blink of the eye, and settle into 'acceptance'. Interestingly, their attention didn't wander elsewhere.

Actors reflecting on this experiment invariably find that, after a brief period of mental activity, they are able to settle into a state of just 'being', although they are very aware of the audience. What becomes apparent is how intense the relationship between watchers and watched can be, without any eye contact or address.

A fourth key element to consider is the architectural arrangement of stage and spectator. The open relationship necessary to comedy for example, is transmuted in other forms of drama, but the relationship does not necessarily have to be any less intense. Grotowski wanted the spectators to confront themselves through their encounter with the actor and thereby experience a kind of purification. However, he asserted the actors 'must not think of the spectator while acting'.[176] To think of the spectator in Grotowskian theatre was to want to act *for* the spectator rather than confront them, and would denigrate the purity of the encounter between actor and spectator that he sought. Although for Grotowski the spectator is not a point of orientation for the actor, s/he must not neglect their presence. But by placing the spectator *alongside* the actors in many productions, he forged a new intensity in the relationship.

Grotowski was reacting to the 'cinefication' of society. He realised theatre could not compete with film and television in replicating the real. Placing living organisms in close proximity meant every action, feeling or spectacle became heightened: spectators could feel the actors' breath, see their sweat. Such exploitation of the visceral nature of theatre emphasises the physical nature of perception and response.

Integrating actor and audience in an act of communion was a major concern for Grotowski, and the dynamics of the space and the positioning of actors and spectators in that space were a vibrant element of his work in Poland during the 1960s. He conducted numerous experiments with the proximity of the spectator and actor in various configurations, always cognisant that 'to some degree the performance appears not on the stage but in the perception of the spectator'.[177]

His work reminds us there is a three-way relationship between actor and spectator and space. And his creation of dramatic space rather than merely a flexible theatre space is quite Artaudian. In Grotowski's work we see a move away from formal theatre structures into theatre-as-environment embracing both actors and spectators: a single all-encompassing space, where even the notion of stage is defunct.

Spatial arrangements of his productions focused on addressing the spectator through the senses rather than words. Grotowski was attempting to 'impose a psychological orientation on the audience that would integrate them in a particular way with each play'.[178]

In *Ancestors* (1961) and *Akropolis* (1962) the actors used the whole hall where the spectators were randomly placed, yet these were two very different experiments: in *Ancestors* the actors included the spectators in the action, in *Akropolis* the actors ignored the spectators as they moved through them, guarding a kind of invisible fourth wall. Next spectators were 'cast' as inmates in a mental asylum and treated by the 'doctors' as ill alongside the actor-patients for *Kordian* (1962). At *Doctor Faustus* (1963) spectators sat on benches surrounding the action on three sides, like invited guests of Faustus, but amongst them sat 'servants', actors dressed like them who had entered with them, creating a kind of 'overlap' between the world of the spectator and the world of the actor – and the play. During *The Constant Prince* (1968) spectators witnessed the torture of prisoners at close quarters, peering down over a wooden 'fence' into a stage that resembled a cock-pit or bull-pen. As they observed the atrocities, clinically/physically cut off from the action, they were nevertheless simultaneously 'cast' as silent accomplices.

The aim of all these strategies was to create an intimacy between the spectator and the action which broke down traditional barriers, increasing the level of audience involvement. This was calculated to maximise the intensity of their relationship to the action, and emphasise the social and political implications of the material.

Feeling that you are sharing the same space with the actors accentuates the sense of being 'present' for the spectator. When spectators can see each other, they become an echo chamber for reactions. This was as true at the Globe in the seventeenth-century as it is in modern theatre-in-the-round. In 1997 the Olivier auditorium at the Royal National Theatre in London was re-configured to in-the-round for a short season when Richard Eyre, then Artistic Director, suggested to Simon McBurney that he mount Theatre de Complicité's new production *The Caucasian Chalk Circle* there. McBurney 'screwed up his face in pain . . . and said "only if it can be done in the round".'[179] The circular space is, of course, central to the art of the storyteller, and Brecht's play is fundamentally rooted in storytelling.

Being in close proximity with spectators, however, is very exposing for actors, although a great test. Doing street theatre in Peru using a circular formation, McBurney recalls that 'wherever the performer looks they contact someone . . . [hence] the performer is singular, unaided, encircled by concentration; or exposed, alone, surrounded'.[180]

Working in-the-round makes the space very intimate, but also makes the performer extremely vulnerable. And, of course, forces them to keep on the move. The following exercise is variously known as 'the plate game', 'Lecoq's disc' or 'plateau', and is a stalwart of physical-based theatre workshops for cultivating spatial awareness and effective positioning. Lecoq developed the game originally to explore the possibilities of choric work.[181] I place a version of it here because in this reincarnation it serves also to give actors some experience of how theatre-in-the-round feels. It works really well after a game of NAME TAG, or CANE DANCING.

The plate game

You need eight or more for this to work effectively. Actors sit around a circular area of approx. 6-8 metres diameter.

Step 1

Firstly invite a volunteer to step into the circle as though entering the stage and make eye contact with everyone before exiting. As they exit they make eye contact with someone who becomes the next volunteer. Each person should ensure that they judge the moment of entry with a degree of dramatic tension, and leave the energy in the space when leaving.

Step 2

Now imagine the circle as a disc balancing on a central pin. (Place a set of keys or a matchbox in the centre if you wish.) Now one player enters the space but this time after making general eye contact they 'invite' another player to join them – purely through the eyes, not by gesture or speech.

The first person is 'leader' and the second 'chorus'. As the leader moves around, the chorus responds to his/her movements and maintains the balance between them. The disc must remain balanced at all times. So that if the leader moves towards the centre, the chorus does likewise, or if the leader moves around the edge so does the chorus, but always opposite the leader to maintain the balance.

As the leader changes the speed, level, direction, or rhythm of his/her movement, the chorus does likewise. Actors should try and keep an awareness of the spectators whilst maintaining eye contact with each other in the circle.

Step 3

When the chorus feels the moment is right s/he stops moving and this is the cue for the leader to leave the circle. The chorus now becomes the new leader and invites another player to join him/her.

Step 4

A further development is to play the game up to Step 3. When the chorus stops moving s/he joins the leader and a third player enters the circle. The new player becomes the leader, and the others the chorus moving in response. Now the disc has to be balanced in relation to one leader and two chorus.

It is the leader who next decides the moment is right to join the chorus and a fourth player enters to become the new leader. We are now playing with one leader and three chorus. You can carry on until you have a leader and a seven-strong chorus. Any more becomes unwieldy in this size of circle.

Try this exercise with actors standing rather than sitting around the circle. When the eyes of the spectator are at the same level as the actors the effect is more intimidating for the actors, and more intimate for the spectators. You can go on to play this exercise with actors and spectators in different configurations; this tests your ability to remain in communication with your partners on stage whilst making contact with the audience.

The idea of keeping events public lies at the heart of opening up the stage-spectator relationship, whatever the material – comic, serious, tragic, absurd. The tripartite focus on self, partners and audience is an essential principle for acting.

Developing such openness is a prerequisite for physical theatre. And the experiential understanding of this will build strong foundations in your ability to draw an audience into the stage-play world on an imaginative level. Involving the spectator at the sensory and visceral levels requires a deeper understanding of the possibilities inherent in somatic work, and the following section deals with cultivating the inner sensitivity necessary.

The Sentient Body

The Sentient Body

The true actor recognises that real freedom occurs at the moment when what comes from the outside and what is brought from within make a perfect blending.[182]

In this section we approach the less tangible dimensions of rhythm, sound, and emotion essential to the actor's craft.

Grotowski and Brook both refer to how a cat's impulse to jump happens simultaneously with the jump, and how performance requires a similar fusion of intention and action (even when that action culminates in speech). The separation of impulse from movement, action, gesture, sound, word is an analytical tool enabling us to break down the process of acting, rather as articulation breaks down an action in order to better understand the physical process. So the separation here of rhythm, sound and emotion is theoretical. They synthesise in the body, and work synergetically on the audience.

'A work of art, understood dynamically, is . . . [the] process of arranging images in the feelings and mind of the spectator', wrote Sergei Eisenstein, and it is this dynamic process which distinguishes a vital work of art from a lifeless one.[183] Rhythm and emotion are at the heart of this dynamic process, sources of energy that fuel vitality and touch us as audience on a sensory plane. And sound, as the elemental vibratory contact between stage and spectator, provides another energy which, through the actor's breathing voice, brings intimacy, collapsing the distance of the purely visual.

The fact that rhythmic, sonic and emotional realms reside in the body and can be accessed spontaneously and directly through somatic rather than cerebral means is a fundamental premise of somatic work.

The practical work in this section takes actors a few steps further, or deeper, than those in the previous sections. Some of the more complex exercises assume both a degree of familiarity between a group, and experience of the earlier practical work. Ideas for exercises here are, as elsewhere, open to modification according to your own ways of working. But for the most part they will bear repetition, not least because every time you do them they will yield something new, not as a product, but as part of the process of discovering a creative self.

Since the study of acting is as much a process of self-discovery as acquiring techniques, self-deception in training will lead to insincerity on stage. Be as honest as you can with every exercise, both in the doing of it and the reflecting on it. We all know when we have cut corners, or held back, or been negative about ourselves or someone else. Good acting requires generosity and humanity as well as a resonant body and a resonant voice.

RHYTHM

Theatre is rhythm.[184]

In theatre, alternating patterns of stasis and dynamism, relaxation and tension, speeding up and slowing down, constitute a constant play of rhythms. Hence Meyerhold's belief that the gift of rhythm was the most important attribute for a director. Rhythm, however, is intangible. Meyerhold used the analogy of a bridge: 'When you look at a bridge you seem to see a leap imprinted in metal, that is, a process, and not something static. The dynamic tension expressed in the bridge is the main thing. The same applies to performing'.[185] Rhythm is there all the time, *in* time; we cannot see it but are affected by it, this play of tensions in the scenic space, between light and shade, sound and silence, and of course between the living bodies of actors, all working together to hold and, ultimately, transfix the audience.

As a musician, Meyerhold recognised a correspondence between stage rhythm and musical composition[186] similar to Appia's: 'When stage pictures take on spatial forms dictated by the rhythms of music they are not arbitrary but on the contrary have the quality of being inevitable'.[187] Adolphe Appia (the Swiss architect and musician who revolutionised scenic space and lighting at the beginning of the twentieth century) saw research into music-as-composition as the basis for rejuvenating theatre.

Influenced by Appia, Copeau harboured a faith in the essential relationship between music and dramatic art, and consequently incorporated music as an essential component in educating his actors. Yet his attempts to fuse the two ran into difficulties.

Copeau was not a musician himself. Frustrated by the lack of a 'master musician' with whom he could work with his actors, he turned to

Dalcroze's Eurhythmics,[188] a systemised approach to the relationship between music and gymnastics designed to promote a common mental and musical rhythm between actors. However, Eurhythmics was too particular a specialism: a musical beat leads movement, and tonal quality inflects it, so that music controls the actor rather than the actor controlling the movement. When music carries the performers their work becomes uniform, they don't find their own internal rhythms. Copeau also found it encouraged actors to invest too much feeling into their movements.

Suzanne Bing, Copeau's principle collaborator, articulates the fundamental problem they were trying to solve: 'The rhythmic sense must come from the inside. Exercises are always unsatisfactory if they do not exercise the outer manifestation of the *inner sense* that one wants to develop'.[189]

Meyerhold encountered a similar problem when he directed his actors to music. The music led the movement. Watching circus acrobats he noticed they use music primarily for rhythmic support, without it there would be catastrophe, but what happens, he wondered, if you take it away?[190] In other words could you cultivate an inner sense of rhythm? His answer was to translate the concept of a musical phrase into movement training, not giving actors music to interpret via movement, but educating them to control the rhythmic shape of *any* movement.

In Biomechanics actors learn a somatic understanding of the potential internal dynamic of any movement phrase through the sequence: '*otkas – posyl – stoika*'. This is the 'form' of every action, movement or gesture. The content can vary, as can the pace. Meaning is modified according to where the accent is placed in a movement, as we shall see. But this basic structure applies to every single action.

The *otkas* is a slight movement in the opposite direction, sometimes translated as 'preparation'.[191] You see a similar effect in cartoons as when Road Runner, for example, swings his whole body backwards before shooting forwards. The *posyl* is the action itself, whether this is as simple as bringing a cup to the lip or as large as a complete trajectory across space. The *stoika* is a definite stop which brings the whole phrase to a close, sometimes more like a comma than a full stop, because the *stoika* has to leave room for the next phrase to begin.

In Biomechanics this tripartite phrasing of movement is taught as a procedure for the whole body as a preparatory exercise. It is then applied to phrasing in the études.[192]

Meyerhold's *otkas – posyl – stoika* bears a striking resemblance to the central principle of 'Jo-Ha-Kyu' in Zeami's *Secret Tradition of the Noh*, the fourteenth-century manual of Noh actor training.[193] Jo-Ha-Kyu is the law of changing quality in every aspect of performance: the play as a whole, each individual scene, every movement phrase, each word: *Jo* is the quality of setting up, beginning; *Ha* is the quality of activity, of doing, which develops and passes into *Kyu*, the quality of apotheosis, or state of climax.

Although it is easy to draw parallels with the Western concept of classic narrative structure in relation to a whole play, or even a scene, there is more to Jo-Ha-Kyu than the notion of beginning, middle and end. The Noh master Zeami derived his concept from observing natural patterns: 'Every phenomenon in the universe develops itself through a certain progression, even the cry of a bird and the noise of an insect follow this progression . . . called Jo, Ha, Kyu'.[194] It is a physical law of unfolding and conclusion.

On the macro-scale this relates to the overall flow of a play within which the smaller climaxes and hiatuses of individual scenes are contained. The whole dynamic pattern can seem like a roller-coaster in a play like *Macbeth* or *King Lear*, yet always moving towards the inevitable 'Kyu' of the final act. Each scene also has its own similar internal structure in condensed form.

On the micro-scale 'Jo-Ha-Kyu' refers to the interior qualitative dynamic of each move and utterance, as the next exercise illustrates.

Lift the arm (No. 2)

Consider the notion that each movement contains a whole story; try lifting your arm from your side to the level of your shoulder and modifying the tensions it contains, accelerating at the beginning, for example, or towards the moment of stopping.

You will feel a different shape to the 'flow' of the movement with each modification. The placing of the tension creates a dynamic, and different rhythmic patterns will inflect the gesture with different meanings, so that each person doing this exercise will generate different 'stories' for what is essentially the same movement. The 'form' of the movement is artificially created, and when an individual then decides on a context for the gesture, it will take on meaning or 'content'. (NB: The same applies to any utterance: try the same experiment saying the sound 'Aaahh'.)

Yoshi Oida states that the principle of Jo–Ha–Kyu 'helps actors to structure their feelings, actions and speeches in a natural way'.[195] Meyerhold's principle of a movement phrase, *otkas-posyl-stoika*, has a similar benefit. The slight move in the opposite direction via the *otkas* also gives actions a sense of an internal impulse which propels the actor into the action/moment. In speech this can be translated as an intake of breath.

This next exercise illustrates the principle of phrasing a movement through space.

Aeroplane [196]

Use a diagonal trajectory across the working area from corner to corner to maximise the length of the 'runway'. It is best to work without shoes.

The first volunteer stands with their arms outstretched like the wings of a plane. They run from one corner to the other. As when you lifted your arm, you are exploring the possibilities of pacing the movement. Here, the idea is to find the optimum moment to accelerate and decelerate so you come to a non-hazardous stop at the opposite corner.

Observing this exercise, you will see considerable variance in both the speed of the 'run' and the point at which the 'brakes' go on and the movement slows to a stop – everyone will fly their 'aeroplane' differently. The ideal is to find a point about two-thirds of the way across where the brakes come on, but this is a suggestion not an imperative. You will find a slight movement in the opposite direction prior to 'take-off' helps to shape the movement.

Some actors plod very heavily across the space. It is helpful to them to point this out. You shouldn't be able to hear the feet in this exercise when done properly.

Repetition is essential. Once players have grasped the intention they find a few practice runs enable them to feel when they over-accelerate, or leave deceleration too late and end up in the wall. Improvement through practice is tangible.

In terms of Meyerhold's principle of a movement phrase, this exercise illustrates the preparatory *otkas,* the action of the *posyl* and the arrival or conclusion of the *stoika.* What it also shows is how the use of the 'brakes' actually shapes the movement: varying the points at which you accelerate/decelerate will render different shapes to the overall movement. You can, of course, play around with this, and that is where the actor's creativity comes into play.

The Russian word *tormos* used in Biomechanics is rather more complex than 'brakes', nevertheless it is about controlling the degree of energy or tension used to modulate the action. This concept resembles Barba's notion of 'energy in time', where a performer holds the dead weight back and creates oppositional tensions, thereby increasing dilation of the body, and magnifying presence. The quality of the control and the choice of placing the climax, or accent, on the movement phrase is the actor's individual creative decision (which can, of course, be negotiated with a 'director'). The idea of phrasing every gesture and action in this way is fundamental to creating dynamic movement on stage.

Although it may sound mechanical to employ the *otkas – posyl – stoika* for every action and gesture it is paradoxically a technical discipline which offers room for individual creativity. The actor acquires rhythmic control of his/her body but, unlike a dancer, creates his/her own steps.

Controlling the rhythmic flow of movement is complemented by working on inner rhythms of the body. Observing the different ways in which the Odin actors strung together a chain of exercises, Barba realised the variations were not due to differences in the ways they executed the exercises but to 'individual differences in rhythm'.[197] The first step towards finding your own internal rhythmic sense is to play around with different rhythms.

Rhythm isn't any more a particular gift than presence. The problem in the West is that by the age of three or four, rhythm is blocked by constant sitting, often in front of a TV, so that many of us are even unfamiliar with our own rhythms of walking. It isn't that we do not have an inherent sense of rhythm, but little in our culture encourages us to use it, so we suffer from rhythmic amnesia.

Activating our rhythmic sensibility, even through simple clapping exercises, is a primary route towards discovering what we have forgotten.

Body rhythms

The heart beats in 'iambs', units of rhythm which have two stresses, which we can represent syllabically as 'di–dum'. Clap the rhythm of your own heartbeat. Notice those of the others in the room but don't allow theirs to affect yours if they seem different.

In pairs, sit comfortably and feel each other's pulse in the wrist. Then clap your partner's pulse rhythm. Listen to any difference between that and when they clap yours. See if you can clap theirs whilst they clap yours without falling into each other's rhythm. If you do, work out why. Is it that your pulses are exactly the same?

Learning to maintain your own, or a character's, rhythm whilst on stage with others is essential. Rhythmic awareness builds concentration, and activates a focus on listening.

Clap-clap

Passing a clap around the circle and attempting to maintain a steady beat is a well-known workshop exercise. It can be made more complex by allowing any player to change the direction in which the clap is going whilst maintaining the beat. You can also send more than one clap round the circle at any one time.

Step 1

A volunteer claps a very short rhythmic phrase which s/he then constantly repeats. S/he is followed by others in turn, each augmenting the previous phrases with one of their own until a clapping soundscape is created involving everyone. (In larger groups you may want to use stamping or other ways of using the body percussively to open up possibilities.)

Step 2

When each person is clapping, the first person changes their phrase, and so on round the circle. Keep repeating this cycle. As you become familiar with simple rhythmic patterns, try to create more complex ones.

Step 3

Now divide the group in half. One half of the group establish a rhythmic pattern on four beats, what we call in music 4/4 time, which is basically a count of one/two/three/four, but they clap only on the first and third beat. You 'hear' the other beats in your head.

The other half establish a pattern on three beats, 3/4 or waltz time, i.e. a count of one/two/three, but they clap only on the first beat.

Start with both on the first beat, clapping together, each group maintaining their own rhythm. If you fall into chaos, start again! When each group is managing to clap consistently in their own rhythm, let them take it in turns to quieten down so that they can hear the other group. Then, when it's working, raise the overall volume, allowing a crescendo to peak, and then let it die down.

Step 4

Next comes the difficult bit! Each player establishes a four-beat rhythm with their feet, by stepping or stamping. Then they clap in a three-beat rhythm over the top of this. You are highly likely to fail – but don't worry, this is normal. Given a good deal of practice, or a genetic disposition to creating polyrhythms, you may be able to accomplish this. If so, try stamping only on the first and third beats with the feet, and clapping on just the first beat of the hands' three-beat pattern. And go on to develop more complex patterns.

Doing things where we fail is important. We are so hung up on getting things right, we tend to focus on the result or product rather than the process. Rhythm is all about process.

Rhythms work in cycles. We are very used to set musical beat-patterns in the West, and consequently our music has developed along those lines. The syncopations of twentieth-century jazz rhythms have their roots in African cultures. In Brazil, Cuba, Korea and India, rhythm is not taught by counting but by talking syllables. So, for example, Indian drummers learn a sixteen-beat cycle, dhin-dhin-da-dhin etc., which becomes embedded in their body; they learn to keep this in them like a poem over which they then improvise.

Despite the seemingly scientific simplicity of Meyerhold's *otkas – posyl – stoika*, a movement phrase should not be constructed mechanically. Absorbed through practice, its tripartite structure becomes embedded, so that rather like the Indian drummer with his sixteen-syllable cycle, it eventually becomes second nature. It works when the actor understands that discipline and technique paradoxically open up channels for creativity. Rhythm has to be felt, not thought.

In addition to the collection of sticks, boxes and bottles used in previous exercises, it's useful to have a range of percussion tools to play with. Instruments don't necessarily have to be bought: anything that can be banged, shaken or rattled can be effective, a jam-jar half filled with lentils is a good substitute for a rain-stick for example, although it's handy to have things like a bell or triangle, the odd drum or cymbal. The cardboard and plastic tubes mentioned earlier can also be played.

The next sequence is a complex exercise which incorporates exercises from previous work before moving on to use percussion. Make sure actors have a strong grasp of the concept of FIXED POINTS and are already familiar with TUBE SCULPTURES (both of these exercises occur in SECTION TWO in BODY IN SPACE and PLAY respectively). Ideally they should have experience of working on COMPLICITÉ, and discovering the alchemy in playing with different partners. And of course the previous exercises in this section are also a useful preface.

Rhythm-scape I

Play the exercise called 'Tube Sculptures', with either tubes or sticks. Work in pairs initially, creating moving abstract sculptures. Try not to let either person lead, but let playfulness generate what happens between you. Let the varying rhythms that emerge carry the movements.

When you construct a sequence of movements from this work, choose units with a variety of rhythmic patterns, for example rolling the tubes, stepping over them and passing them will all have different tensions and tempos.

Once you have a sequence, go back over each unit of action and construct these as individual phrases of movement, applying the otkas-posyl-stoika. Advanced groups may be able to modulate each phrase using tormos, if they have grasped the concept. Then mark the moments between each unit of action, i.e. the stoika, with a fixed point, so wherever the tubes are at that moment they become still, making a brief pause in the overall sequence.

[NB: I find it more productive to use the Russian terms rather than their translations. The English equivalents (preparation, action, stop and brakes) do not have the same impact or resonance. Student actors soon learn to incorporate the Russian words into a common vocabulary which they use in reflecting and critiquing their work.]

Don't rush this exercise. The results, when shown, will demonstrate a whole spectrum of rhythmic variations, and the fixed points mark the shift between each rhythmic change. You can work in larger groups once the foundation has been laid between two players, or swap partners, and the results will be different again: the chemistry between players will influence the outcome. And whilst you may find individuals have a predilection for certain rhythmic patterns, working with new partners opens up the possibilities of finding others.

The internal dynamic of these rhythmic sculptures correlate to the notion of scenes, each with its own individual Jo-Ha-Kyu.

Following on from this work, distribute various items of percussion. Groups of three to five are about right for this next development.

Rhythm-scape 2

Actors now improvise with the instruments to create a soundscape containing a variety of rhythmic patterns. Use the 'template' of the previous exercise to create these step by step, first exploring the sound of each instrument before playing them together. The secret is to let arbitrary improvisation develop before attempting to choreograph the whole piece.

When you have selected several units that please you, go back over them and employ the otkas-posyl-stoika principle to structure each one into a complete phrase. Modulating the phrases here (using tormos) can be done by increasing and decreasing volume and/or the intensity of the rhythm. When you string the phrases together mark the transition between each one with a slight pause, i.e. a fixed point.

Play each composition and discuss the results. It may be that some groups create very busy soundscapes. Encourage them to remember that rhythm still underpins a pause, just as when hearing (counting) the beats between claps in the earlier exercise.

The sentient understanding of moments of transition or shifts in rhythm gained through this work is immensely valuable. Firstly, it prepares actors for sensing the moment at which an improvisation needs to move on. In improvisation 'as important as the actual material thrown up by the scene is the moment chosen for breaking it and beginning another. There is a moment in almost every improvisation where things reach a head and are moving quickly towards a resolution. If one can trigger off the new scene at just that moment, the actor's energy-equipment is instinctively brought into play. Improvisations like these feed on . . . their sense of danger'.[198]

This is true also in text work, where beats and units of action constitute the internal dynamic of a scene, and actors need to be able to recognise and play the shifts between them. This exercise can therefore be applied to text work.

Secondly, the application of the *otkas – posyl – stoika* principle to sound rhythms as well as movement leads actors to a keen understanding of the importance of structuring speeches as well as actions.

An ability to play in rhythms other than your own relates to neutrality and working outside the habitual. Stick work is a useful avenue for developing rhythmic sensitivity in actors. As you play with the stick you discover a rhythmic relationship with an object. When working with a partner, as in CANE DANCING, you discover a rhythmic relationship with another actor.

Observation and analysis of rhythms in nature is endemic to the work of many practitioners. It is the core of Lecoq's philosophy: he advises acting students 'never to lose their curiosity . . . about the structures of life and life's phenomena'.[199] Working mimetically to discover the internal energy and rhythm of elements, animals, any living form, is central to Lecoq's teaching. He calls it 'identification', and he regards this dimension of mime as a primary method of acquiring knowledge: 'Corporeal impression is more important than corporeal expression'.[200]

The aim of mime in Lecoq's philosophy is for the actor 'to identify himself with the world by re-enacting it with his entire being'.[201] Like Copeau's actors, Lecoq students re-enact not only people, but animals, plants, trees, colours, the elements. Lecoq's maxim is 'everything moves', even the apparently static mountain. The actor must go beyond the literal image to find the inner dynamic of matter in terms of space, rhythm and breathing.

The earlier neutral mask exercise invites the masked actor to walk through mist and convey that s/he sees the sea.[202] The aim is to sense the rhythms of the sea in the body, as though the sea lives inside you, and to breathe *with* the sea. Identifying somatically with the rhythms of matter and transposing these into breathing, action and sound is a fundamental exercise of Lecoq's which can be applied to virtually any material thing.

Lecoq has investigated the dynamics of nature in movement terms in considerable depth, and you are referred to his book, *The Moving Body* (2000), in which he describes the methods he uses for practical analysis of nature, for a more detailed exposition of his theories and practical work. Very briefly, he designates water as: 'a moving, resisting force, which can only be experienced by struggling with it'; fire as both combustion and flame, whose 'dramatic justification lies in anger'; air, he says 'is found through flight' and is 'an element which gives support', whilst earth is clay which can be compressed, smoothed and stretched.[203]

Bear these definitions in mind when you undertake the next exercise.

Earth/fire/air/water

In this exercise actors search for somatic identification with the four elements within a collective. Nevertheless, the responsibility lies with each actor to display their own identification with the elements, rather than imitate another actor.

Designate each of the elements to four corners of the space. A group of actors move in a clockwise direction. They must keep close in a pack, rather as in the exercise 'Shoal of Fish', with the leader changing as necessary on the turns. As they pass through each designated element they become earth, fire, air or water. The rest of the group observe.

At the zenith of each element they should convey their impression with the greatest intensity. And as they move towards the next element, the previous one lessens in degree before the new one embraces them.

In your feedback, discuss which actors gave a more convincing impression of each element. Sometimes there are two or three equally remarkable renditions of an element which are individually very different.

Then another group circumnavigates the room in the same way. Each time you discuss the exercise, try to come to a consensus on what 'works' and what doesn't. And each group that follows should try and put this into practice.

Provided you have an experienced group, invite individual actors to find the dynamic of any element and progress to exploring other material things. To do so with inexperienced actors is counter-productive as this is a difficult exercise which can induce the 'inhibition factor'.

Most practitioners use analogies with animal movement. Laban suggests that actors 'consider and compare' the movement rhythms of animals in order to observe the variations in intensity of energy spending. He points out how each genus of animal is 'restricted to a small range of typical qualities', whereas humans are much more varied. Cats appear relaxed and flexible when jumping, a horse will be more tense and concentrated. A man can jump like either, or at least imitate both dynamically.[204]

Observing the rhythms of different animals forces us to be more accurate when imitating them. And the more accurate the mimicry, the more precise the use of the body. When actors played a shed of cows, a thicket of blackberries or a squealing pig in Theatre de Complicité's *The Three Lives of Lucie Cabrol*, the accuracy of their work was not showily athletic, but rhythmically convincing.

It is important to be equally accurate when imitating people.

Copy walk

Work without shoes for this. Walking round the room, criss-cross the space. Notice how you are walking. Find your own natural rhythm, the pace and flow which feels most natural and comfortable, as though you could walk all day. Now exaggerate your own walk, emphasising points of tension, whether you place more weight on your left or right foot. And return to normal walking.

Now in pairs, X walks behind Y. Observe how your partner's body gets involved in the process of walking. What happens in their hips? Do they swing their arms? Does the ball or heel of the foot go down first? Begin to imitate them. Be precise.

Now start to exaggerate their walk-mannerisms. Again, be as precise as you can. Don't invent anything that isn't there, and don't accentuate one thing more than any other, particularly if it has comic potential. Gradually all the Ys drop out and watch the room-full of crazy walks!

Then swap over and replay.

Rhythm is clearly a primary factor in character creation. And also in speaking text. The foundations laid in the practical work in this section can be followed up in relation to character and speech.

'Rhythm seems to be a language apart, and the rhythmic language conveys meaning without words'.[205] The place where this is clearest is comedy, what we call 'comic timing'. Comedy wastes no time, situations are set up very quickly, and an audience 'reads the rhythm'.[206]

The next two exercises follow on from COPY WALK. It is also useful to have done clapping rhythm work, particularly on syncopated rhythms.

Foot-steps [207]

You are working here to a rhythm of four beats, i.e. 1/2/3/4. Here you need your shoes on so that we can hear the beats of the steps. The volunteers do not speak, although they may make eye contact.

Step 1

Two people walk across the space diagonally in the same beat, ie 1/2/3/4. They appear to be in tune with one another!

Step 2

Now X steps on the beat, and Y on the off-beat. Now there appears to be some conflict between them.

Step 3

Now X walks on the beat, and Y starts out, but then suspends one step so as to go onto the off-beat. Alternatively Y can speed up a step to go onto the off-beat. This time they started out in tune, and then conflict developed.

The next improvisation picks up on the idea of alternating the beats to create different scenarios from the same material.

The interview – in four beats[208]

The following text is learnt by volunteers and played according to the three rhythmic versions given below. Don't add anything, and keep to the given timings.

The dialogue runs as follows (insert your own real answers):

X	Your name is?
Y	Says name
X	And your age?
Y	Gives age
X	Where do you live?
Y	Says where
X	Do you drive?
Y	Answers yes or no
X	Do you own a car?
Y	Answers yes or no

Now play this 'text' in the following versions:

- *Version 1   X speaks on the first beat. Y speaks on the third beat.*
- *Version 2   X speaks on the first beat. Y speaks on the second –*
  almost over the first.
- *Version 3   X speaks on the first beat. Y speaks on the fourth beat.*

Each rhythmic pattern will generate different characters and relationships. There are also hilarious moments when actors try so desperately to come in on the right beat that they trip over their words and say something inappropriate. And it is worth noting that comic moments frequently arise from 'mistakes' rather than from attempts to be funny.

This exercise is not only good fun but teaches very simply the principle that rhythm is a governing agent of meaning.

SOUND

Do not think of the vocal instrument itself, do not think of the words, but react – react with the body.[209]

The majority of practical work suggested so far in this book takes place in silence, although always, of course, accompanied by the sounds of people 'doing' – and breathing while they're doing! Part of the difficulty with the 4:33 exercise at the end of SECTION THREE is that it heightens the actuality of silence, for there is no tangible 'doing'. We seem to find silence intensely uncomfortable. Perhaps because we are so accustomed to noise in our lives, especially if we live in a city.

In order to appreciate sound we need to recognise the power of its counterpoint, yet real silence is never really silent, as this next exercise demonstrates.

Living silence

Take your time with this exercise. Make sure people are warm.

Lie on the floor and relax from feet up to head by contracting and releasing the sets of muscles in each 'zone', eg feet, calves, thighs, etc. Close your eyes.

Listen to the sounds in the room, others breathing, a clock ticking perhaps, the workshop leader padding round, a window rattling. Really absorb them, become as familiar with them as the surfaces of the room in the earlier exercise on controlling the space in section one. Pinpoint exactly where each sound comes from.

Now extend your aural field to what lies beyond the room in the same building, footsteps on corridors and stairs, doors opening and closing, computer keyboards tapping, pipes gurgling. Try only to listen to the sounds rather than imagine the corresponding activity.

Hear as much as you can, whilst still acknowledging the breathing and other sounds in the room.

Next go beyond the building. What's outside? Traffic, birds, people, an ambulance siren in the distance? It's as though you're stretching your ears. Hear them all. But don't lose aural touch with the sounds in the building and in the room.

Finally bring your attention back to the room and concentrate on the sounds there once more.

Just as in the exercise CONTROLLING THE SPACE, you notice things that normally pass you by. Focusing on sounds in this way is another aspect of awareness, and such work aids concentration. And if there is extraneous noise at any point, groups are more able to absorb it without being distracted if they have done this exercise regularly.

You have to train your ear in theatre as well as your body and voice. Aural awareness must be developed alongside visual and sensual awareness. Listening is, of course, fundamental. But we feel and respond to vibrations as well as hearing actual noise. It is worth noting that the Latin root of the word 'percussion' means 'through the skin'. A drum beat is an obvious example here, and in primal cultures the drum is a means of communication rather than simply a musical instrument, working on sensory as well as auditory wave-lengths.

The next exercise explores the idea of the body's own percussive possibilities and how we 'hear'.

Orchestral manoeuvres

Remain on the floor to begin with, and keep your eyes closed. The leader taps someone who then makes a sound using any part of the body, and the floor if they wish. The leader will tap people gently to indicate when they should join in (or hand out numbers before starting) with another sound. Keep it simple and gentle, a tap on the thigh or a click of the fingers is enough, until the whole group creates a quiet chorus of percussion.

At this stage, the exercise is deliberately low-key; the emphasis is on listening to the different sounds rather than energising them. When everyone is fully involved ask for a gradual increase in volume and then let it die away slowly. Enjoy listening to the final shreds of sound.

Now, eyes open, come to standing, and repeat the exercise making a new range of sounds. Keep them percussive rather than vocal at this stage, maybe stamping a foot or clapping hands. This time energise the sounds you make by using the whole body, and seeing how loud and soft you can make the 'orchestra'.

Differences in the two stages of this exercise relate to the degree in which listening changes, and how we respond when we see as well as hear, and also when we feel vibrations. Invariably a steady beat emerges to which the sounds conform. More advanced groups who have worked on rhythm may be able to work less rigidly with a beat, allowing sounds to be made more arbitrarily and punctuating the 'composition' with silence.

Reflect on the two stages and discuss them. Did either give the group a sense of unity? When did you forget to listen, or only hear part of what was going on? Be honest in your responses.

The following game activates more acute somatic/aural awareness as players listen for a specific sound.

Homing pigeons

In pairs decide on a sound each, abstract rather then literal, and very simple. Make them quite different, whatever springs to the mouth or fingers, no matter how daft. Make sure you both know each other's sound. Decide who is X and who is Y. Now blindfold the Xs and then ask the Ys to spread out around the room well away from their partner. As Ys stand still, they each whisper their sound or 'percuss' very quietly, and the blind Xs have to locate their partner through the sea of whispers.

Swap over and replay.

Sometimes it is quite difficult to distinguish your partner's sound from the others. And what is fascinating about this exercise is the way the bodies of the 'pigeons' seeking their partners become so alert in their listening. This is partly to do with being blindfold, which of course activates a more acute sensory awareness. But it is a useful corollary to that notion of being 'alert in stillness', that state of readiness so essential to performance.

Suzanne Bing's mask exercises for Copeau's actors were often accompanied by vocalisation and bodily sound effects. Even Etienne Decroux, the mime purist, recognised the symbiotic relationship between movement and sound despite his insistence on vocal silence in mime: 'audible breathing, the pounding of heels, the click of the tongue against the roof of the mouth or against teeth, seem always to have been a part of Decroux's mime performance'.[210] More recently in dance, which we generally assume to be irreversibly locked into using music as accompaniment, Christopher Bruce (Artistic Director of Ballet Rambert) choreographed a piece, *For Those Who Die Like Cattle,* which dispensed with music and used only the sound of the dancers' feet and the percussive sounds of their bodies as accompaniment.

The concept of vocal mime takes the sounds naturally emitted during the course of moving and develops them into expressive forms. You will find when you do an action and release a sound simultaneously, the action becomes stronger. Abstract movements work better than behavioural gestures, such as nodding the head or pointing a finger, which are gestures emphasising a thought rather than purely somatic impulses.

Action sounds

Move spontaneously and discover what sound is released. Doing something energetic like a squat jump will provoke a different sound from rolling on the floor, for example.

Discovering a sound as an extension of movement in this way is a method of exploring the route from impulse to action to sound, and to word eventually. Don't worry about how bizarre the noise is. Sighs, cries and groans are all part of vocalisation and, as Artaud recognised, sometimes these can express more than language.

Laban's observation that 'sounds accompanying working actions are the audible result of an inner mood'[211] is relevant here. For Laban, the inner attitude of an action or person can be accessed through the external: copying a physical manifestation and letting the voice out will release an inner attitude. Freeing the voice via the body was the approach of Littlewood's Theatre Workshop where voice training was allied to movement training: everything was done through Laban. And Jean Newlove, their movement coach, has a useful chapter in her book *Laban for Actors and Dancers* (1993: 99-107) which provides exercises for exploring sound and gesture through Laban's 'eight basic effort actions'.

Sound tag

You can apply the idea of action releasing sound to a game of tag in which players make a sound when they tag someone. Making several players

*'taggers' will liven up the proceedings and create plenty of noise. Adapting
'Pass the Tag' (from section three: the body in space) to incorporate sound is
a further variation.*

A game of NO-BALL TENNIS (from SECTION THREE: PLAY) in which
physical reactions are accompanied by vocalisation which comes out of the
movement, is another playful way to begin work on freeing the voice. We
are used to hearing tennis players grunt and sigh after all.

Just as physical training can lead to a mechanical approach, voice training can trap the actor in technique. Technical proficiency is frequently
attained at the expense of the emotive and intuitive self, wedding the
actor to rules and strictures about breathing and voice production. Play-
orientated vocal work is a less mechanical avenue to discovering the power
and spirit of the voice.

Operatic musical chairs[212]

*Use opera as the music for the game – something like the 'three tenors' or
Lesley Garret will do nicely. Play a game of musical chairs with the added
proviso that when you lose your chair, i.e. when you are out, you sing an aria.
Imitate the vigour and verve of the opera singers. You may be ecstatic or
desperate that you've lost your chair.*

Many practitioners see voice as an extension of movement and, as such,
vocal action rather than simply the articulation of speech,[213] for the voice
is produced by bodily movement, however slight: both respiration and
movement originate in the pelvic region. Sounds that tennis players make,
for instance, are allied to expulsions of breath accompanying physical effort.
Vocal action means working on the voice as an expressive channel alongside movement rather than training the voice *per se*.

'Proper voice work is very physical,' asserts Patsy Rodenburg, Voice
Coach at the Royal National Theatre: '[It] makes use of the whole body
from head to toe . . . speaking and singing are really the end results of a
whole series of reflexive physical actions and body placement which you
simply must become aware of to gain mastery and control over your vocal
instrument'.[214] The common denominator is breathing.

Most actors are familiar with preparatory exercises which alternate the
three breathing states of in, out, and held, drawing the air into the lower

lungs by expanding the diaphragm (abdomen) and into the upper region by dilating the rib cage (thorax). These are a beneficial method of relaxing the body as well as preparation for vocalising, and can be effective in warm-ups. The most important thing is that actors breathe using 'total respiration', i.e. both abdominal and thoracic, and have an awareness of how their own breathing operates, how to place the voice and amplify it using the natural bodily resonators.[215]

Just thinking about voice as action and the notion of its having a spatial dimension gives us another zone to play in. We can all recall testing an echo in a cave or tunnel with a shout, the wonder of hearing our own voice reverberate. Sending sounds into imagined spaces encourages you to think of sound in terms of shape, and helps in training to place the voice. Sending a sound through a wide tunnel or a narrow tunnel, across the sea or up a mountain, makes different demands on the breath and facial muscles. And the idea of sound as action can be harnessed in trying to overturn a chair or sweep the floor. You won't succeed of course, but invoking the imagination in voice work is as important as in physical training, and you may discover something about the way volition affects the voice. Always be aware of what happens in the body. Generally if the body is static the sound will have less power. Let the body accentuate the sound produced.

Both Grotowski and Lecoq encouraged actors to use mimicry, always rooted in the principle that any sound must pass through the whole body. Accuracy is just as crucial here as in mimed actions. Try mimicking the sound of dripping water, shovelling gravel, starting a car, any animal. It is the reciprocal relationship between voice and movement which needs to be playfully explored, fed by visual and aural observation.

Decroux's one-time collaborator Jean-Louis Barrault, repudiated the rule of silence in mime, pointing out that sound is the result of breath. He went on to implement Artaud's theory of the *Kabbale*, a respiratory process from the Hebrew Kabbala, and it was this which prompted him to designate the navel as the focal point for movement, in contradistinction to Decroux's emphasis on the spine. Fusing Decroux's grammar of mime with this respiratory technique and his own concept of character creation enabled Barrault to develop work which epitomised the notion of the 'total actor'. His mime pieces exploited the organic link between sound and action, so that as performers struggled against waves created physically by others, for example, they also vocalised the sound of water.

Steven Berkoff frequently emulates this way of working, for example in the opening sequence of *Hamlet:* 'We hear the wind tearing round the turrets. It is the breath of the actors. They make the wind. They act as orchestra, both physically and psychically'.[216] Similarly, when Dario Fo performs the starving Zanni, conjuring up an imaginary feast, he creates all the sound effects himself: 'syncopated sounds of gurgling stews and sizzling oils' . . . and 'musical vocalisations that resemble a jazz singer scatting his way through a song'.[217]

One way of approaching sound effects is to start by exploring individual words physically in some depth through the body, which is what happens in the next exercise.

Wind and sea

The aim of this exercise is to create a sense of a ball being swept along an empty beach. First of all, experiment with playing 'Ball on the Wind' (from section three: the body), and attempt to create the sounds of the wind as the ball is wafted round the circle, and the sea washing in and out on the 'beach'. This is likely to prove difficult, and you may find actors are tentative about making sounds.

Put the ball aside for the time being. Spread out around the room and remind yourself of the exercise of running from one side of the room to the other to displace the air (section three: the body in space).

Step 1

Imagine the air in the space moving as wind and move against it, finding where the resistances occur in the body, then let it blow you from behind. Play with this idea, surprising yourself by altering the strength of the wind and its direction. Notice what effects this has on the body and the breath. Be as precise as you can – as though your 'outside eye' can tell which strength and direction you're playing with at any time.

Let half the group watch and discuss the level of accuracy achieved and vice versa.

Step 2

Now attempt to 'be' the wind. This means finding what Lecoq calls the dynamic of wind, its internal energy and rhythm. Remember to involve the whole body. The more extreme your movements become the better at this stage.

As you begin to express the dynamic, emphasise your breathing, allowing sound to come with it. Explore the possibilities of that sound whilst continuing to move.

Let half the group watch again and discuss the results.

Step 3

Now repeat the exercise with the word sea. Imagine the air in the room moving as sea and explore how you move with or against it. Avoid any pretend swimming! Notice what happens to the body and the breath, and try to be precise.

Then progress to 'being' the sea, finding its dynamic in your movement. And finally let sounds emerge from your movements. Try to be as honest as you can with these. If you find yourself slipping into clichéd 'sea noises', which you might have made sitting in a chair, stop and repeat the previous steps.

Then split the group in half. One half vocalises the wind and half the sea whilst passing the ball between you as in 'Ball in the Air'. Try to maintain your own rhythm, so that wind and sea remain separate. Notice if there's a difference between this and your previous attempt at making the sound effects. Break up the circle so the ball is passed in a more arbitrary manner, to capture the idea of a ball blown along a beach.

Work like this takes time to develop, and requires a lack of inhibition. Many young actors are highly 'voice-inhibited'. Without words, they can be extremely expressive; as soon as they open their mouths they either clam up or mutter or gabble. What is worse, they seem to shrink physically too, and risk undoing all the previous work they've done.

To a certain extent with physical work, actors cannot see how well or badly they are performing an action; yet when they speak their auditory feedback tells them immediately. If we are self-conscious about our bodies we are even more self-conscious about our voice.

Hayley Carmichael puts her finger on the problem when she recalls her early training: 'I was quite happy to just be on stage and I could believe in anything that happened as long as I didn't open my mouth . . . as soon as I opened my mouth it was just Hayley . . . [I thought] it doesn't sound like another character. It sounds just like me'.[218] We identify *ourselves* with our voice, it represents us, our personality, our identity. The neutral mask might help erase habits and traits from the *body* yet there is no equivalent neutral mask for the *voice*.

'Never listen to your own voice,' says Grotowski, ' . . . if you listen to your own voice you block the larynx and block the processes of resonance'.[219] His vocal training taught actors to set in motion the whole system of resonances within the body, directing the voice towards the ceiling (from the mouth) or the wall (from the chest) and listening to what comes back, rather than what goes out.

The notion of liberating the voice in this way rests on the fact that vocal range is not limited to sounds produced by the larynx and vocal chords. Grotowski developed his actors' voices by using the body's natural resonators. The existence of these has been known in the East and Africa for centuries, but only recently rediscovered in Europe by Alfred Wolfsohn. Working with these resonators, Wolfsohn was able to extend the range of 'singers, actors and ordinary people . . . from two to eight octaves, and even nine'.[220]

There are five main resonators: the mouth, chest, stomach, the top and the back of the head, which all act as amplification chambers to carry the voice. Learning to compress the air into different resonators at will, and exploit inactive ones to swell the sound, was a focal point of Grotowski's early research and he acknowledged his debt to Wolfsohn. Grotowski's *Towards a Poor Theatre* (1975: 121-134) contains detailed exercises for working on the resonators and placing the voice, which can be practised individually. (These techniques are primarily about releasing the potency of the voice, the focus is on the voice in the whole body not merely the throat and larynx.)

Wolfsohn's research led him to the conclusion that 'the voice is not the function solely of any anatomical structure, but the expression of the whole personality',[221] which is why, of course, we identify so strongly with our own voice. His gifted pupil Roy Hart developed this research and founded The Roy Hart Theatre, which moved from London to France at around the same time as Peter Brook moved to Paris – both as a result of an invitation from Jean-Louis Barrault. In fact, it was Brook who took Grotowski to see Hart's work in the 1960s. Hart, Brook and Grotowski have all made significant inroads into the relationship between liberating the voice and psychic energy. Through using the body's natural resonators their actors have been able to tap 'a fuller and richer range of sound and emotion'.[222]

The Roy Hart Theatre's ideological approach lies in the way they have 'redefined the word "to sing" ',[223] recognising voice as the manifestation of the psyche, and an ethos which lies in confronting psychological difficulties through the voice. However, the voice is not separated from the body as the work embraces a high degree of physical involvement.

Ugly sounds are as valuable and valid as beautiful sounds: screaming and raw emotional expression are integral to the process. Consequently, their work challenges hegemonic acceptance of what is natural and pleasing. Performers not only seek to liberate their own tensions through sound, but also those of the audience. The Artaudian overtones are evident, and, like Artaud, members of the Roy Hart Theatre often receive a mixed reception. Enriquo Pardo, one of its members, performed *Hymn to Pan* in Stockholm in 1982, a piece which involved exploring his voice with sudden switches from animal to human, bestial to spiritual, with screams and cries. This succeeded in alienating some members of the audience, yet one review stated '[he] has created a mythological and poetic language'.[224]

You can't suddenly liberate the voice in an afternoon's workshop. Like mask work, the best route is to undertake a course run by an experienced practitioner. The next sequence of exercises gives a small taste of this sort of work, and is adapted from a workshop given by Guy Dartnell (who has trained with Roy Hart) which had a profound effect on a group of my student actors. The earlier exercise SPINE TAPPING is a good preface for this. But do also use breathing exercises first, paying attention to filling the lungs from both the diaphragm and thoracic areas.

Pass the note [225]

Playing a game of 'Sound Tag', and/or 'Ball on the Wind', with the addition of releasing a sound as you tag or throw the ball will help free up the voice first.

Step 1

Stand in a circle. One person sings a note and passes it to the next and so on round the circle. Make sure you look into your partner's eyes as you pass and receive the note. Think of it as a present being given.

You might notice how males and females tend to alter the octave, men lowering a note passed by a woman, and women raising one passed by a man. We have in-built cultural conditioning that causes us to use our vocal range according to perceptions of gender, males using the lower register and females the higher.

Step 2

Pass the note again and this time try to keep it in the same octave. Men may have to find their falsetto voice, and women their contralto or baritone register. This may cause laughter, partly out of embarrassment. Actors may be surprised at what comes out when they go beyond the normal limits of their range. It is extremely useful to find the extent of your whole range and be able to utilise it, women especially, as many young female actors have a tendency to overuse the higher register.

Step 3

Once you have completed a few circuits, invite actors to change the note by sliding up or down the scale before passing it on. So an actor takes the note from the previous person, and explores it to the whole group as s/he alters the note before passing it on to the next person.

Allow the notes to be 'impure'. The aim is not to create a perfectly sung note, but to play with the note in a spontaneous manner as a vocal sound, and let the idiosyncrasies of your attempts to change it shine through. You may find a break in the voice creates something interesting, for example. Exaggerate any peculiarities that emerge and develop them. Each person may therefore take a minute or so to receive, play with and pass on the note.

The energy required for this is quite intense, don't let it flag. Try to feel you are filling the space with the sound, in a similar way to your work on presence. This may mean increasing the volume, but it is also about releasing the latent power of the voice.

Step 4

In the next round, exaggerate the body movements that have started to accompany the note/sound. The leader may stop individuals and encourage them to explore the possibilities inherent in the sound in relation to its emotional qualities. This is difficult to describe in print, but will become apparent if you have followed each step through.

As the sounds produced become more complex, they acquire an emotional resonance beyond the everyday which can be developed. It has nothing to do with what an actor might be feeling, and everything to do with the spontaneous creativity of the moment. In some instances, the essence of a character can start to emerge, as voice and movement synthesise.

The following extract from a student actor, writing after this exercise, describes the effects:

We found ways of making noises previously undiscovered, and began to tap into hidden meanings and impulses which get obscured by words with literal meanings. Often the sounds which seemed as if they were going wrong created the greatest emotional depth. These were particularly powerful if they occurred on the break of someone's voice, a previously unused sound which they would have normally thought of as embarrassing, but proved to have the greatest emotional qualities.

In sound-making exercises like this we are searching 'to discover how the human voice can vibrate in a manner that matches certain emotional experience'.[226] Freeing the voice in this way not only alerts us to its inherent physicality, the way it can move through the body like a wave, but just as crucially its psychological impact, how a wave of sound flowing through us awakens deeper sensibilities. When the voice then meets language, it becomes an emotional probe, seeking sonorities and vibrations beyond literal meaning.

Acknowledging the para-linguistic properties of language leads us into the realm of sound as poetry. Poets recognise that the fabric of language has emotional codes and threads beyond the personal or even public. As Ted Hughes points out, the *tone* of a sound transmits more than its semantic meaning: 'a simple syllable can transmit volumes'.[227] Hughes suggests there is a 'common tonal consciousness' which operates in the same way as the Jungian collective consciousness.

It was this idea of a universal language of communication that dominated Peter Brook's experiments in the early 1970s.

The first year of Brook's International Centre of Theatre Research, based in Paris, was devoted to the 'study of the structures of sound',[228] which culminated in the project *Orghast*, performed at the ancient tombs of Darius the Great at Shiraz in Iran (then Persia). During the rehearsal process, actors were given fragments of archaic languages to work on, including Ancient Greek and Latin, and Avesta, one of the atavistic Persian languages. Brook writes of how the actors brought an emotional faculty to bear on these alien linguistic patterns 'scanning them with . . . sensibility', so that gradually hidden rhythms and 'latent tides of emotion swelled up and shaped the phrases until the actor found himself speaking . . . with increasing force and conviction'.[229] Semantic meaning still evaded the actor, but 'every actor found it possible to play the words with a deeper and richer sense of meaning than if he had known what they were meant to say.'[230]

As part of this search into the somatic roots of language Brook brought in the poet Ted Hughes to invent a new language, called Orghast, which exploited the possibilities of tones and sounds without being dependent on meaning. (A.C.H. Smith has written brilliantly about this and the whole project in his book *Orghast at Persepolis*.) Hughes's task was to find sounds corresponding to abstract ideas; he knew that 'the deeper into language one goes, the more dominated it becomes by purely musical modes, and the more dramatic it becomes – the more unified with total states of being and with the expressiveness of physical action.'[231]

Dialogue is not simply to explain but to express. Playing with the tonal potential of language and its sonorous and rhythmic qualities is vital to finding channels of expression.

Invented languages, such as those used in STICK STORIES, have a fulsome tradition in European theatre via the commedic legacy. The touring Commedia troupes routinely combined a number of different Italian dialects, and the physicality of the performance in foreign countries was helped along by the use of *grammelot*.[232] Dario Fo is a modern exponent of this kind of made-up language, defining it as a 'babel of sounds which, nonetheless, manages to convey a sense of speech . . . *Grammelot* indicates the onomatopoeic flow of a speech, articulated without rhyme or reason, but capable of transmitting, with the aid of particular gestures, rhythms and sounds, an entire, rounded speech'.[233]

Invented languages offer a degree of freedom and licence. And Dario Fo points out their usefulness when performers – or writers – want to escape the censors. He cites an incident when Molière flouted the censor's edicts concerning an anti-Jesuit passage by using an actor who was a *grammelot* expert, 'capable of delivering a whole monologue in phoney French, using no more than a dozen genuine words and filling out the rest with onomatopoeic inventions'.[234]

In *Min Fars Hus* (1972-74) Barba's Odin actors used a fabricated language 'based on tonal and rhythmic variations rather than on linguistic signification'.[235] There were odd Russian words, but mostly the language comprised nonsense words that 'sounded Russian'. A similar experiment occurred when Trestle Theatre collaborated with a Rumanian theatre company: the result was a language which used some Rumanian words but, more importantly, 'sounded' Rumanian, which the actors spoke in *Beggar's Belief* (1998). Although the actors in this production were masked, voice and sound-language added a corroborative dimension, giving out emotional signals too.

Copeau and his nephew, Michel Saint-Denis, and their associates, experimented with what they called *grummelotage* or 'the music of meaning'.[236] This form of expression 'attempted to transmit states of mind by cries, murmurs and chanting all related to the dramatic moment' but lacking any semantic logic,[237] and, predictably, when Artaud heard about it he was impressed. Believing the tone of the voice was more important than conventional notions of 'elocution', led Michel Saint-Denis, (who took over as director of the Compagnie des Quinze from Copeau and later founded key drama training outlets in London) to work without them too. He wrote: 'If we dispense at first with words, it is only to make clear that words are the result of an inner state, an inner physical state, related to the senses, which conditions the spoken word.'[238]

A rather more prosaic way of approaching the sonorities and physical expressiveness of language is to use the following exercise.

Swear-speak

Swear words in most languages are strong and forceful, frequently with hard consonants and short vowels, and charged with sonic energy. It is important in this exercise that actors use a word they do not know. However, most groups are able to come up with a range of swear words from languages other than English which serve the purpose. Get them to teach one of these phonetically to others who are unfamiliar with it. Don't spell the word or translate its meaning. Simply teach it sonically.

Once everyone has a word, they then investigate it vocally, allowing the impulses it generates in the body to provoke actions and movements through exploring every dynamic of its sound. For example if the word has an 's' in it,

*accentuate it so that you really hiss it. Find what kind of energy the word
gives you. Explore the word fully, and don't settle on one action or gesture,
but find as many as you can.*

*Move around the space, discovering how expressive you can be with this
word.*

*Find new words, again from an unknown language, perhaps one from the
Eastern or Southern continents where the spelling is more alien and you
have to approach them phonetically. This time choose words which have less
force. They may still have an onomatopoeic resonance. Break them up into
syllables, so that actors learn them phonetically with no understanding of
what they mean. Run the same exercise as with swear words.*

Like Artaud, Brook came to recognise the incantatory and ritualistic
qualities of language. The previous exercise reminds us that sounds work
on us physically just as movements do, conjuring feelings. Certain qualities of sound affect us even when we don't know the language, charging us
emotionally or spiritually. Humans also, in times of great elation or
trauma, express themselves in sounds rather than words. As the Orghast
experiment seemed to prove, *in extremis* language is close to music, and
music, like myth and dreams, transcends articulate expression.

In the African experiment which followed *Orghast*, Brook's search was
for musical sounds which could communicate beyond words and across
cultures. The encounter with the nomadic Peulh tribe (superbly docum-
ented in John Heilpern's account of that African journey, *The Conference
of Birds*) and the subsequent 'meeting' of the actors and tribesmen in a
single 'ah' sound, taught Brook that 'a universal language might be as
simple as one note repeated many, many times. But the right note must be
discovered first'.[239]

Brook's work illustrates how getting away from the notion of taming
the voice and seeing it as a creative instrument, indissolubly linked to our
emotional and spiritual core, can lead us into new territory. Just as so much
physical work on the body is about stripping away, so too with the voice: it
is a question of shedding not only inhibition, but habits, clichés and
personal mannerisms to find a heightened state of vocal perception.

During the last thirty years a new breed of voice teachers, influenced in
some degree by Wolfsohn's research, have developed methods designed to
erase the multiple blockages which curtail the actor's voice. Cicely Berry,

Voice Director at the Royal Shakespeare Company, and Patsy Rodenburg, Head of the Voice Departments at the Royal National Theatre and Guildhall School of Speech and Drama, have both published immensely useful manuals which contain a wealth of exercises for actors (Berry,1973 and 1987; Rodenburg,1997). These are especially valuable for making that vital connection between voice, text and emotion.

Other teachers work through song, for singing is a fruitful avenue for exploring the connection between voice and emotion as well as releasing hidden potentialities in the voice. Laughing and crying are the instinctive roots of singing. In all cultures, the singer represents the capacity to celebrate joy and sorrow. There are several key practitioners in this field, including Helen Chadwick for example, who works with songs gathered from Eastern European folk traditions. Singing together also promotes a complicité with a spiritual edge.

Without any tune or song, choral singing can uncover tonal and melodic potency in the collective voice. The next exercise is like an old friend which many actors may already know. Yet it is unerringly fresh with each acquaintance.

Choral hum

Lie on the floor and get comfortable. Contract and release the muscles from feet to head, as in 'Living Silence', and close your eyes. Everyone breathes deeply, initially breathing in and out with a beat of four or so, and holding the breath in between in unison. Then each actor finds their own rhythm of deep breathing.

Gradually, let the air passing the larynx make a sound. Develop this into a note you can sustain, taking in breath to fuel it. Don't alter your note to mimic anyone else, nor to create harmonies at this stage. When everyone is happily producing their note, invite them to increase the volume, letting the sound swell to fill the room. When this chord reaches its zenith, let it gradually die away.

This may be enough for those encountering it for the first time.

In further trials, move on to developing the sound so that individuals vary pitch and tone, exploring the resonators in their bodies when producing the sound, and responding to the collective sound of their partners. This is most

effective when no-one attempts to lead or impose any preordained idea of
harmony or melody on the sound.

Each group will find their own chemistry in creating this sound, depending
on the varieties of voice within the group. It has never failed me yet as an
exercise which has a profound effect on actors as an uplifting experience.

The way the sound swells and reaches towards a climax before dying
away in this exercise demonstrates the principle of 'Jo–Ha–Kyu' discussed
in the previous section on RHYTHM. And once actors have a grasp of the
otkas – posyl – stoika explored in that section, it can be applied to shaping
a sound, whether percussive or vocal, to give it an internal dynamic.

E-MOTION

Words were rarely the starting point . . . Out of the physical action would come
the feeling.[240]

If training in rhythm and voice serve as pathways to sensitivity, where
does emotion fit in? It is perhaps easier to relate rhythm and sound to
movement. Yet emotion is also an active force, an energy which provokes
movement. Hyphenating the word 'e-motion', as I have done in the title of
this section, alerts us to its active nature.

Actors often expend large amounts of energy attempting to pump up
emotional states by calling up personal memories to provoke the symp-
toms of a feeling. Intentionally seeking psychic states or regurgitating the
memory of emotion, will produce at the very least an imitation of an emotional state, at worst hysteria. What causes actors to do this is a misinter-
pretation of, and over-emphasis on Stanislavsky's concept of 'emotion
memory'.

The actor Vasily Toporkov's account of Stanislavsky's rehearsals for
Tartuffe (1938)[241] is enlightening and should be compulsory reading for
actors. By this point in his career, Stanislavsky was nearing the end of his
life and wanted to ensure that those he trained understood that the foundation for his system was *physical actions*, 'the chief element of stage
expressiveness'.[242] When asked in rehearsal about 'emotional states',
Stanislavsky replied '"Emotional states". What is that? I never heard of
it',[243] which was clearly a denial of his own earlier work. And when an
actress said she had 'kept detailed notes of all the rehearsals in which she

had taken part under his direction' and asked how she should use them, Stanislavsky replied, 'Burn them all.'[244]

Toporkov reminds us that early on in his career Stanislavsky had called for 'control, clarity and completeness in even the most insignificant physical actions',[245] and that he always insisted on 'good diction' in his actors' physical actions. In fact he always started with the physical line of actions for any scene: 'It was considered the highest achievement if an actor could reveal the scheme of a scene by means of purely physical actions or with a minimum number of words.'[246]

The point about Stanislavsky which is reinforced in Toporkov's account, is that he demanded action in rehearsal not discussion, discussion came *after* the physical exploration: 'When actors start to reason . . . the will is weakened. Don't discuss, just do it.' He worked meticulously on the tiniest details by provoking the actor's imaginative response to the 'given circumstances' to uncover physical actions. As to feelings, Stanislavsky 'refused to let us play *feelings*', writes Toporkov, and insisted that 'we must play *images* . . . feeling will come of itself as a result of our concentration on live action in the given circumstances.'[247]

The essence of Stanislavsky's system was that once the physical actions were uncovered, every action had to be justified by a rational and logical analysis in behavioural terms. He worked on characters through analogies to 'real life', as though they had an existence beyond the text. In fact, Stanislavsky's 'physical actions' are really psycho-physical actions, a response through the sensory body to imagining someone in the given situation. And he was, of course, preoccupied primarily with naturalistic texts and fourth-wall realism, which demanded a literal replication of human behaviour. Nevertheless, his advice to his actors to conduct daily exercises in rhythm and voice is instructive: 'Every physical action is inseparably linked with the rhythm which characterises it.'[248]

Meyerhold, one-time pupil of Stanislavsky, came to reject the psychological approach of his teacher's middle years, which he thought unhealthy, preferring instead a physiological route. Emotional expression was a by-product of intensely detailed physical choreography; Meyerhold was more concerned with moving the spectator than what went on inside the actor.

Ha-ha-ha

A simple demonstration of the physical nature of emotion is to smile and repeat the phrase 'ha-ha-ha-ha-ha'; it is more than likely you'll begin to laugh and feel momentarily 'happy', turn your mouth down and squeeze your eyelids together and you reproduce the sensation of being near to tears – for no other reason than you are activating muscles used for laughing and crying.

As both Meyerhold and Lecoq have pointed out, the muscles used for laughing and crying are the same, yet you will feel differing rhythms of breathing and muscle movement with each of these in the following exercise.

Face masks[249]

Line up half a dozen actors facing the rest of the group as audience. Each actor walks forward as though into the 'mask-maker's workroom'. On their left sits the tragic mask, on their right the comic mask. They try on each in turn, using their facial muscles initially to represent the features of each mask.

They must go from one to the other, as though they are looking in a mirror, and develop a separate stance for each mask, laughing bodily in the comic mask, weeping bodily in the tragic mask. The facial expression acts in the same way as a training mask, releasing dramatic expression through the body. Actors who have undertaken mask work will find their ability to do this effectively is enhanced. Try also to find the somatic rhythms of each 'mask' through your breathing.

After a few minutes each actor finds that the comic mask is stuck. S/he cannot remove it no matter how hard s/he tries. S/he is fixed permanently with the smiling face of the comic mask, and the internal despair of the trapped mask-maker.

The principle here is that you can recreate the appropriate muscular tension and, in finding the shape of the body or facial muscles and related breathing states, emotion becomes apparent. You are internally passive and externally active, focusing only on the *doing* of the task.

Actors who try to play the feeling first will invariably be less successful than those who find the physical configuration of the face and body. That is not to say that the physical manifestation will not provoke feeling, but the starting point is the physiological, not the psychological. When the starting point is the transformation of the body, the feeling gains authenticity through the palpability of action. Instead of chasing elusive feelings through the mind, the body traps them in the muscles.

The idea of stimulating emotions through physiological means has recently undergone intensive research by Susana Bloch, Pedro Orthous and Guy Santibañez-H.[250] They suggest that actor training should include systematic psycho-physiological exercises in expressing emotion.

The technique they developed for simulating emotions trains the actors to adopt specific breathing patterns to control muscular tensions which are integrated into 'dynamic or static, bizarre postures',[251] and control eye and facial muscles. Actors were able to reproduce specific emotions at will, and learned to vary their intensity through these 'effector patterns': 'When an . . . observer . . . watches the correct execution of an emotional effector pattern, s/he considers the observed emotion as 'true' as a spontaneous one', although the performers 'had not 'felt' the emotion and had concentrated only on executing as precisely as possible the instructions given by the experimenters.'[252]

In a controlled experiment, actors trained in this method of switching on and off emotions by use of effector patterns performed a scene from Chekhov's *The Seagull*, and made a more convincing impact on an audience of seven theatre directors than those who had worked on the scene in a conventional manner.[253]

A period of psycho-physiological analysis of the play preceded this work, and this is what distinguishes it as a potentially rigid method rather than a creative pathway to working on emotions in text work, for an 'emotional baseline' had to be outlined for the scene through intellectual analysis before it could be rehearsed. Nonetheless, the actors' discovery that the correct execution of the effector patterns triggered corresponding feelings in them demonstrates the effectiveness of provoking emotion by physiological means. What is more impressive is the way the actors were trained to switch on and off various emotional states so they could shift between them.

There is, though, a huge danger in standardising emotions rather than allowing a free play of emotional registers. Bloch maintains that 'the psychological language used in the theatre to denote emotions is too imprecise'.[254] And she may well be correct. But any attempt to notate texts with emotional behaviour is akin to suggesting art can be created by joining up the dots.

One of the interesting things to emerge from Bloch's experimental research is the way pure emotional states need to be blended together to achieve mixed emotions. So, for example, mixing joy and anger gives you pride – anger generated from tensions in the back and neck, and joy from 'laughter breathing'. Each mixed emotion has a similar recipe of basic ingredients in different proportions; irony uses different degrees of joy and anger, for example, with tension in the limbs rather than the torso, and the degree of 'joy breathing' is turned up a notch. This is, I think, a useful concept for actors because it promotes the idea of emotional complexity.

Breath is the key: altering the rhythm of breathing generates a powerful link between patterns of movement and emotional expression. And Bloch discovered that using only the breathing patterns would create the desired facial expressions in the actors.

Artaud's ideal of the actor as an 'athlete of the heart' was rooted in a breathing system designed to elicit emotions: 'Since breathing accompanies feeling, the actor can penetrate this feeling through breathing providing he knows how to distinguish which breathing suits which feeling.'[255] Based on the points of Chinese acupuncture, the idea was that certain breathing patterns release suppressed feelings held in various organs. So, for example, drawing and directing breath from/to the kidneys in the small of the back produces sorrow, and from/to the solar plexus produces anger. Long sustained breaths create subdued reflective emotions, whilst short accelerated rhythms induce agitation.

The idea that suppressed feelings are embedded in the subcutaneous regions of the body is reminiscent of Freud's belief that suppressed desires reside in the subconscious. And Feldenkrais reminds us that our bodies reflect and project inner states: 'Every emotion is, in one way or another, associated and linked in the cortex with some muscular configuration and attitude.'[256] This means 'each phase of movement, every small transference of weight, every single gesture of any part of the body reveals some feature of . . . inner life.'[257]

It is clear that muscles remember. Actors and dancers remember the physical score of the action just as the pianist's fingers remember the notes. Therefore, concluded Grotowski, 'memories are always physical reactions'.[258] In other words, the body will do its own remembering.

Rather than using will to provoke a particular emotion, he encouraged his actors to allow the mind to become passive, thereby unlocking the body's own way of accessing feeling.

The following exercise encourages actors to discover this in relation to a personal memory. There is no necessity for them to articulate the memory orally, or describe what happened. Participants will need to be familiar enough with each other to touch them.

Memory sculptures

To begin with everyone lies on the floor in a relaxed state. Feel the back spread over the floor, and contract and release all the muscles as on previous occasions. Close your eyes.

Recall any incident in which you felt very passionate. It can be something that happened to you from any time in your life, but it is important that it is an incident you feel is significant in some way.

Gradually allow your body to respond to the memory. Keeping your eyes closed, let your body find a position that corresponds to how you felt at the time. (NB: This is not a literal replication of how you stood or sat.) Again, like the previous exercise, this is rather like mask work but don't over-contort your face. If you find you're doing so, try and revert to a blank expression and re-route any tension down through the body.

Exaggerate this position to maximise every point of tension. Really contract the muscles and extend your limbs to the maximum reach. And work out what rhythm of breathing accompanies the stance.

Now relax. Keeping your eyes closed, go back and forth between the relaxed lying position and your 'memory position' making sure you know where every point of tension and bodily accent is.

When everyone has developed these positions to their maximum expression, gradually relax again and stand.

Now work in pairs. Without verbalising, each actor 'sculpts' their partner's body into the position they themselves created. Your partner will cooperate rather like a rag doll, willingly contorting his/her body to your tactile instructions. Make sure you convey where the tension points are, and to what extent the limbs should reach. Try not to demonstrate. The work should be conducted in silence.

When you are being 'sculpted' by your partner, try to be as helpful as possible but do not try and interpret the movement. You will begin to feel points of tension, and need to exaggerate those as you did previously. Closing your eyes from time to time will help you focus. Notice what internal state the sculpting has on you. Does it prompt any particular breathing rhythm? Do the tensions imposed provoke any feeling in you?

Once each pair has completed their sculptures, they are presented individually to the group. The rule is that you can never ask an individual what the incident was, nor should they reveal it. That would be drama therapy. However, in my experience, the results demonstrate some intensely felt passions, which are frequently very 'readable' in terms of emotion if not context.

Those who are 'sculpted' report back on the degree to which the physio- logical impulses impacted on their breathing rhythms and feelings. The work should be evaluated in terms of what the actors have learned about the relationship between feeling and the body from both creating their own memory sculpture and 'modelling' someone else's.

The use of somatic memory was a cornerstone of Grotowski's practice, and his disciple Eugenio Barba carried this on with his Odin actors. Both agree that pumping up emotional states is very damaging. At the same time, both demand a deep level of honesty and sincerity from actors, constantly paring away habits and clichés through a *via negativa* approach, i.e. not directing the actor towards something but away from their own physical and vocal mannerisms.

Grotowski believed that 'by means of concrete details it is possible to attain what is personal.'[259] He advised drawing on the most intimate and private memories we secrete within us to use at high dramatic moments: 'In the most important moment in your role, reveal your most personal and closely guarded experience.'[260] The example he gives is that an actor required to kill an animal in a play might recognise that 'killing an animal in a scene [would] give them a thrill, a sort of climax', and therefore recall his personal experience of 'intense physical climax . . . so intimate, so little meant for the eyes of others' so the 'shock of sincerity' will inform the fictional dramatic moment.[261]

Just as the actor working on presence has to remember that s/he is training an actor's body larger, more resonant than her/his own, s/he has to remember that any character is more intense. The distinction between daily and extra-daily movement applies to emotion: 'If he is playing a jealous man, that man's jealousy is beyond his own jealousy . . . if he is playing a violent man . . . the violence he is playing has a greater charge than his own . . . if he is playing a man of thought and sensibility . . . the finesse of that man's feeling is beyond his everyday capacity.'[262]

The actor needs not only a capacity to feel beyond the 'daily', but also to cultivate and appreciate a range of emotions, 'from the crudest to the most refined'.[263] And then s/he has to be able to move from one to another, often extremely quickly. The question is how?

One strategy is to undertake what Susan Sontag refers to as an 'education of the heart', that is reading novels.[264] Far more beneficial for theatre actors than watching movies, where the imaginative work has already been done, reading novels is an education of more than just the heart. Reading a novel requires you to create a world from words on a page, imagine characters, hear their private and public voices. Enough said.

By far the most important strategy is to take the verb 'to feel' out of the actor's working terminology: 'If you begin by feeling something, then all you can reach afterwards is a tense, stressed expression. A feeling cannot be forced out – it is the result of many factors'.[265] Torgier Wethal, one of Barba's Odin troupe is referring to the fact that feeling arises from the integration of imagination and technique: these are the actor's primary tools.

In performance, actors require 'methods which will produce a believable "human" performance every single night, irrespective of what the actor is actually feeling.'[266] The way Yoshi Oida describes combining imagination and technique is instructive. He suggests that you try and perform a particular emotion with maximum physical expression and then, having achieved this, 'attempt to keep the emotion at the same level whilst reducing the physical action', which will intensify the expression.[267] So it is not more feeling, but less physical expression which intensifies the emotion. Eventually, the actor learns to reduce the outer movement to zero whilst maintaining the inner emotional movement.

This is reminiscent of Artaud's belief that 'any true feeling cannot in reality be expressed. To do so is to betray it. To express it, however, is to *conceal* it. True expression conceals what it exhibits'.[268]

SECTION 5

Devising

Devising

Actors must learn to create their own theatre.[270]

All the key practitioners mentioned in this book stressed the importance of somatic improvisation in their training, and all of them rebelled against established theatrical convention. Yet there is little evidence of practitioners dispensing with the singly-authored text until well after World War II.

Meyerhold, for example, believed in movement as the primary element in theatre, but he always worked with written texts, although he cut them up and re-ordered them on occasion. He was concerned with training his actors to serve his visionary stage compositions rather than follow their individual creativity. And Copeau, despite his innovative use of improvisation in training, was essentially a classicist who never really relinquished his reverence for the text, though his company did work collaboratively with the writer André Obey to produce *Noé* and *Le Viol* in 1933, after a spell of creating their own 'new commedia' in rural Burgundy. Even Artaud, who called so vociferously for the end of theatre's subjugation to the word, wrote scripts for his surrealist productions, albeit strangely surreal ones. But he never advocated the pursuit of the individual or collective imaginary potential of the actor.

It is with the mime artist Etienne Decroux that we find the first call for actors to take control of the creative process. Decroux wrote his 'order of composition' in 1931, which is virtually a blue-print for what we now call 'devising', putting the 'responsibility squarely on the shoulders of the new actor for the creation of a new text and a new theatre'.[271]

Seventy years on, the singly-authored text continues to be an *idée fixe* for mainstream theatre managements, in spite of the variety of devised work on the touring circuit. The constant call for 'new writing' in contemporary theatre frequently means a play by a young (preferably twenty-something) writer who may have little or no experience of the medium of theatre, and consequently fails to exploit the imaginative power of the medium. Even the Royal Court Theatre, bastion of innovations in playwriting, has been known to turn down devised work from highly regarded physical-based companies on the grounds that there isn't a text or a playwright. Like the censor they once resisted so strongly, they want a script first – though not, of course, for the same reasons.

Without going into the history of devising in depth, it is worth noting that Theatre Workshop's *Oh What a Lovely War* (1963), which transferred to the West End of London, was essentially the most significant piece of devised theatre to reach the mainstream British stage. It was closely followed by Brook's experimental *Theatre of Cruelty Season* at LAMDA (1964), which included both improvised and text pieces, and his production of *US* which, like Littlewood's, was developed with actors through a research and development process, with a writer working alongside the process. This was Brook's first original collaborative piece.

Both *Oh What A Lovely War* and *US* were ideologically grounded pieces which did not conform to the idea of the well-made play but used a more fluid collage-like structure, where contrast and juxtaposition worked like cinematic montage to create political meaning and dramatic effects. Both were born out of a need to convey outrage; aesthetic decisions and dramatic effects served the political points. These were pieces unified by theme and style rather than narrative. Significantly, creative ownership belonged to the actors not merely through performance but in the making process. And this was due, particularly in Theatre Workshop's case, to the fact that the companies had worked together for a considerable time, facilitated by gifted directors. Through training and rehearsing together over an extended period of time, they had a shared physical and imaginative vocabulary.

The more general proliferation of devised work in the post-sixties has as much to do with the post-modern repudiation of the hierarchy of text as the emergence of a new breed of actors or practitioners challenging the idea of the actor-as-interpreter and reclaiming the notion of the actor-as-creator. On a broader canvas, the newfound freedoms of the 1960s permeated theatre as much as the other arts, not least because once censorship ceased in 1968 there was no longer a requirement to submit a script to the Lord Chamberlain prior to performance. Performance artists, 'happenings' and a new generation of (sometimes self-taught) actors began making use of spaces not designated as theatres (arts centres, pubs, clubs etc.) to present performances which challenged the traditional notion of a 'play'.

The seventies was the era of 'alternative' theatre, fuelled by politically impassioned theatre-workers who reinvented agit-prop to startle audiences into taking notice of social and cultural issues. The new radicalism was finally ground down in the mid to late eighties by Thatcherite policies designed to reduce state support of the arts in favour of private sponsorship. A combination of political disenchantment and precarious funding resulted in many companies and studio spaces closing, and the re-emergence of conservative text-based theatre designed to put bums on seats so as to maximise the box-office income needed to replace lost subsidy. For the most part, the radical devised theatre of this period was more concerned with form and style as carriers of ideological messages rather than exploring a new aesthetic or championing the notion of the actor-as-creator. More often than not, improvisation was a creative tool serving a political purpose.

Frost and Yarrow suggest that 'actors and directors have been taught to regard improvisation only for its developmental value in actor training, and for its occasional usefulness in the rehearsal situation.'[272] They claim improvisation is put to the service of interpretation in most drama schools so that the idea of the actor as the servant of a written text continues to prevail, despite the influence of Michel Saint-Denis and maybe even because of him.[273] Like his uncle, Jacques Copeau, Saint-Denis came to view the actor-as-creator as part of a training process leading towards interpretation rather than towards the goal of autonomous creation. And while Copeau's pupil, Decroux, called for actors to make their own work, he was essentially a mime purist who taught silent cerebral mime rather than acting.

It was another line of Copeau's heritage that eventually brought the notion of the actor-as-creator to fruition. For it was with Jean Dasté (Copeau's son-in-law and one of his actors) that Jacques Lecoq trained after the war, and when Lecoq set up his school in Paris in 1956 it was with the express intention that pupils should develop their own creative personalities in order to be able to make their own art: 'The aim of the school is to produce a young theatre of new work, generating performance languages which emphasise the physical playing of the actor.'[274]

Lecoq can be seen as a visionary, training actors for a theatre that did not exist: 'Lecoq's school is one of those theatres that, rather than being a resumé of what has happened, has helped young performers find new directions and so revitalise the theatre'.[275]

Unlike Decroux, who also ran a mime school in Paris, Lecoq taught his mimes to speak. And just as importantly, he encouraged them to discover their own performance identity as a necessary adjunct to becoming autonomous theatre-makers. This is sometimes painful, as some students relate: 'Lecoq strips you completely and gives you your true identity; for the first months I was on the verge of tears . . . you go through a long process during which he reveals you to yourself.'[276] Rather like Grotowski's *via negativa*, Lecoq works on the principle of steering the student away from the known, the clichéd, the easy solution, to pare away any falsity in the acting.

This is different from excavating the self in a Grotowskian sense, for the students' focus is more outward looking. They are more concerned with what they see around them than what they find within. The Lecoq school gives students a grounding in improvisation orientated to observation and analysis of the world around them, the objects and people in it. The founder members of Theatre de Complicité met at the school, and Simon McBurney says of their early work, 'Everything was based on observations of things we could actually see and feel, combined with wherever our imaginations would take us.'[277]

The study of past traditions through practical exploration is a crucial dimension of training for devising, and in the second year of Lecoq's programme students explore a range of different theatrical styles (including Pantomime Blanche, Melodrama, Tragedy, Bouffons, Clown and commedia dell'arte) in order to 'ground the students in the different traditions so that they may use them as a point of reference for new work'.[278] In commedia work, for example, they learn to integrate slapstick and acrobatics with mime and use these 'as a vehicle for emotional expression and not just a demonstration of physical skill'.[279]

An impressive number of Lecoq graduates have been successful, and influential, in making their own work (Steven Berkoff, Ariane Mnouchkine, Julie Taymor, Theatre de Complicité), and more have been touched by the school's teachings through the work of his colleagues (Monika Pagneux, Philippe Gaulier) and the school's multi-national alumni. Lecoq's ideas of training through play, with somatic improvisation as the primary method of creativity, have fed into physical-based theatre by osmosis through the working practice and training workshops conducted by many ex-students.

Devising is the dominant mode of creating work in millennial physical-based theatre, despite notable exceptions, such as the work of Steven

Berkoff,[280] and Theatre de Complicité, who regularly mount productions of classic texts (*The Visit*, *The Chairs*, *The Caucasian Chalk Circle*) and apply the devising process to adaptation (*The Street of Crocodiles*, *Three Lives of Lucie Cabrol* and *Light*) whilst continuing to make devised work (*Mnemonic*, 1999). There are indications that this may be changing as companies with a track record in self-generated work have begun tackling classics (The Right Size's collaboration with the Almeida to produce *Mr Puntila and His Man Matti*, 1998; Kaos Theatre's *The Importance of Being Earnest*, 1999, and *Volpone*, 2001; Trestle's revival of Besier's *The Barretts of Wimpole Street*, 1999), and commissioning new work (eg Told By An Idiot's production of Biyi Bandele's *Happy Birthday Mister Deka D*, 1999). Some companies include writers as part of a collaborative team (eg Frantic Assembly for *Sell Out*, 1998; *Hymns*, 1999), and in some cases an actor or director is the writer whose script is rehearsed in a similar manner to a devised show, and undergoes considerable change during the process due to the creative input of the actors (eg Kaos Theatre, Reject's Revenge). But by and large, most physical-based theatre is devised by companies whose core members train and play together.

STARTING POINTS AND PROCESS

It is from the blot that inspiration is born.[281]

The function of training and improvisation is to set in motion the creativity of actors so they not only improve themselves as performers but also make their own work. Familiarity with physical-based devising means actors are less inhibited and more inclined to take risks; they can also perceive the more complex aspects of the relationship between text and word. Above all, they develop an understanding of how theatre works.

All the suggestions for practical work in the preceding sections are aimed at actors discovering their somatic impulses, and developing a physical articulation of the imagination. A shared vocabulary is what fuels devised work: the way you train and play will inevitably inform the style of work you produce, even what you produce. Simon McBurney was able to put 'half an hour of the show together in fifteen minutes' because he had spent three weeks developing a common language between the people working on *Out of a House Walked a Man* (1994). 'Where you begin is where you . . . prepare the ground' he states, 'I prepare them so that they are ready; ready to change, ready to be surprised.'[282]

Chaos is a necessary aspect of devising, not least because truly creative work makes use of chance. Dario Fo quotes Picasso who, rather than viewing an unintentional blob of paint as a mess which might spoil a painting, would watch the stain spread and 'deeply moved, begin with sheer delight to take advantage of that accident'.[283] When everything comes from the actors, what happens in performance is determined by what happens in rehearsal, and accidental discoveries are part of that.

Any group wanting to devise a piece has to discover what they want to say. Devising is 'a way of working to find out and develop ideas . . . that involves stepping out of the conventional roles of playwright, designer, director, actor or production manager in order to become part of an ensemble.'[284] The prime motive for making a piece may be a desire to create something with a specific group of people rather than a piece about anything in particular. Given a committed group, you can make short pieces of theatre from more or less anything – as you have already discovered on occasions during the practical work undertaken so far. Making a piece that sustains itself over more than a few minutes requires the ability to develop improvisational work, to build and broaden the focus and eventually to edit and structure material to elicit a response in an audience. But it does not necessarily mean knowing what your intended outcome is at the start.

Devising is really collaborative writing in the broadest sense of the word 'write'. Training exercises offer a way of working that places actors in a perpetual state of discovery in much the same way as writing exercises. The analogy with writing is pertinent: poets, for example, often create phrases or word patterns and search for the meaning afterwards, and I know several writers who have written short stories and even whole plays from the starting point of a creative writing exercise. Contrary to popular belief, writers don't necessarily start at the beginning and work through to the end, especially when writing for performance. And they research their characters while they are writing them, exploring who they are and discovering what they want as they progress with the writing.[285] The process is one of developing ideas and continual redrafting.

Some companies, like some writers, begin with developing characters; others start with research that gets transposed into theatrical ideas. There is no definitive method or starting point. Each group finds its own way.

Devising is rooted in the concept of the creative actor developing ideas from tasks. It is usually the director who both translates ideas into tasks (which may be games or improvisations) and operates later as an editor, an outside eye, a shaper of the whole, in essence as the dramaturg. Increasingly, companies who devise their work in this way refer to the product as a score, borrowing the musical term to indicate that the principle of creation is one of composition rather than linear plot construction.

Marcello Magni (a founder member of Complicité and a freelance director) believes the role of the director and designer is 'to service the actors',[286] and both he and John Wright (founder of Told By An Idiot and a freelance director and workshop leader), describe directing as facilitating. Few directors have hard-and-fast methods. Each play is different, and each group of actors have different needs. But the process frequently follows three stages: a pre-production research period, a 'making' stage where the 'text' is generated, and a final phase of rehearsing that text.[287]

Many companies use video to record improvisations, and sometimes a 'scribe' to log what is said. These fragments are scrutinised, some ideas will be jettisoned while others go on to be developed. It is not dissimilar to the editing process in film, except the material is re-made each day.

Etienne Decroux's compositional plan posits a progression from impulse to movement to action to gesture to sound to word, and it is this paradigm which we find operating in physical-based devising. Companies speak of how their ideas come from a range of sources fermenting over a period, but they work on these through physical improvisation. What the final outcome of the piece will be is the result of this developmental process. The (researched) starting point might be a theme, concept or even a story but imaginative responses and ideas are tested through performative channels rather than worked out round a table in advance. Research is a collective responsibility. It is from research, whether book-fed, style-fed or life-fed, that theatre is made. But action arrives before word.

The first base of Decroux's plan is a visual scenario, and this is what the commedia dell'arte actors constructed and built upon for their performances, incorporating prepared *lazzi* and acrobatic tricks into the scenario framework. They began with a set of masked characters, but you can develop situations through improvisation which allow characters to evolve through interaction rather than deciding who they are first. Mask work (see SECTION TWO) is an excellent starting point for creating visual scenarios and seeing how characters can develop through interaction with other masks and objects.

I include the following examples of scenarios for those who perhaps have not come across one. The first is adapted from an original commedia scenario which tends towards farce, the second is much more open and can be explored from a number of perspectives. Both are deliberately incomplete, springboards for invention rather than fixed outlines. If you have too fixed a scenario the process is less interestingly creative because you spend time working out how to get information across.

Commedia street

Cast groups of six as three couples: X1 and X2, Y1 and Y2, Z1 and Z2.
The X and Y couples have lived in this street for years.
X1 has a long-standing affair with Y2. They meet behind the backs of their partners.
The Z couple move into the middle house.
Y1 falls madly in love with Z1. The feeling is mutual. They begin an affair.

Set up the playing area as suggested in 'Working with Commedia Masks' in section two. You may wish to designate entrances and exits as specific houses for each couple – the audience could be the third one – but it is not essential. The only other item you're allowed is a dustbin or laundry basket – big enough to hide a person in.

If you start knowing this much, it is quite straightforward to let improvisation develop the rest of the story so that different groups have different outcomes and decide on different endings. The scenario is simply a framework. You may decide to incorporate particular games to get the ball rolling for individual scenes. 'No-Ball Tennis' is a good one for meetings between couples-in-lust, for example. And adapting 'Sock-Tag' as in section three: play, is also a useful generator.

Make a decision about whether to work in a silent universe, or use gobbledy-gook, or whether you want to incorporate 'real' language. A combination of expressive sound based on the idea of the 'Yes/Yes' exercise and a smattering of language works quite well. Remember to keep the action exaggerated and use visual strategies rather than resorting to verbal explanations.

Invite actors to play this scenario with a time limit – say five minutes – and ring a bell to alert them to the fact that they have one minute left to conclude the piece. Alternatively, you can allow preparation time so they produce a piece of work-in-progress.

The next scenario is a complete contrast, yet it operates on the same principle of giving a framework within and from which a host of possibilities present themselves.

Game of straws[288]

Four/five children play the ancient game of straws.
One hides the ends of the straws in their fist.
The others pick a straw.
The one who gets the shortest straw must ...
Eventually we see the children are sitting on a ...

If you fill in the gaps first and then work the scenario you will probably find you are creating action that 'joins up the dots'. This is a good starting point for those who have never worked from scenarios before. However, if you leave the gaps open, in other words wait to see what evolves out of playing the scenario and allowing the person drawing the short straw to invent what happens, you will get a sense of surprise – and perhaps a more imaginative result.

Once again different groups will invent different outcomes. Showing pieces to each other is an important dimension of the devising process with larger groups. It sparks new ideas in the rest of the group, and consequently work develops organically.

The early work of Theatre de Complicité was based on 'universal themes' grounded in those of the commedia dell'arte, for example: Death (*A Minute too Late*, 1984), Hunger and Poverty (*More Bigger Snacks Now*, 1985), Love, Sex and Jealousy (*Please, Please, Please*, 1986), Fear (*Anything for a Quiet Life*, 1988), testimony to the founder members' training with Lecoq, where they had studied past forms.

McBurney and his colleagues set up their rehearsal room as a play-ground: 'We played together and we looked at the world and it would make us laugh and it would make us cry,' and out of this playground 'fragments would emerge'.[289] Eventually the fragments were jacked together to create the whole.

At this juncture their work had a knockabout visual and physical style which operated in the realm of absurdist comedy. The performers were adept at 'externalising the internal trauma of character', so although hysterically funny, they also touched on the tragic isolation of characters.[290] For example in *Anything for a Quiet Life*, Mr Pellici (Marcello Magni) and Ms Box-Cooper (Annabel Arden) signalled their mutual desire through gorging on raspberry cream sponge cake, since they were unable to articulate their feelings.

The characters had arrived from exploring the theme rather than by design: 'We just dressed up and Simon took photographs of us. Then, when we looked at the photographs, we said, 'They [the characters] are arriving. What are they going to make us do? It was a while before the plot was of any importance at all. What was important was to let those characters roar round the rehearsal room.'[291]

Escalations[292]

This is one of the most useful exercises for devising, especially if you are working in a comic or grotesque realm. It works in much the same way as 'Changing Gears' (see section three: play), where each actor increases the level of energy/tension on a scale of 1-10. You can play this as actors, or use a set of characters you have developed through mask work.

Follow exactly the same template as changing gears, but decide collectively on a theme first. If you play the escalations of fear, for example, you still play the level of tension but in relation to 'fear'. Make it the responsibility of the last person to invent the reason for the highest escalation, which could be 'they're going to kill us', or even that they themselves are the object of the fear, such as 'make way for the child-snatcher'.

Characters may emerge, or rather characteristics that you like to play with that can be developed into 'personae'. If you're using a set of characters, you'll deepen your knowledge of them. As you become more skilled, use the highest point of escalation to trigger the next scale, so everyone might become resigned to dying, or cunning in escaping the child-snatcher: this way the highest escalation point acts as a transition between 'scenes'.[293]

Sometimes the chemistry of performers and how they play together enables them to work purely from play. The sole purpose of The Right Size partnership, Hamish McColl and John Foley, is making people laugh and as a duo they operate rather like a double-act in the music-hall tradition. The surreal worlds they create include hilarious characters and situations, such as a waiter on elastic (*Stop Calling Me Vernon*, 1994) and two strangers stuck in a bathroom for twenty-five years (*Do You Come Here Often*, 1997). There was no reason for the elastic, apart from its inherent absurdity and comic potential, and the two strangers end up playing Grandmother's Footsteps the wrong way round and getting trapped in each other's memories as they try and work out why they are in the bathroom.

Comic tomfoolery is a hugely liberating way to work, but its success is as dependent on technique as inspiration. The exercises on 'timing' (towards the end of SECTION FOUR: RHYTHM) offer some useful groundwork for comedy, and playing NO-BALL TENNIS (SECTION THREE: PLAY) is good preparation for this next exercise.

The waiter[294]

You will need a table and chair and a tea-towel. Two volunteers play this game, one is the waiter, who carries the tea-towel over their arm, and the other is the customer who comes to eat at the restaurant. Actors do not speak. Everything apart from the table, chair and tea-towel, is mimed. It is a posh, upmarket restaurant.

Do not decide anything else. Just play the game.

How the waiter carries/uses the tea-towel, how a particular actor enters spark ideas. Try not to impose anything. The humour emerges from the fact that both actors try very hard to get things right (including the mime). They fail of course!

When actors try to impose an idea on the situation the improvisation usually flounders. When both customer and waiter play their role as seriously as possible, the scene finds its own development through what happens between them and comic moments arise from 'mistakes'. It's exactly the same as being 'in the moment' in a tennis match.

Different chemistries between new pairs of actors will generate fresh
scenarios. Allow the improvisation to continue until one pair of actors
completely run out of steam, then invite two more to play.

Design is incorporated here as part of an image system: table, chair and
tea-towel are basic elements contributing to the 'world'. The earlier you
work with potential design elements, the more they will become integrated
into the whole – they may even inspire the work.[295]

Bouge-de-la are a company whose founder members, Aurelian Koch
and Lucy O'Rorke, took Lecoq's course at the Laboratoire du Etude Mouve-
ment (L.E.M.), which relates movement to architecture, in addition to the
two-year programme for performers.[296] Their work is design-led, in the
sense that they begin by exploring and playing with design concepts,
usually sparked by research into a theme or story. 'All our shows are
fundamentally about humans and their environment,' says Koch, whether
that is an arctic environment (*The Man Who Ate His Shoe*, 1994) or the
solitary bedsit of an autistic woman (*Underglass*, 1996).[297] Frequently
there are no words, although a sound-track is integral, and more recently
they have worked with dancers as well as actors .

Their shows focus on the performer(s) and a 'living' set, which is integral to the action, so that walls open up or a model boat runs into an iceberg. Ideas have to be tested in rehearsal, where things change and evolve.
In *Evolution: Body* (1998) the focus was on the relationship between 'set as
a costume and costume as set' for this interrogation of modern genetics:
'The original idea was to make something free-standing that the performers could wear, but also step in and out of, so that the costume became
the set. But this was technically too difficult – we made suits lined with
chicken wire which the performers couldn't move in! You couldn't play
with them. Then we made suits with rings so they could be hung on
bungees, and as the suits got messed around and became more alive they
looked like distorted bodies, like pieces of meat hanging and this kind of
felt right because they looked like bodies and flesh. So then we lined them
in red and made bags to hang them in.'[298]

Evolution: Mind (1999) was about 'the relationship between us and
technology, our dependence on it and the impact of it in the way it extends
your potential and drives you round the twist.'[299] The computer came
'alive' in this show, like a cinematic special effect, as a grey alien emerged
through the rubbery keyboard to haunt the performer.

The game called JUMBLE PLAY (SECTION THREE: PLAY) comes from Bouge-de-la and offers a fascinating insight into how objects can lead movement. Extended improvisations developed from this game can lead actors to create characters and scenarios through play. This game also works as a solo improvisation (see JUMBLE SOLO, p 174).

Organising the space is a key factor, as it will affect the style and design. Ridiculusmus began the process for one show in a room with three white boxes: 'We were working on improvisations which started in a room with three white boxes and after two days we realised we were in a gallery. It wasn't preconceived.'[300] And so the art gallery setting for *The Exhibitionists* (1997) arrived by accident, and the company have since performed the piece in art galleries as well as theatre spaces.

Rejects Revenge played on stepladders and a plank during the rehearsal process for *Crumble* (1994), which Tim Hibberd states was half the fun: 'You swing them about and you stand on them, you stand under them, you pick them up, you make a boat, you make a plane . . . almost the entire show [was] based on the fact that we picked up ladders and played with them.'[301] With *Peasouper* (1996) they decided on side-screens and a back-cloth, but as the work progressed the back-cloth became a box because they needed to stand on it, and then that became hollow so they could crawl through it.

Rejects Revenge are unusual in that they begin with a devising phase and then Tim Hibberd writes a script from what has developed, which then goes back into rehearsal. The three actors employ a freelance director to facilitate their work from the beginning. The director is 'an audience member with prior knowledge', who tells them what works and what doesn't, acting like a mirror for the actors.[302]

Other companies rely more heavily on a director to 'provoke' a text, working on the basis of an agreed idea. In Told By An Idiot (which consists of two actors, Hayley Carmichael and Paul Hunter, who hold equal artistic control with director John Wright), for example, the actors are actively involved in imaginative play and have considerable input at every stage, but in rehearsal they develop the work via the instigation of the director: he orchestrates their physical play. A designer is involved at an early stage and so a set is integrated into the play/rehearsal process. What is clear from the actors is that their notebooks are a key factor, both in the generation of ideas and the continuous reflection on the process.[303]

Their work treads a thin line between comedy and tragedy; the aim is to make 'visual poetry' rather than tell stories in a conventional narrative mode. *You Haven't Embraced Me Yet* (1996) for example, has echoes of Beckett where 'delicious absurdity and theatrical economy'[304] meet in the telling of a tale about a man torn between two women.

And in *I Weep At My Piano* (1999), the company took the friendship between Lorca, Dali and Buñuel as their inspiration to produce a moving tribute. The piece worked independently as an evocation of love and loss rather than being a direct biographical account, the research operating as a springboard for the actors to create a piece which evolved organically out of their imaginative responses to the material.

Foursight Theatre begin with research, and performers are set specific research tasks which fuel their character creations. They worked with the set and the songs from the start of rehearsals for *Six Dead Queens and an Inflatable Henry* (1999), and even though the directors (two on this occasion) had a clear idea of the style they wanted: 'the creative impetus comes from the actors, [the directors] worked from images the cast bring alive'.[305]

Many pieces of devised theatre are based on extant stories or scripts. The most inventive are imaginative responses of the collaborators to the source material rather than straight adaptations. This is the way Theatre de Complicité approach source material. Work on Bruno Schulz's *The Street of Crocodiles* began with a workshop at the Royal National Theatre Studio in 1991 and went through a series of evolutions and productions with different ensembles from 1992-1994 and a revival in 1998-1999, with the input of each new company member affecting each production. This is an important element of devising. The personal and cultural experiences of the collaborators inform the work, are part and parcel of it.

The choice of material is crucial. Ideally, whatever it is, it has to matter to everyone involved. At the very least, everyone needs to be able to respond imaginatively and bring their personal skills to the process.

The key point is that whether your starting point is a style of performance or an idea about content, the process begins with generating visual material: characters, action, images, all from physical improvisation. In *The Street of Crocodiles* the major focus was finding the kind of images that reminded them of the world of Schulz's stories, images which Mark Wheatley, the company writer, says 'we believed . . . to be the most important aspect of the piece . . . they had to summon up this lost world'.[306]

The notion of creating 'theatre of images' is important. But the images need to be a step away from the everyday. Bim Mason (who runs the Circomedia course in Bristol, and who directed Rejects Revenge in *Crumble* and *Peasouper*) suggests that working in a pantomimic dimension allows the work to go into 'that non-realistic world, that switch into fantasy', which he believes is an essential feature of physical theatre.[307] Visual metaphor arises from what he calls 'semi-abstract work', where you create 'telling images' through making a concept visual.

IMAGE AND GESTURE

We do not go to theatre to understand but to experience.[308]

However you start, it is essential to grasp the principle of moving from impulse to action, and to acquire primary compositional techniques. Solo work is important: discoveries can be made individually and through working with a director which are equally as valid as those made with acting partners. Such work is particularly useful for developing characters.

Barba's concept of collective creation eschews collaborative work in the initial stages. He argues that when improvisations involve two or more, 'actors tend to focus on the interactive process rather than the theme of the work', i.e. they are more concerned with 'reading' their partners and responding to them than 'exploring their own physical dialogue with a theme'.[309] For him, the individual actor's responses are the major resource he works with; in the final production they are like soloists brought together through his vision.

The following sequence of exercises focuses on individual responses with the aim of exploring the route from impulse to gesture and image. View them as experiments through which you further your own creative understanding and development.

Actors need to be comfortable working in their own defined area of the space and able to ignore others around them. In terms of showing their work, they need to have reached a degree of confidence and lack of inhibition with the group and/or director. With the following exercises, it is assumed you are familiar with practical work from the previous sections, or similar work. They all take place in a 'silent universe'.

Working with objects is fundamental to the Odin actors' training; their improvisations with objects lead to character creations. In the following exercise, the idea is to develop your engagement with the object at a more than superficial level so you and the object become partners in evoking imaginary worlds.

Jumble solos

Set up a collection of items as suggested in 'Jumble Play' in section three: play. Actors let any of the items choose them, and, as in Step 1 of 'Jumble Play', conduct a motion study of the item. Ensure this is a thorough investigation of each item's properties: how heavy it is, its texture, how it moves, whether it has any moving parts, and most importantly, how it makes you move.

Let the object lead your movement and experiment with moving at floor level and ways of travelling across the space. (Split the group if there is limited space.) Don't take the object at its literal level, let it surprise you; a handbag over the face becomes a kind of mask, for example, or a fur coat a flag. If a music-stand presents problems, explore how you constantly fail to control it.

After an initial exploratory period, each actor takes about ten minutes to choreograph a solo piece which incorporates these early discoveries, or examines one particular idea provoked by their response to the object. Try to remember the principle of structuring phrases of movement via the otkas-posyl-stoika, so each piece has rhythmic shape.

When presented, these solos will appear as a series of image-based performances. Those watching then select which sections of each performance worked most effectively. These are then rehearsed again and re-presented. At this point, those watching become directors (or designate a small group as directors) and decide which solos have some kind of aesthetic correspondence, perhaps by virtue of their line or rhythm of movement, the texture or colour of the objects themselves, or some other reason. Experiment with playing various solos in tandem or consecutively and observe the results. As in the earlier stick-work, 'meanings' emerge which may or may not correspond to the performers' intentions.

A similar process can be applied to a controlling idea or theme – the simpler the better. Single words are often very productive, 'boredom' for example, or even something as basic as a colour. Giving individual actors a level of intensity on a continuum from 1-10, rather like the escalations exercise, will give group work a compositional dimension.

Ideographs[310]

Once you have decided on a theme, each actor develops a physical response to what this conjures in them, producing a gestural image, what Herbert Blau calls an ideograph. Like a Japanese brush painting, an ideograph is an abstraction of the essence of an image, a pared-down form that contains the essence of an action. It carries a concentrated meaning, expressing the kernel of an idea, not its realistic outer illustration.

The action condenses the image without offering any distracting detail. Try not to think! Allow your body to respond spontaneously, in a similar way to the 'memory sculptures' exercise in section four.

If you find yourself starting with an everyday behavioural gesture remember you are working in a more symbolic or surreal realm, searching for a physical expression for your inner response, connecting the inner and outer to concentrate meaning rather than producing an illustrative mannerism. This is what Bim Mason means by stepping away from the everyday into the 'pantomimic dimension' and creating 'telling images'.

Clarifying and exaggerating the movement and tension points will help to make a gesture more powerful. Like the sighs and cries emitted in the sound exercises, an ideograph may be quite abstract. It is your honest imaginative response, expressed in physical terms.

The gesture you produce may be static. Try to find a way into it and out of it that gives you an action you can modify according to the otkas-posyl-stoika principle, with a point at which the dynamic shifts through employing tormos.

Present the ideographs to the group and, as before, let them decide as directors which ones are most effective. Once you have made a selection, try stringing them together, or perhaps actors can learn some of each other's and attempt to string them together. Do they work as complementary facets of a theme? Are they just weird? What ideas and feelings do they provoke in the spectators?

Remember this is a training exercise leading to a grasp of compositional techniques, not a 'how to devise' lesson! What you arrive at one day will be different on another. What you deduce about the impact of your work on spectators, whether you fail or succeed in affecting them, is part of your self-development. Avoid asking 'what does it mean', or 'what did you mean' to any actor. It is more important at this stage to discover what communicates and what doesn't at the sensory and aesthetic levels.

Not all actors have a talent for directing, nor are all directors actors, although I would argue that a good director has to understand the chemistry of acting. However, the role of an outside eye is essential in the devising process, whether taken by an individual or shared by members of a company. Without this dramaturgical input, work lacks shape and potential dramatic moments remain unexploited.

Building on the foundations of the previous two exercises, this next one approaches the relationship between research and impulse. You will need copies of random pages from a biographical dictionary to distribute.

Character katas [311]

Distribute random pages of a biographical dictionary so each actor has information on one person to work with. Read the material and then explore the physical responses it evokes in you in terms of 'ideographs'.

Once you have found three or four, work on them to see how you can move between them, and then structure a short sequence of actions that is repeatable. When you have a repeatable cycle, work on it to shape its rhythmic structure. It might appear like a 'kata' from a martial arts discipline, a kind of abstract gestural dance.

It is important in this exercise to channel the feelings or associations that are conjured in you by the material into your actions, so that the kata becomes a composite of the original stimulus and your personal response. This does not mean identifying with the person, but letting your emotional response feed into the work. You might feel angry, for example, at the indignities suffered by your 'biographee', or sympathy for them. You might even feel indifferent to their riches and success. Try to incorporate these into how you colour your performance of the kata.

When you present these, spectators may like to suggest what kind of person they 'see' in the kata. They are not meant to guess who it might be, but often some connections to the original person are made. Notice how any emotional colouring is interpreted.

These exercises work on the individual actor's personal responses to objects, ideas and people to produce images and gestures. Finding a breathing pattern to accompany them and working on what sounds might complement them is a further stage of development. Starting points for devising work may emerge, although that is not the primary intention. A more important outcome is the way in which you begin to see how meaning can evolve in response to a stimulus, how image and gesture can be arrived at without first deciding on character or situation, and, in the final exercise, how personal feelings can inform movement.

Grotowski's students were asked to make two columns in their notebooks and write in one everything they had *done* during an improvisation, and in the other everything they had *associated* inwardly.[312] By associations he meant all those things that arrive in the mind unbidden during improvisation. Recalling both columns would enable them to repeat the improvisation before working on structuring it and perfecting it for performance.[313] This was during the final phase of Grotowski's research, when students produced 'acting propositions' from working on personal memories and through which they found new relationships between gesture and voice, between the inner imaginative world of the actor and outer physical manifestation. These were then developed into a 'line of physical actions' and eventually presented in-house as individual compositions.

Thomas Richards, who documents his work on physical actions with Grotowski in his illuminating book *At Work With Grotowski on Physical Actions* (1995), writes that it is important to choose memories which touch the actor at some deep level. S/he must define the situation, make the line of physical actions clear and, when performing, think only about what s/he is doing and the associations. Grotowski insisted that actors *always* structure their improvisations. Reliance on chance and 'the moment' led to superficial work, he found.

Torgier Wethal recalls working with Eugenio Barba along similar lines in the sixties. These 'studies', as they were called, worked on the principle of a guided fantasy through which the actor fixed a sequence of actions supported by inner visualisation: 'Nature and all the details of the

experience were to be seen with the inner eye'.[314] Some actors will see
images on an internal 'movie screen' and then show them in space, others
'live' the experience and their body carries out what happens. The crucial
thing is that 'the improvisation must not illustrate this world,' says
Wethal, 'the actor must simply react completely, both physically and
emotionally, with respect to what is happening, to what he is doing'.[315]

This process of creating individual compositions is applied by the Odin
actors to character work for their productions. They frequently work from
objects or costume items chosen by themselves. Else Marie Laukvik began
working on a stilt character who appeared and developed over three
productions (*The Book of Dances, The Million* and *Anabasis*) by working
with a prop, 'a fringed flag on a staff: a butterfly. When I held it up in front
of my face there was a person in the butterfly. The character went up on
stilts shortly after it got a white dress ... Then I made a wig of long, black
silk fringe and attached it to my head with a red headband. Even the
butterfly had a headband'.[316]

The character is developed through solo improvisations, using props
and costumes, and shown to the director, Barba, who makes suggestions. In
further shows, Laukvik's stilt character acquired a red and black dress with
white Rangda-inspired trousers, roses from Thailand, an English umbrella
and Kabuki-style hair – and a puppet-daughter, which was incorporated
into *The Million*; all these additions were made by the actress herself.

Several things are worth noting about the Odin actors' working process.
One is that the characters grow out of their training (they started training
outdoors – hence Laukvik's stilts, for example), so there is a 'continual
exchange of impulses between the two: ideas about a coming production
take ... training in a new direction; a discovery made in training can inspire a [new] scene'.[317] Secondly, their characters are sometimes played by
another member of the company; in other words, once the character is
created it becomes a 'text' another actor can play. Drawing on personal
experience and imagination, connecting the interior psyche to the exterior
world is an integral part of their devising. They are inspirational both in
the ways they develop characters and themselves through their work, and
in the way they retain their individual performance identity within Barba's
unique method of creating montage.

Odin's work, like that of most other companies, arises from research
and source material. Like Grotowski, Barba is attracted to myths, and many
of the characters his actors create are rooted in archetypes. His interests

lie in historical perspectives, such as the destruction of the Indians, or Brecht and the situation in Nazi Germany (*Brecht's Ashes*, 1982). Source material is transposed into theatrical ideas via the creations of individual actors and their dialogue with the director. Music is an important feature too, and the eventual 'performance text' is 'a polyphony of the actors' actions, use of text, changes in the lights [and] space'[318] woven together in a labyrinthian structure which puts the onus on the spectators in constructing meaning(s). Words are one dimension of a whole spectrum of performance elements, as in the work of many other companies. In physical-based devising, spoken language is on an equal footing with all the other performance elements, and is frequently the last thing to be set.

GENERATING TEXT

Words are a pattern on the canvas of movement [319]

Physical theatre is more than choreographed movement, and even though there are examples of purely visual theatre (usually accompanied by a sound-track), speech is more often than not a component. Language for the actor-creator (actor-author) is one of the tools of the trade and it is important to get it right even though it is not potential literature. The best praise is when an audience don't seem to notice it, when the language is so much part of the piece that it seems knitted in.

Few companies employ a writer. The post-modern distrust of language seems to have spread into a distrust of writers. Yet frequently the textual aspect of physical-based devised theatre – both the words and structuring that are the writer's craft – is its Achilles heel. Performers are trained in the poetry of space but not in the poetry of language and the rhythms of structure.

The exercises in SECTION FOUR offer a foundation in working on sound and voice. Having accomplished that work, you can return to some of the earlier exercises, such as CHANGE THE OBJECT, or JUMBLE PLAY for example and play them again with sound and speech. What you may find is that once people start speaking they tend to think first and block the spontaneity of the impulse. Trying to marry action and speech so that one is indivisible from the other is the aim of the exercises that follow.

The half-masks of commedia are excellent catalysts for generating speaking characters from a physical impulse. When actors allow the masks to lead them, there is no gap in which to think before doing; consequently speech accompanies action.

Rather than attempting to play the masks as the original commedia characters caught up in archaic scenarios, let each actor find his or her own character through working a mask, using it as a catalyst in the creation process. The characters produced may resemble the originals, but it is surprising how many variants these masks can spawn. Remember that the cut of each mask will influence the way the character speaks and the physical stance the mask provokes will release the character's voice.

Commedic characters may speak in heightened or grotesque voices, but they operate in quite prosaic worlds where motivation tends to be quite basic. Working on the simple notion of knowing what a mask wants (see SECTION TWO) offers considerable mileage in developing improvisations. The scenario exercise in the previous section is also a useful starting point.

You can play this next game with characters you are exploring, or purely as actors creating something on the spot.

The letter

A blank sheet of paper folded into an envelope is the only prop you need. (Have a few ready as they sometimes get crumpled or torn.) Place the letter onstage. A volunteer enters. S/he sees the letter and reacts and plays an imaginary situation physically and verbally. The letter isn't necessarily addressed to the recipient. It is entirely up to the actor who it is for and what is in it. The 'world' you create does not have to be realistic.

Try to avoid telling us what is in the letter: "Oh Wow! I've won the lottery. Great." or "She's leaving me. Oh god. I can't live without her." Dialogue is there to intrigue as well as inform. The less you let us know, the more you will arouse curiosity and create suspense, as in the following examples: "I don't believe it. No. Yes. It says ... It's true," or "No. Please. Don't. Don't leave." This leaves the meaning open to possibilities.

The danger with this exercise is that actors decide on what is in the letter before they get to it and produce a preconceived reaction. Trying to be inventive often backfires. It is more productive to wait until you pick up the letter, and keep your response to a simple idea and work that honestly. This means trusting the moment, letting an idea arise unbidden. The exercise is

*not about succeeding or failing but unearthing a moment of truth. Ideally
what is in the letter should be a surprise to you as well as the audience.*

The most important questions at this stage are: Did we need any words?
Did the words gloss the action or surprise us? Do we want to know any
more? What happens next?

If we can 'read' the action then the words need to do something else.
When words do not need to carry the action, speech may add a sonic
dimension or serve another purpose.

The three principle functions of dialogue are: to embody action, move
the story along, and reveal/conceal character. In STICK STORIES (SECTION
THREE), gobbledygook language carried the action and moved the story
along, and actors were storytellers rather than characters. Telling stories is
in itself a highly productive way of developing yourself as a creative actor,
providing you realise that storytelling is not recitation but a reinvention of
the story – in effect a solo improvisation where the actor is him/herself as
narrator, but plays characters in the story, acting out the action and
dialogue. Storytelling also requires you to cultivate an open and direct
relationship with your audience.

Once actors start speaking, a common problem is saying too much.
Learning to condense language is as important as acquiring economy of
gesture. Theatre distils life; a conversation that would take three hours in
real life may take less than three minutes on stage. And in life we frequently reveal more by what we don't say than by what we do say. Implication not statement governs our exchanges. The most effective dialogue
is unpredictable, so lines that elicit predictable answers, or duplicate
gesture, are redundant.

Yes/yes

*Work in pairs. Each duo plays an improvisation, along the lines of 'No-Ball
Tennis', integrating speech and movement but the only words you can say
are 'Yes' and its variants, e.g. 'okay', 'uh-huh', 'yep', 'yeah' etc. Again it is the
reaction that's important rather than a preconceived idea. Limit the number
of exchanges – ten is enough.*

*Situations emerge out of actions and speech, sometimes with a clear sense
of potential development. More importantly, you realise that words in theatre
are the tip of the iceberg.*

When you have a situation, dialogue has to serve more specific objectives in conveying information and moving events along. The following two exercises foster an understanding of this.

Who and where

It is situation that makes language come alive, more particularly situations that demand action. Location is a good starting point: knowing where you are generates situations and contexts in which characters and storylines can be explored.

You need a set of people/occupations for this exercise, such as: baby, zoo-keeper, witch, trapeze artist, dentist. The odder the mix, the better. Make up your own and write them on slips of paper and distribute them. Actors do not reveal who they are.

Now split into pairs and give each pair a location. Again, the more bizarre the better, such as: canoe, top of a building, far-away planet, bath.

Each pair knows where they are, but not who each other is. To begin with improvise only the situation and allow who you are to become apparent to your partner, i.e. don't state who you are but imply it through action and speech. Once you realise each other's occupation then go back over the material you have generated and compose a short performance which conveys to the audience who and where you are without stating it.

There is no reason why the characters should not already know each other nor why they should be living in present time. Try to ensure that each character has a distinctive speech rhythm as well as a physical stance and gestural language. Limiting the number of exchanges (lines of dialogue) helps to promote economy of speech; with less to say actors focus on other performative strategies and when they do speak what they say carries more weight.

When you show these pieces, notice how effectively actors are able to convey who they are without resorting to literal gestures or dropping big hints. Is it clear where they are? Is where they are integral to the action of the piece? Work out which particular detail, either in action or word, gave the spectators the necessary information. How subtle was this? You may also like to think about when the who/where became apparent, and what effect that had on the spectators' interest.

The notion of subtext is usually associated with naturalism, but arche-types and caricatures are also driven by desires which frequently reside under the surface. Sometimes it is useful to realise that what a character says is not transparent. They may say one thing and mean another. Contradiction keeps characters vital. And internal conflict is as important as conflict between characters and their environment, or each other.

For an audience, knowing everything about a character renders that character lifeless. Audiences want to be involved in working out the char-acters. Although, eventually, you will need to know far more about your characters than will be revealed, knowing what they want, and discovering how or whether they get it, is far more productive than knowing their shoe-size (unless that is integral to the plot). Revealing or concealing motivation through language is what the next exercise plays with.

Roundabout

Work in pairs. Decide on (or distribute) a situation which demands action, such as grave-digging, putting up a tent. Develop an improvisation in which X gets what s/he wants from Y without stating it. Limit each actor to a maximum of ten lines.

As in the who/where game, the characters may know each other and they need not be in present time. You can use characters you are already exploring, or from a fairy tale or myth, or start from scratch.

What becomes interesting here is how the speech can be removed from the action (unless you retreat into the obvious, eg X wants the spade or guy-rope from Y) allowing the words to meet the action as a surprise.

The point that all these exercises bring out is that very often you don't need to say very much. The more economic the speech, the more powerful if – like the right gesture – it's the right word.
There are one or two useful tips:

- avoid explanations which tell the audience what's going on or who you are
- find a speech style for characters through exploring their movement
- value silence.

A useful way to practise generating verbal text is to use fairy tales, as their structures and characters are malleable and situations are presented in only their essential elements. If we unravel *Little Red Riding Hood* we find the following components:

- *people*
- one mother
- one daughter
- one grandmother
- one wolf
- one woodcutter
- *places*
- two houses
- one wood
- *objects*
- one basket of food
- one red cape
- one axe

This gives you a set of characters, locations and objects, in effect a scenario on which you can build images, gestures and verbal text. In literal terms, the journey of the story travels from one house to another through the woods, whilst symbolically (and emotionally) Little Red Riding Hood travels from innocence to experience. Telling the story chronologically means following a linear path so that the consequence of each event promotes the next. But a consideration of structuring from a compositional perspective means these components can be shuffled and stitched together in other ways.

STRUCTURING TEXT

Composition is organising chaos.[320]

Structure is, essentially, the architecture of a piece. An architect draws up a pattern or template for buildings without which they would fall down, but is aware that different shapes have different functions and give different pleasures. So, for example, the arching cathedral might give a feeling of spiritual uplift, square houses might signify safety. Similarly, different structural patterns yield different theatrical experiences.

The spectator is not aware of the existence of structure; it is the invisible map on which the journey of a piece travels. Yet although invisible, there are definite transitions which guide the spectator. In narrative terms these are the turning points of the plot. Certainly not all theatre is plot-driven, in fact at the turn of the millennium narrative is under threat and, as I have already pointed out, physical-based devising is more often compositional in structure. Narrative does, however, offer a useful starting point.

Classic narrative is recognisable as the paradigm used by Hollywood screenwriters. Commercial cinema demands a beginning, middle and upbeat end – in that order. We are all familiar with this restorative three-act structure, with its logic of cause and effect and its linear progression punctuated by twists and turns in the plot. We call it story, yet there is a fundamental distinction to be made between story and narration. Story is the raw material of the events, narration is the way those events are organised.[321] Devisers, like writers, need to understand this distinction so they recognise the need to organise the raw material in a way which tells/invites an audience how to construct the story/stories, and infer meaning(s).

Stories can be told in different ways, and they offer different experiences depending on how they are told. Separating story from narration enables you to see how the story is *assembled*, in other words how it is structured. It is not dissimilar to taking an engine apart to see how it works.

The most immediate way to get to grips with this is to consider time. In plot-driven drama, the material is traditionally organised in chronological order, hence its linear progression. The fact that the story appears to be 'going somewhere' is reinforced by the time-structure which is also moving forwards. However, the necessity for time to work in tandem with chronology has been challenged and there are increasing numbers of plays in which chronological order is disrupted, for example Caryl Churchill's *Cloud 9* and *Top Girls* where the time-structures are disjointed, and Pinter's *Betrayal,* where time moves inexorably backwards. Perhaps theatre has been influenced in this respect by the cinematic device of the flashback. You could lay out the raw material, i.e. re-assemble the jigsaw pieces of these plays in their *correct* chronological order to create a more conventional narration. But the way Churchill and Pinter play with time offers an alternative experience.

Cut-and-paste time-structures still have plot embedded in them, but it is not the controlling mechanism; the disruption of time is not gratuitously chaotic but operates as a layer of meaning so that the spectator has to piece the jigsaw together and, sometimes, search for the sense in it all, seeking connections through poetic resonance and implication. The primacy of the story is qualified by the reshuffling of events, reducing the focus on upcoming events and suspense and refocusing on other areas. Rather than being passive spectators, transported and 'carried away' on the wings of the story and by an empathetic response to characters, the act of piecing fragments together makes spectators more actively involved and more questioning of the relationship of one thing to another.[322]

Experimenting with *Little Red Riding Hood*, or any familiar fairy tale, and working out alternative time-structures in which to present the story will generate a host of different ideas. The skeleton of the story and its components remain unchanged, but their treatment can be altered by playing about with the chronology of events and the time-structure.

As long as you have a sequence of events to work from, i.e. you have constructed an outline scenario, you can begin to play with time as a structuring device. Remember too that you can also suspend time. Theatre has always been aware that suspending story time allows you to go into dream time, inner world time (someone's mind), or theatrical time (addressing the audience). A word or two of warning, however. Playing around with time structures is only possible once you have a sequence of events in place. Otherwise you are putting the proverbial cart before the horse.

At its most basic, structure relates to capturing the attention of the audience and hanging on to it. However amusing or intriguing the characters, however lyrical or punchy the dialogue, if interest and suspense are absent the audience's attention will wander. The strategies you employ in organising the material are closely linked to how you control or manipulate the spectator, and how much freedom you give them to interpret. In plot-driven drama the most obvious of these is the manipulation of suspense or tension: the spectator is hooked by wanting to know 'what will happen next?' The structure here becomes a series of small explosions detonated by events. The journey of the story is 'plotted' to maximise the effect of each explosion.

In *Little Red Riding Hood*, for example, the key plot-moments are when she strays from the path and meets the wolf, when he kills grandma and dresses up in her clothes, and when Red Riding Hood assumes he is grandma with devastating results.[323]

Martin Esslin reminds us that interest and suspense 'need not necessarily be aroused merely by devices of plot', for interest can be roused by visual images, and there are many kinds of suspense. He elaborates on the potential questions raised in the spectator's mind by structure: 'What will happen next?' generates one kind, but equally, knowing what will happen might generate the question of *how* it's going to happen, essentially the premise upon which Greek drama was built for spectators who knew the stories in advance. There are also the questions 'what *is* happening', or even 'there seems to be some kind of pattern to what's going on, I wonder what it is?'.[324]

Esslin refers to Beckett's *Waiting for Godot*, where suspense is more reliant on these latter questions. It is a play which marks a significant shift in modern theatre away from narrative into more poetic structures. In *Waiting for Godot* interest and suspense are embedded in the underlying uncertainty of waiting whilst we are 'entertained' by Vladimir and Estragon as they kill time. Beckett's play reminds us that structural considerations are bound up with where you situate the audience in relation to the construction of meaning, the degree to which your audience will experience a common view or interpret meaning(s) in a more individual manner. It is more akin to the experience of reading poetry than reading a story.

Rejecting the concept of the dominant story is a distinguishing feature of postmodernism, summed up by Simon McBurney in his programme note to Theatre de Complicité's 1999 piece *Mnemonic*: 'We live in a time where stories surround us. Multiple stories. Constantly. Fragmented by television, radio, print, the internet, calling to us from every hoarding and passing us by on every street corner. We no longer live in a world of the single tale.'[325]

Disruption and fragmentation tailor the assembly of *Mnemonic*, reflecting its theme of memory. The sequence of events is governed by the theme of the piece, which does in fact contain stories, but is not overtly dependent on one single story as the binding agent. It travels back and forth across time and place, dwelling on moments, jumping track, just as in life where the brain is involved in solving problems out of sequence: 'The shards of stories we have put together, some longer, some shorter, collide here in the theatre, reflecting, repeating and revolving like the act of memory itself.'[326]

Borrowing the idea of memory as the structuring principle for *Little Red Riding Hood* opens up possibilities for telling the stories of the mother, the woodcutter, the wolf, grandmother and Little Red Riding Hood from the interior perspectives of each character's memory of the events. These can be worked on imaginatively to create a new telling of the tale. You could even depart from the tale and simply use it as a springboard from which to create a series of story-fragments connected more obliquely. To do this, you retain the characters as archetypes, and open up the creative possibilities of exploring them via the the thematic concerns of the original story, in this case 'from innocence to experience'.

Do we need story at all? This was the question raised by Gertrude Stein when she started writing plays: 'Everybody knows so many stories and what is the use of telling another story.'[327]

Stein's own work is enormously challenging for performers and audiences and, perhaps as a consequence, rarely performed. Yet her attempt at getting beyond story to a presentation of the relations between things in their essence is insightful. Her concept of the play as landscape enables us to cut loose from the idea of story: just as a landscape 'has its formation' so should a play, since landscape does not move yet always presents things 'in relation, the trees to the hills the hills to the fields the trees to each other',[328] in other words detail by detail without the need to rely on story. The journey/experience is connotative, metaphoric or symbolic rather than event-bound.

Invoking the idea of a play as landscape reduces the necessity for story and embraces the significance of texture and detail as binding agents, creating an image network which opens up material to more individual interpretations.

Improvised material and ideas thrown up from collaborative responses to story, theme or political/cultural concern become the basis of this kind of work. Using an image network, rather than a plot, weaving these together offers alternative *textural* (as opposed to *textual*) threads to follow. Spectators are less concerned with cause and effect (character-orientated or plot-motivated) and more involved in interpreting what they see. Without a dominant narrative, the onus shifts towards the spectator as the constructor of meaning, and frequently away from the notion of a common view of what is happening.

The opening of Bouge-de-la's *Underglass* is an illustrative example. The show was based on a book about an autistic woman whose obsession with routine dominated her life: 'We spent twenty minutes repeating the same routine over and over again and in doing that we altered the audience's perspective on how they see things. They watch the opening and they think they've seen it. Then they have to watch it again and they notice more things. Then again and they start to zoom in like a close-up camera and focus on certain details. Then I change the colour of the shirt I put on and suddenly you can *feel* them there. There have been occasions when people applaud and shout out at that moment. Ah she's taken the yellow shirt instead of the green one.'[329]

The idea of repetition that is eventually challenged is reminiscent of minimalist music. Steve Reich, Arvo Part and techno-music all use similar strategies, building a cumulative effect out of patterns of repetition and small changes.

Presenting something which uses an essentially visual language to an audience activates a certain part of the brain and puts them in a more meditative and reflective mood of reception. Leaving space for the audience 'to invent and dream while they're watching' is part of Bouge-de-la's philosophy, but at the same time the progression of things is very clear: 'The pictures are very readable very quickly,' says O'Rorke, 'but they can also write their own version. Some people saw themselves in that character, some people saw relatives they had, some people saw all sorts of different things. We want it to be a very individual experience.'[330]

Bouge-de-la have found that gradually audiences find their own way of reading their work: 'Some audiences find it difficult at the beginning when they don't understand that kind of concept. But when they've seen more of our shows they really enjoy that aspect . . . [and then they say] you can just let it wash over you, and then images come back to you afterwards.'[331] It is important to remember that thematic concerns govern their work, that they have 'something to say' and are not merely creating aesthetically interesting patterns of images. Their trilogy *Evolution: Body* (1998), *Mind* (1999), *Spirit* (2000) is underpinned by a deep concern for contemporary problems confronting humanity, and their work is grounded in considerable research.

The choice of source material lies outside the parameters of this book. But by far the most successful pieces of devised theatre are those inspired by a shared passion for the subject matter. Heartfelt passion can, however, divert you from thinking about the audience. And it is the experience you want to give your audience that should guide structural decisions. If you are adapting a story then that story must be told. If you are exploring a theme then that theme must be clear. If you want to make them laugh then the mechanics of laughter must be evident.

In the previous section you were encouraged to create visual images through engaging with objects (SOLO JUMBLE), themes (IDEOGRAPHS) and biography (CHARACTER KATAS). And when presenting these solo pieces I suggested those observing might work directorially to sift out correspondences between them and perhaps put them into sequences, selecting colours, textures, or gestural style which offer similarities and contrasts to create counterpoints and balance. Perhaps also there were moments when repetition, or the reincorporation of a previous image/gesture created an effect, when one thing became more interesting through variation. These are likely to generate image networks which operate on an aesthetic plane, rather in the manner of contemporary dance.

Images do not have to be aesthetically pleasing, as the recurrent 'ideograph' of burning in Brook's *US*, which culminated in the onstage immolation of a butterfly, demonstrates. When Brook and his collaborators were searching for a new language of acting during the process of preparing *US* (a highly controversial devised piece about Vietnam, which prompted questions in the House of Commons), they came to the conclusion that the complexity of the material was such that 'it could only be done through a flow of imagery, with actors who could move backwards and forwards between several different styles.'[332] There was no dominant story; styles were mixed, as in montage,[333] to create effects through contrast and juxtaposition.

An image network generated from source material (whether story, theme, political, cultural and/or personal concerns) can be developed to incorporate spoken text and/or music. You will end up with a wealth of images, scenes, ideas, stories which need to be consolidated and organised into a coherent whole.

If you regard the images or scenes you create as 'cells' that form a network, these have to be selected and then placed in relation to one another just as a film editor cuts and cross-cuts in the post-production room. It is how the cells relate to each other and the cumulative effects of them in sequences or in counterpoint which determine the spectator's experience. This is an ongoing procedure. Unlike film, where such editing occurs in the cutting room after the images and scenes have been fixed on celluloid, in devised theatre choosing the cells and deciding how they fit together occurs as part of the developmental process. In this sense, structuring is daily decision-making. It requires taking the spectator viewpoint and deciding which of Esslin's questions you are provoking and what experience you want to offer your audience. Be prepared to reject material. Scrapping scenes and ideas is part of the editing process.

Transitions between cells become signposts in structural terms. Just as the twists and turns of plot provide transitional moments in narrative, the shifts between scenes and visual images serve to provoke transitions in compositional structures. You need to find bridges and links between them, or ways of putting them together to create desired effects.

Some of the exercises suggested earlier in this book incorporate foundation work for this aspect of structuring. In particular, the RHYTHM-SCAPES in SECTION FOUR encourage an instinctive sense of 'feeling the moment' when an improvisation is ready to move on, the point at which a shift into a new scene is needed. Similarly, ESCALATIONS foster a sense of the contrasts between different dynamics and how shifting through the 'gears' deepens the intensity. The sentient understanding acquired though such work is useful preparation for structuring material where you need to be able to sense moments of change.

Finding transitions which push things in a different direction, when a fresh idea takes over and moves things on, is the key to creating fluidity. As you develop work on your raw material, try moving between different styles. So, for example, act out *Little Red Riding Hood* by starting quite realistically and moving the action into the surreal, exaggerating the fantastical elements and finding ways of moving between different styles. Do you jump between surreal and real or slide gently from one to the other?

These acts of choosing and placing images and scenes are fundamentally the craft of a writer: 'This is the largest part of a writer's job whatever the working method: not dialogue . . . but the choosing and structuring of the scenes.'[334] This is the most problematic area of structuring, finding the best order so as to create a coherent whole. If you are not working with an experienced writer, the outside eye of a director is essential.

I have moved away from the idea that theatre is about story to emphasise that narrative is not the only way of structuring text but merely one particular structuring device, just as naturalism is as much a particular style of theatre as melodrama or commedia dell'arte. Narrative is, in some respects, one of the most difficult, for although it is often easy to generate material for the beginning and middle of a narrative, unless you have an ending which is both inevitable and surprising, structuring the latter stages can present problems. There are many excellent sources for advice on narrative structure in screenwriting manuals, and if your material falls naturally into that mould you may find consulting such manuals extremely helpful.

Story structures have much to offer, not least a given internal dynamic which shapes material. It is not just the cause-and-effect logic of story that holds an audience but the emotional journey of characters. This is where Zeami's law of unfolding and conclusion comes back into play, for the principle of Jo-Ha-Kyu (which is dealt with in SECTION FOUR: RHYTHM) is extremely useful in thinking about structure. And indeed, rhythm is at the heart of structure. Even films are predicated on rhythmic structure; it is the edit-rhythm in particular which governs the levels of tension we feel.

As I explained before, Jo-Ha-Kyu is more than simply beginning-middle-end; it has more to do with the interior dynamic, the flow of the whole. Just as the flow of water is determined ultimately by its final destination, the flow of a devised piece is determined by its conclusion. That ending may be a return to the beginning (creating a cyclical structure as in *Waiting for Godot*), or the resolution of a problem posed at the start of the piece, or a point at which characters come to a new realisation through what has happened. The more definite the ending, the more closely everything that happens has to lead towards it. This is easy to see in narrative structures where the logic of cause and effect is the governing principle.

By contrast, in circus the experience is governed by the variety principle: the clowns are followed by trapeze artists and then by the strong man and so on until perhaps the clowns return. Like a theme-park ride, there are varying degrees of thrill and tension, and plateaux in between. Each individual act has its own interior dynamic, its Jo-Ha-Kyu, and the whole is bound together by spectacle. The conclusion is the end of the event, not of any interior journey.

A central preoccupation of modern theatrical exploration is that the spectator *experiences* theatre as an event. As Jos Houben puts it, 'We don't go to the theatre to understand, we go to experience.' Although the sense of communion that comes from the collective presence of the audience is valued, a common view is not necessarily the aim. So the experience can be closer to circus than narrative satisfaction. However, it is still necessary, I believe, to take the audience on a journey that has more than simply spectacle and visual excitement as the outcome. Theatre is able to probe the human condition. Circus is not.

In traditional narrative structures, the spectator's attention is held by the cause and effect and linear progression of story where meaning is set, and every spectator will receive and decode the signs in a similar fashion and from similar (visual) points of view. In compositional structures, the spectator's attention is held by fascination with spectacle and the experience of the whole, where meaning is not particularly set and the performance may have in-built ambiguities so that spectators are invited to construct individual meanings from different points of view.

The (literal) repositioning of the spectator in Grotowski's experiments (see SECTION THREE: AUDIENCE) gave them differing visual perspectives, but essentially he was working with narrative structures rooted in myth which focused on a central character. Although Eugenio Barba has followed suit (placing the spectators in the scenic space is always integral to the Odin performances), he has developed a distinctive way of using montage to structure improvisation work so that an audience has an active and individual response rather than a collective empathy for a central protagonist.

Barba will suggest a theme to actors; they create improvisations from their personal response to the material, which he then reworks. He does not enter into any dialogue about the actor's motivations, but orchestrates their solo improvisations into 'actions', sequences of action, and scenes, re-ordering and structuring according to his own intuitive sense of tempo and rhythm. Meaning is virtually shunned. It is the experience of the spectators which counts. In fact they cannot always follow a scenic whole but must choose where to look as different and apparently discontiguous events occur in various corners of the scenic space. This is closer to the idea of circus spectacle than narrative unity, yet Barba's work is much more than variety acts. What unifies the work are deep philosophical concerns rather than simply entertainment, plus a desire to affect the spectator on a primal level.

Here is Meyerhold's idea of reaching the spectator in the sensorial plane, where the rhythms of stage composition provoke responses rather than engagement with the inner psychology of character or the narrative drive. For Meyerhold 'the spectator's impression is richer when it's perceived subconsciously.'[335] Artaud too felt this. His vision was of a theatre which touched spectators on a visceral level, where their unconscious response was the heart of the experience.

In this sense, structure is very much bound up with directing. A director is the eyes and ears of the potential audience, and structural decisions are bound up in how s/he wants them to 'read' the work. And a directorial vision is what ultimately provides coherence. It is not arrived at by chance but is the organisation of chance elements and collective creativity.

Structure is complex. It can seem like a crossword puzzle with no clues in the rehearsal room! One way of ensuring you are clear about the way the piece hangs together and its potential effect on the audience, is to write each scene – however small – on a 5x3 card. If you lay these out on the floor it is easier to organise the material you have created into a coherent journey. Inviting people to view the work before production night is always a useful way of testing whether it works.

Given time, and a commitment to experimenting with ways of structuring material, you may arrive at the point where you make structural decisions on an instinctual level. However, it is vital to consider the experience from the audience's point of view in the process of devising. Structural decisions inform how audiences will interpret and respond to your work, and the art of theatre demands that you communicate with your audience.

SECTION 6

The physical text

SECTION 6

The physical text

We have to . . . make words part of our whole physical self in order to release them from the tyranny of the mind. [336]

Although it may appear very different to work on a play rather than the collection of fragments and scraps that you have when devising, the starting point is very similar. The difference lies, of course, in the fact that the words and structure are already there. You meet the story and characters through language, rather than arriving at them through from playing with ideas. However, as with devising, using instinct rather than reason lies at the heart of a physical approach to text. Too much thinking can stifle the creative process, as Berkoff puts it: 'Too much analysis, like too much choke, can make you stall.' [337]

Text work requires exactly the same preparation as devised work: a company needs a common physical and imaginative vocabulary. The process is organic. The responsibility of the actor is to work creatively as part of an ensemble and contribute ideas. If you have no ideas in rehearsal you will end up doing nothing interesting on stage.

Although texts do, to some extent, determine the style of a production, a company's way of working is also a key factor, and physical approaches to text from contemporary companies reveal a range of styles as the following examples illustrate. The distinctly energised delivery of Steven Berkoff's work has a magnitude reminiscent of Meyerhold's concept of the grotesque. Kaos Theatre deploy an acutely stylised physicality, which moves beyond the illustrative into the surreal (*The Importance of Being Earnest* 1998, and *Renaissance* 2000), and also veers towards the 'grotesque'. Trestle Theatre's *The Barretts of Wimpole Street* (2000) exploits the company's distinctive handle on visual storytelling – a highly legible gestural language rooted in their explorations of mask work. Theatre de Complicité's forays into extant plays (*The Caucasian Chalk Circle* 1997 and *The Chairs* 1998, being the most recent) have capitalised on the highly imaginative and playful ensemble skills that are the company's hallmark.

What binds these disparate styles is the way the physical life of the actor is the imaginative conduit of meaning, narrative, and character, so what is said is simply one layer in the multiple layering of meanings. In other words, they encourage a complex seeing. It is largely through the eye that the spectator's imaginative sensibilities are drawn in.[338] But the actors do more than merely illustrate the text.

Games and play foster imagination and spontaneity within a framework (the rules of the game). A play supplies a framework, and the situations and words act as a stimulus for the actors' creativity. The ability to enter into imaginative worlds, to make transitions between worlds – those momentary fleeting worlds of emotion as well as the environments of the play – is vital. Ultimately it is your imaginative response to the text that allows character and style to emerge.

Joan Littlewood had a masterly grasp of the relationship between games and text, and led her actors into the imaginative world of the play itself through games allied to situations in the play. Consequently, the actors made discoveries about the characters and events in the text through playing games. Quite frequently too, Littlewood left casting until later on in the process so the ensemble had a grasp of the whole play before being assigned specific tasks/roles. Although this is virtually impossible to emulate in the commercial theatre, it is an immensely valuable method of working. Even if a play has been cast, beginning the rehearsal process with a collective exploration of the whole play kick-starts the process of mutual collaboration.

Actors' imaginations can be stimulated by ideas adjacent to the text in exactly the same way as a devising process uses research. So paintings, photographs, music, history – all the items sparked by a play but additional to it – are part of the cauldron of ideas that fuel the process. It is every actor's responsibility to research the play as well as the role s/he might undertake; that is how true collective ownership of the process and performance occurs.

Berkoff frequently uses actors as a chorus, who transform themselves into environments as well as other characters. In *Agamemnon* and *The Trial*, a chorus created the design, manipulating sticks and rope in the former, and door frames in the latter to conjure the worlds of the play. In *Hamlet* ten actors not only doubled the thirty roles but also sat on chairs around the stage-area as a chorus, watching and commenting on the action via their body language: 'They change like chameleons, or sometimes become a mirror for the events in the centre . . . neutral observers, sometimes staying within their characters, but often as people caught up in the environment – as in religious paintings where the subsidiary figures enhance the whole by focusing on the centre.'[339]

Multiple role-playing, or doubling of roles, is a common strategy. This is not simply economic necessity, for it can also be seen as a tangible acknowledgement of the duplicity of acting: the actor can be simultaneously storyteller, character(s) and member of a chorus creating environments, or commentating on the action. In other words, there is a demonstrable awareness and execution of transitional acting. Character is something arrived at and conveyed through predominantly physical rather than intellectual or psychological means, and the actor's skill lies as much in an ability to shift between characters as well as between worlds.

Doubling enables actors playing smaller roles to become genuinely involved in the whole play. And, in terms of technique: 'Doubling presents a great opportunity for an actor to work around the range of their talent.'[340] The richness of some of Shakespeare and Brecht's silent roles, for example, (which are frequently cut in the mistaken belief that they are unimportant) offer considerable challenges to actors.

Although many practitioners have ditched text as an 'authority', they are often still drawn to classical texts. All great texts embody something universal or profound. Like myths in the ancient world, they explore the human condition yet leave the door to interpretation open. Asked why he chose texts from the 'great tradition', Grotowski replied: 'These are like the voices of my ancestors . . . [they] fascinate me because they give us the possibility of a sincere confrontation.'[341]

For Grotowski, his encounter with a text is similar to his encounter with an actor: 'The author's text is a kind of scalpel enabling us to open ourselves . . . to transcend our solitude.'[342] By confronting it, the actor and producer confront themselves, their beliefs, experiences and prejudices. The concept of being open to the text, of allowing it to work on the actor and, perhaps, reveal something new to him/her, challenges the notion of being true to authorial intention. Instead of approaching the text as sacrosanct, with the actors as servants of a work of art, the actor's respect for the text is that of a craftsman for another craftsman's material; s/he meets the 'author' on equal terms.

There is no foolproof method of physicalising text. The danger lies in thinking that physicalising means simply illustrating. Although visualisation plays a central role in animating a text, a physical approach has as much to do with searching for the underbelly of a play, so that communication with the audience happens on the sensory as well as visual and auditory levels.

Energy is crucial – what kind of energy does the play demand? To think of the text itself as a physical entity, brimming with energy, with patterns and colours embedded in it, means starting from a position of not-knowing, of innocence if you like, so that meanings emerge rather than being imposed.

To cover the possibilities of physical theatre in relation to text in real depth deserves more space than can be dedicated here. It is, however, absolutely vital that text work does not start without prior training. You won't get very far without establishing a common physical vocabulary, and the notions of play and complicité and other concepts illustrated in this book are as essential to working on scripts as they are to devising.

The aim of the exercises in this section is to offer some routes to searching out meaning, story, character, through somatic encounters with a text. They build on exercises used earlier in this book in order to provide some continuity. It would be pointless to attempt the exercises here without exploring those in the earlier sections. This is not to suggest a rigid method, but rather to indicate how preparatory training feeds into the process of interpreting text.

Many of the following games and exercises approach text from abstract or tangential angles in the belief that 'the sudden surprise of discovery can often reveal more about a text . . . than approaching it directly'.[343] They are not designed to forge a particular style, but simply offer a physical approach to unlocking the text.

The text examples used here are predominantly from Shakespeare for one very good reason: the heightened language of Shakespeare encourages the exploration of the limits of expression, and lays a foundation for approaching modern plays with a respect for the playwright's choice of words. The tendency to render modern prose (or even Shakespeare) as 'everyday-speak' belies the fact that any writer worth their salt uses language deliberately to resonate with more than surface meaning. In Cicely Berry's words: 'Work on Shakespeare opens our awareness to language in modern writing by adding to the resonance of the words we speak, even when they are rooted in a modern reality.'[344]

IMAG(IN)ING THE TEXT

I want them to hold the piece in their hands; but that understanding is not an intellectual process, it is a physical one, they have to feel it.[345]

Whilst the spontaneous reactions demanded by improvisation can help to teach the necessary honesty of performance, in improvisation everything is happening for first time; it is more difficult to get that same sense of truth with a script when the outcome is preordained. To get 'behind' the text, to find the impulse behind word and action, you need to tackle the rhythmic and sonic patterns of a text, to find the underlying dynamics, and allow them to provoke your imagination.

In RHYTHM-SCAPES and SOUNDSCAPES in SECTION FOUR, tubes and then percussion were used to create abstract, or free-form, pieces using the *otkas – posyl – stoika* as a structuring device. The following exercises follow on from this work, applying the same idea in principle to text. Prefacing the next exercise with those earlier ones will enrich the work.

Scene-scape[346]

Scenes I, IV and V from Act I of Hamlet *work very well for this, provided everyone knows the play.*[347] *Distribute a collection of percussion tools and/or instruments – home-made ones are as effective as the orchestral varieties – anything that can be shaken, rattled, banged or chimed will do, but ensure you have a variety of sounds.*

Each group reads a scene through and pinpoints the major moments of tension, using these to subdivide the scene into smaller units. Once these are agreed, the group should attempt to label these using an active verb. Act I Scene IV for example, might end up in six sections labelled: Waiting/ Debating/ Seeing/ Beckoning/ Fighting/ Following.

Having established these units, each group uses the percussion to improvise a soundscape of the whole scene. This will go through a few 'drafts' to create a final piece. Try to avoid the literal, such as replicating the sound of footsteps. Be careful always to be concerned with capturing the ebb and flow of tension rather than mimicry – it's a soundscape not a sound-picture.

Another point to bear in mind is how to move between units. The principle of a 'fixed point' is useful here, in other words punctuating the moment of transition from one unit to the next.

These compositions are played to the other groups. Those working on the same scene may well find points of similarity between their soundscapes, and although it's quite common to find that groups will inflect the same scene slightly differently, the units usually fall into a similar overall pattern.

Remember the importance of silence. In the early stages, many soundscapes are too busy. And the discovery that 'less is more' is a valuable lesson.

Action-scape

Now create the action of the scene in movement using the previous exercise as a basis. In other words find physical equivalents for the sounds in terms of the ebb and flow of tension. Actors may represent characters, but you may decide to work as a chorus, or a combination of both, and the movement can be quite abstract. The aim is to capture the rhythm of the scene in physical terms rather than mime the scene's action. Use no words. Present the scenes as choreographies using only percussion to accompany or punctuate the movement.

This work encourages actors to recognise the underlying pattern of a scene, its peaks and troughs, where one unit ends and another begins, from the intuitive perspective of rhythm.

It is a variation on the (Stanislavskian) notion of scoring the action, which operates by stripping the text to a small selection of key words and building the action around them, a method which depends more on analysing language than sensing rhythm but is nonetheless a useful way of getting to the action of a scene, discovering what is happening.

If you move on to creating a more literal action-scape after the previous exercises, i.e. playing out the situation on the battlements, you will find that actors render the scene more vividly than if they had simply attempted to portray the action from a reading.

Any scene can be presented as dumb show, with no words, in the manner of visual storytelling, sometimes called *tableaux vivants*. Dumb shows and scenarios reveal the skeleton of a scene or story and serve to bring the narrative into focus. They are a highly effective way for actors to grasp the story of a scene, and bring an awareness of how an audience reads what's happening through the physical interaction of actors. However, in order to work beyond the merely pedestrian and illustrative, you need to work on the transference of energy.

The earlier exercise, STICK-STORIES is a useful corollary here.

Stick-scenes

Building on your shared understanding of the rhythmic pattern of the scene, present it now as a dumb show using a stick to pass the energy between players. Try to keep as much space between you as possible, so that the moment of passing the stick gains urgency.

Adding gobbledeygook in place of dialogue (along the lines of the exercise stick-stories) brings it into the realm of storytelling. The important thing is not to use gobbledeygook to paraphrase the dialogue, but for its sonic and tonal properties.

Passing the stick forces actors to interact – you have to look someone in the eye to pass and receive the stick! It also promotes an understanding of how focus shifts, and how important it is to keep every moment alive onstage. When the stick 'dies', so does the scene.

Another way of using the stick is to pass it before you speak. The person receiving it has to react to what is being said.

By now you will have a deeper knowledge of the scene you've been working on. And you'll start to see how the possibilities of your own imaginative interpretation open up. Once you have the lines (see p. 205 for advice on line-learning in DEALING WITH WORDS) and you return to this scene, re-play this stick-passing exercise. You'll find it energises the scene and offers you choices for where to place the focus. You can then play with modulating the energy along the lines of the game CHANGING GEARS in SECTION THREE.

Thinking visually in theatre does not mean thinking pictorially. Playing with different configurations of audience to stage, e.g. in the round, traverse, thrust, is a valuable deterrent. It serves to energise performance, even if you know you will eventually play the piece end-on.

At the heart of 'imaging' a text lies the art of suggestion. Peter Brook remarked that if you furnish the stage, you furnish the mind of the spectator. Metaphor can be far more powerful than reality. In Brook's *Marat*

Sade, the actors poured buckets of red and blue paint to represent the blood of the peasants and monarchy shed in the French Revolution. Brook's work is awash with such vivid images, from the red ribbons dangling from the mutilated Lavinia's arms in *Titus Andronicus*, to the arrows carried across the stage in *The Mahabharata*. CHANGE THE OBJECT is a good exercise for laying the foundations of creating images and worlds through physical improvisation.

Berkoff makes an interesting point about props, saying that in *Hamlet* the cast would use props in rehearsal, but if they got in the way – or in the way of the inventiveness of the actors – they would mime them instead.[348] He recalls getting very tired using fencing foils to rehearse his fight with Laertes at the end of *Hamlet*. One day he suggested rehearsing all the moves without the foils, with the beat of a drum marking each move; they fought with a new power and agility. This 'fight without foils' became part of the production, the audience 'inventing' the steel blades flashing through the air and the blood they drew, which made the scene far more horrific.[349] Such moments of collective imagining are the very essence of theatre.

Sound effects serve as an imaginative support for the suggestive power of mime, and working initially with percussion encourages a sensitivity to the relationship between the audio and visual that feeds the spectators' experience. Sound, like design, should be part of the process of exploring and imag(in)ing the play rather than something tacked on. There is the added pleasure and fascination of watching sound effects being made. Watching an actor shake a thunder sheet as King Lear hurls abuse at the sky, or hitting the timpani as Pericles struggles to keep his ship on course in a storm, adds another dimension to the spectator's experience and involvement.

Using musicians who respond to and react with the actors in rehearsal, as Berkoff and Brook do, developing the musical score along with scoring the action, is an increasingly common strategy. Using musicians, or actor-musicians, working to create an integrated musical score during rehearsals is an ideal which some companies pursue, Kaboodle Theatre, for example, whose musicians share the stage with the actors, and sometimes play small roles in performance. Then there are companies like Commonground, whose actor-musicians create and play the music as part of the making process, integrating the two in performance.

Even if you have no musicians, actors can work on exploring text through rhythms and sound. Just as we need an extra-daily body on stage, using different energies to those we use in everyday life, we need to recognise that language in theatre is removed from the daily. We need to see language as charged with an alter-energy. Rhythm and sound work are a route to discovering the hidden energies in a text.

DEALING WITH WORDS

Be conscious of the action behind the words.[350]

Because we meet texts as words on a page, our first reaction is to approach them in terms of their meaning. Yet, as Peter Brook has pointed out, 'a word does not start as a word – it is an end product which begins as an impulse.'[351] And, as we have already noted, Brook has found the secrets of text are hidden in the sound, rhythm and texture of the language as much as in its meaning.

For Brook movement *is* meaning. The actor does not need to analyse whether they are interpreting the meaning though their actions; nor do they need to understand how the words, or the rhythm and sound of the words, beget action and/or meaning through them. They need only to trust their physical response to rhythm and sound via the suggestions of the director. It is not a state of identifying with the character that Brook is working towards; it is a state of 'being' which allows action and meaning to become inseparable, actor and character to become so entwined, that the actor's body is a conduit of meaning(s) for the audience to read.

Voice work is an obvious starting point, and the exercises on sound in SECTION FOUR provide a basis. Beware of working only on voice-and-text; in 'total theatre''all the elements of the human being are brought into motion'.[352] You need to get inside the words physically. Working somatically on text reveals the semantic: feeling the movement of the language is a route to understanding. As Cicely Berry puts it, you have to 'feel the language knocking around inside you'.[353]

Joan Littlewood's actors recount that they never seemed to learn the lines, they were fed in during rehearsals for the most part. She also employed the French practise of using a *siffleuse*, another company member whispering the lines in the actor's ear as the rehearsal progressed. Although many find it a distraction, it is worthwhile pursuing this strategy as it helps actors realise that they do actually know the lines, and are hanging on to their book as a 'security blanket'. It is also a co-operative way of working and enables actors to become more familiar with the whole text.

Some companies use the technique of recording the lines as neutrally as possible on tape. As actors work on the rehearsal floor, the prerecorded tape is played and eventually the actors take over – the lines have become embedded.

You cannot act with a book in your hand. However, learning lines before rehearsals creates its own problems. Actors have a tendency to learn lines in a manner which is already inflected; they work out what they think the character is saying, and why, and inflect the words accordingly. Rehearsals then become a battleground as the actor has a set meaning which s/he finds difficult to relinquish in order to explore new ideas which suggest different inflections.

To explore the possibilities inherent in a text requires learning lines in as non-inflected a manner as possible. Cicely Berry offers some excellent advice for both solo and group work in Chapter 8 of *The Actor and the Text* (2000). As she points out, being involved in an activity whilst speaking lines takes the actor's attention away from trying to remember them. Disarming actors through games and activity prevents them from becoming too head-based.

Sometimes great physical effort can release the voice, partly because it takes attention away from speaking, as in the following exercise. Use this for working on prepared speeches.

Squash the speaker [354]

A volunteer lies face down on the floor. Two or three other actors lie on top, crisscrossing the prone body, and others stand around and watch the fun. As the volunteer starts to speak s/he tries to lift the others off her/his back and get up.

Lying on the floor releases your voice to some extent, but since energy is directed to the effort of pushing off the bodies squashing you, the voice finds alternative pathways and the words take on a fresh energy and urgency.

Few actors succeed in getting up; cheer them if they do.

Seeking a primitive, uncluttered response to language is not dissimilar to seeking neutrality in the body. You have to allow language to work on you, rather than you controlling the language. Exploring the sonic and rhythmic properties of language is a way of discovering the impulse behind the word(s).

A somatic route is essentially holistic and is based on the premise that exercises in physical consciousness affect the actors' psychological awareness. The temptation with text is to seek intelligible meaning, to make sense of what is being said. In somatic training the actor has to suppress this desire in favour of attending to the sonic value and rhythm of language which leads to a deeper understanding at sub-lingual level. The true connotations of the word are the end-product of the process rather than the starting point.

Finding the sonic value as a celebration of words releases textures, feelings and moods suggested by their sound. It enables the colour of the word to lead you rather than you colouring the word. Words have a physical root. See them as a potent force. Language can restrain or choke hidden depths of meaning when looked at semantically. This is why Brook approaches text like music – the last thing he looks for is feeling – for that will come through exploring the way the voice 'moves through a word' finding connections between consonants and vowels just as a musician searches for relationships between notes.[355]

The exercise called SWEAR-SPEAK towards the end of SECTION FOUR is a good preface for the next exercises.

Lingo-physic

Find a selection of alternative spellings or unusual words from any good dictionary, either phonetic or deriving from another language. For example, the word guinea could be written gini, the word arcade could be written ah-kaied, the word tuatar is simply very unusual! The idea is that the words look unfamiliar, i.e. we can create their sound without knowing their meaning. Scrawl several of these up on a board so everyone can see them.

Taking each word at its phonetic level, learn them and then play with the sound of them, tasting them on the tongue, exploring what happens to your mouth when you say them – and what happens when you try to express them physically. You are tapping the energy of the word rather than trying to impose any meaning.

The trick here is to find pleasure in exploring the extremes of the sounds, feeling the vibrations of each syllable and letting the body move in response.

Yoshi Oida explains that in Kyogen training, actors learn how to communicate laughter by making the sound 'ha–ha–ha'; in a similar manner the sounds 'shaay, shaay, shaay' are used for sadness.[356] Apart from the purely technical (descriptive) aspects of words we use in ordinary life, many words 'carry an emotional resonance in their sound'.[357] Good writers choose words for their sonic value and it is important to respect this when working on text: the principle here is that exploring the sound of the words can lead you towards the feeling.

Text-physic

You can extend the lingo-physic exercise to clusters of words, or even phrases from unfamiliar languages short enough to learn quickly. I came across the following example in a workshop run by Kenneth Rea:

Tane muhata
Te mutate
nghere[358]

Once again, write this up on a board so that everyone can learn it. And as in the previous exercise, explore the sound of the phrase through the body, allowing the muscles to respond physically. You are making a relationship with the text on a sonic level, connecting with it at a visceral level.

Follow this with a few lines from any Shakespeare play, such as the beginning of Caliban's speech about his homeland: 'This isle is full of noises, Sounds and sweet airs that delight the ear and hurt not', or a line or two from Gertrude's speech on the drowning of Ophelia 'When down her weedy trophies and herself / Fell in the weeping brook'. These two provide a clear contrast in terms of their emotional resonance. Again, put them up on a board so that actors can learn and refer to them and follow exactly the same process as before.

With these Shakespeare phrases, let the sound lead your movement, so that you are echoing the sound with your own physicality, forming motifs, making 'conversations' within the body.

Negotiating text in this way allows you to discover nuances of meaning contained within sounds of words and the relationships between them, their assonance and dissonance. Sound imagery lends weight to the text's concealed emotions.

Action precedes analysis in working on text. And seeing words as an active force feeding the imaginative process rather than a preordained template for presentation opens up more possibilities for interpretation. The imaginative encounter between the actor and the text is more than illustration; it should be an illumination. Language has its own muscularity, musicality, and magic. Once again we come back to rhythm, for every word, phrase, sentence has its own internal rhythm.

Stick-lines

Each group has a stick to pass between them around a circle. Take a line from Shakespeare, such as Miranda's 'O brave new world that hath such people in it' or Gertrude's 'Her clothes spread wide, And mermaid-like awhile they bore her up'. As the stick passes round the circle, the group speak the line one word each at a time. The aim is to try and find a rhythmic flow to the line. Practise allows them to keep the speech moving in an uninterrupted manner.

How each earlier word is inflected will, of course, dictate how you inflect yours. So this becomes an exercise in listening as much as speaking. See what difference it makes if you can marry the rhythm of the line to the rhythm of the stick going around. Then try passing the stick the other way, so the line comes back in a new direction. And then see if the stick can have its own journey whilst the line travels at a different speed.

Actors love this exercise. The level of concentration deepens within the group as they realise the range of possibilities in delivery. One group invented a version where members stand with their backs to each other. They said this emphasised the listening and made them more aware.

Focusing on something else whilst speaking releases surprising rhythms and inflections. When concentrating on something else words adopt new patterns.

Ball-speeches

Four people take it in turns to speak a speech they have learnt whilst throwing a ball to each other. At first what happens is they adopt the rhythm of the ball. If you break up the pattern of the ball, by playing piggy-in-the-middle, or by trying to stop the person speaking from getting the ball, new patterns emerge in the speech.

Similarly, using the exercise CANE-DANCES with two players who have learnt a section of dialogue generates physical insights into the relationship between characters. Gertrude and Hamlet in Act III Scene IV is great for this. Remember to use only a short exchange of dialogue – a 'unit' along the lines of the first exercise in this section. And be sure that actors are familiar with playing the game first before using it with text, otherwise you will cause confusion.

This helps prevent actors from presenting the result of thought rather than the process of thought, a common tendency which means there is no surprise either for the actor or for the listener. Words need to be seen as thought in action. Naturally believable, truthful utterance in life is unclouded. It is married indivisibly to actions. And actions are physical responses to situations. You have to discover the character's responses through exploring what they do and say.

Peter Hall suggests viewing words in the same way as you would a mask, so that a role, like a mask, becomes like another skin.[359] In good playwriting the movement and intonation patterns of language are reflections of character. Paying attention to the internal dynamic of words, their inherent musicality, how consonants and vowels are balanced, and the pauses, stops and breaths, will give you a rhythmic pattern on which to develop the inner life of a character. Blank verse, for example, will discipline the delivery (via the breathing) in the same way as a mask disciplines the body, once you observe its demands.

CHARACTER

As if they were craftsmen given a piece of clay to mould . . . [they] show their mind in their body at every stage of the events.[360]

Mask work is a wonderful foundation for character work, because it teaches you to perform something other than yourself whilst at the same time investing yourself deeply in the performing.[361] Actors who have undertaken mask work are less dependent on their own personalities in acting, more sensitive to the text as a 'form' which acts as a catalyst on them, allowing a character to emerge rather than be imposed. Working on counter-mask is a fruitful pathway to realising the multi-dimensional nature of characters, how (as in life) characters are full of contradictions.

If you start with an idea of what a character 'is like' you are likely to end up in a conventional and clichéd portrayal. The audience are the ones who must decide what a character 'is like'. The art of creating believable characters lies in never quite knowing who they are. As soon as you think you've got them, they disappear. You can only remain responsive to the possibilities of what they might be. This doesn't mean indecisive acting. On the contrary, you have to make decisions about them, how and where they move, how they speak, what they do. But those decisions should emerge organically through somatic investigation. The effect is arrived at cumulatively.

The idea of the 'fully rounded' character can be misleading, inviting the idea that they are a fixed entity. Characters change during the course of a play, and a sense of surprise at their actions has to be constant. You cannot play descriptions. Too often, actors come up with a generalised overview of a character, such as 'she's a perfectionist' or 'he's a pessimist'. Playing generalisations is a recipe for tedium. In real life people are full of contradictions. They act and speak according to the situation they find themselves in at the moment. The art of conveying character lies in finding the right action for each moment – starting with details and allowing these to accumulate. Stanislavsky understood this; it is the basis of his concept of 'physical actions'.

Stanislavsky also emphasised that the physical and verbal life of a character are outward manifestations of their inner life. Whether you find it more conducive to begin work from 'outside' or 'inside' a character, what you must enable the spectator to do is 'read' them like a weather vane. And for this to happen, the psychic and physical life of character have to connect. This is where you exploit your development of inner awareness with the capacity to work externally, and the control you have acquired over your body.

The suggestions for exploring text-based characters here are ideas for provoking the actors' imaginations through physical means, since that is ultimately how they will project the fictional constructs of the play-wright(s): 'The theatre is the meeting place between imitation and a trans-forming power called imagination, which has no action if it stays in the mind. It must pervade the body.'[362]

Playing around with the idea of characters as animals is highly productive. Preface this next exercise with the game ANIMAL PAIRS in SECTION TWO. Actors will need to have learned a speech for a particular character for this.

Animalistics

Invite actors to think of an animal that a character reminds them of. For example, Gertrude could be a leopard, Ophelia a swallow. (NB: Don't ask actors to justify their choices – the point is to give them free rein on the idea sparked in them, not come up with an analytically-based interpretation.) First, let them explore the extreme limits of the physical characteristics of these animals, so the room resembles a zoo.

As they are doing this, ask them to speak the speech (or any extracts that pop into their mind), using the physical movements they are engaged in to colour the words, repeating words and phrases at random, relishing those that seem to work in tandem with the animal's movement. (The idea is not to speak the speech word-perfectly.)

Next, invite the actors to think of another animal for the character – prefer-ably in complete contrast to the first, for example Gertrude as a crow and Ophelia as a rabbit. Repeat the physical explorations, creating another wild-life park, and then ask them to speak the speech again as in the previous step.

This is a great way of releasing the actors physically and fostering the idea of the 'otherness' of characters. It often gives actors starting points for the gestural language of a character and can reveal quite surprising discoveries about them too.

The exercise CHARACTER KATAS can also be adapted for working with text. In SECTION FIVE this was used in relation to biographical information and engaged you in feeling and thinking about characters to render them as creative ideographs. You can use information gleaned from the text about a character, from what they do, say, and what others do to them and say about them, in exactly the same way as you used the biographical information, to develop physical characterisation. The important thing is to ensure you incorporate your response to the information.

This exercise helps you avoid working with clichéd mannerisms, those thousands of conventional gestures which we use in day-to-day communication. These are, in Dario Fo's words, 'banal, well-worn stereotypes which do not indicate the presence of an intelligent imagination', for in theatre 'it is as essential to re-invent gestures as it is to re-invent words'.[363] The gestural language of theatre is not simply an exaggerated stylisation of the everyday.

You frequently come across young directors cajoling actors to 'make it bigger' in the mistaken view that enlarging the gesture is the route to a more intense theatricality. Firstly you have to establish the right correspondence between the inner dimension of character and its exterior expression. Then you can begin to play with scale. Sometimes a simple movement of the hand will say as much as a movement of the whole body – but only when the whole body is involved in that small movement of the hand. Clarity is as crucial as exaggeration.

Connecting the inner dimension with the outer expression is a clumsy way of talking about the alchemy of acting and polarises 'inner' and 'outer', when in fact the two should work together, one feeding the other, to create the final incarnation of character. Actors work in very different ways to achieve this, and one actor's preference may well be poisonous to another. You will find your own way through a process of trial and error, and through whatever training you undertake.

Berkoff draws a distinction between the idea of playing characters rooted in 'personality traits so beloved of the naturalistic school' and playing the essence of characters as archetypes.[364] For him, television and film acting 'celebrate the burying of personality into stereotypes', whereas theatre revels in the archetypal.[365] Training in neutral and archetypal masks enables actors to envisage character in more than behavioural terms, to work on finding the essence of a particular type. Exploring characters through a range of archetypes, for example tackling Gertrude (in *Hamlet*) through both 'wicked stepmother' and 'wise crone', is one route to finding their inherent contradictions.

Working on colours is related to work on archetypes. Colour conjures particular responses in us. Yet beyond the conventional relationships between red and anger/danger, blue and melancholy, green and jealousy, lie a spectrum of physical attributes.

Colour-katas[366]

Call out individual colours with the simple instruction to move blue, or yellow or purple, for example. Each actor responds individually. And go on to add a sound to that colour, a sound that is prompted by the movement. Compare the results.

In physical terms, the essence of each colour produces similar dynamics in movement terms. Red is short and contained – on the spot if you like. Yellow has a short but vivid span, whereas blue seems to go on forever. Intellectual attempts at trying to reason this out generally fail. You just feel it.

Applying this is not simply a question of identifying what colour relates to a character, but using the dynamic properties of colour as an exploratory device for characters at a particular point in a play where their mood seems identifiable with a colour, or shifts through a colour palette.

Finding gestures and movement of characters is analogous to finding the dynamic of elements. You are searching for gestures which reverberate through the anatomy so the whole personality is imbued with them. Artaud noticed that the stylised gestures of Balinese dance-drama are always aimed at 'the clarification of a state of mind or a mental problem'[367] and he found the horde of ritual gestures deployed by performers penetrated the mind in a similar fashion to music. He called for a 'physical knowledge of images' maintaining that it is necessary to find 'correspondences between a gesture in painting or on stage, and a gesture made by lava in a volcanic eruption'.[368]

The next exercise demonstrates how to explores this notion in relation to character, using the Ghost in *Hamlet*.

Fire/mountain [369]

Walk around the room in the same way as 'Stop and Go' in section one. Keep your own pace and criss-cross the space. As you walk explore the element of fire in your body, first in the arms and legs, then the hands and eyes until you are moving as fire.

Now walk with that same sensation of fire within but show it only in your eyes. When you pass someone allow your eyes to meet and momentarily 'fizz' with them.

Then stand, and in the same way, find the quality of mountain in your body. First of all remain in one place. Once you have found the mountain explore how the mountain might move. How would it travel across space? Develop this into walking as the mountain, commanding the space. Think about the fire within the mountain, so that you might have moments when lava oozes slowly, or erupts, or a rock-slide occurs.

Acting is a process of imaginative and physical transformation. The inner conviction of the actors is what creates and sustains the imaginary world – and peoples it. That inner conviction is a marriage of technique and imagination, the one supporting the other to create convincing incarnations.

When working with text-borne characters it is important to work in a playful way. Playing games in character is great fun. Get the court of Elsinore playing GRANDMOTHER'S FOOTSTEPS, or BALL IN THE AIR, and you will have an instant, interactive, character-development session! Similarly, the constraints of performing improvised situations in character provide enjoyable ways of finding out how to play the characters. Never forget that 'theatre must always retain its playful dimension',[370] and working through the body is fundamentally about enjoyment.

Appendix

MASK MAKERS

Ninian Kinier-Wilson
32 Moscow Drive
Liverpool L13 7DH
tel: 0151 259 5422

Michael Chase
The Mask Studio
The Glasshouse
Wolleston Road
Amblecote
Stourbridge
West Midlands DY8 4HF
e-mail: mask.studio@virgin.net
internet: www.mask-studio.co.uk

Trading Faces
2 Bridge View
Bridge Street
Abingdon
Oxon OX14 3HN
tel: 01235 550829

Trestle Theatre Company
Birch Centre
Hill End Lane
St Albans
Hertfordshire AL4 0RA
tel: 01727 850989

TRAINING COURSES IN PHYSICAL THEATRE

Circomedia
Centre for Contemporary Circus
and Physical Performance
tel: 0117 947 7288
email:
  info@circomedia.demon.co.uk
internet: www.circomedia.com

Dell'Arte International School of
Physical Theatre
P.O. Box 816
Blue Lake
CA 95525
USA
tel: +1 707 668 5663
email: dellarte@aol.com
internet: www.dellarte.com

Desmond Jones School of Mime
and Physical Theatre
20 Thornton Avenue
London W4 1QG
tel: 020 8747 3537
email:
  enquiries@desmondjones.co.uk
internet: www.desmondjones.co.uk

Ecole de Mime Corporel Dramatique
Unit 207
Belgravia Workshop
157-163 Marlborough Road
London N19 4NF
tel: 020 7263 9339
email: infoschool@angefou.co.uk
internet: www.angefou.co.uk

École Internationale de Théatre
Jacques Lecoq
57, rue du Faubourg St. Denis
75010 Paris
France

École Philippe Gaulier
St. Michael's Church Hall
St. Michael's Road
London NW2 6XG
tel: 020 8438 0040
email: kba31@dial.pipex.com

Hope Street International Arts
Training and Development
Hope Street
Liverpool
tel: 0151 708 8007

International Workshop Festival
(annual)
66 Theatre Street
Lavender Hill
London SW11 5TF
tel: 020 7223 2223
email: i-w-f@i-w-f.demon.co.uk
internet: www.i-w-f.demon.co.uk

The School of Physical Theatre
3 Mills Media Centre
3 Mills Lane
Bromley-by-Bow
London E3 3DU
tel: 020 8215 3350
email:
   school@physicaltheatre.com
internet: www.physicaltheatre.com

Short courses are advertised
regularly in *Total Theatre* magazine.
Information available from:
Total Theatre , The Power Station,
Coronet Street, London N1 6HD
(*tel:* 020 7729 7944, *email:*
magtotaltheatre@easynet.co.uk)

Endnotes

Where books are cited by author and date of publication only, fuller details will be found in the Bibliography.

Introduction

[1] Hayley Carmichael, 'My Theatre', in *Total Theatre* ,12 (1) Spring 2000.

[2] Lecoq, 2000:9.

[3] In 1984 an organisation called Mime Action Group (MAG) was formed in Britain, associated with the European Mime Federation, and over the next decade this grew into an umbrella organisation for mime, physical theatre and visual performance, renaming itself 'Total Theatre' and producing a periodical of the same name.

[4] He later complains about the way it has been overused to describe 'anything that isn't traditional dance or theatre', (from the Bound to Please programme 1997).

[5] Gradually the company have moved towards multi-media performance, (incorporating video and holography in *The Happiest Days of Your Life* (1999), for example, alongside an onstage swimming pool), with dance as the primary mode.

[6] Brook, 1968:72.

[7] From *The Actor and The Ubermarionette* (1907) in Walton, 1983:85.

[8] From *Thoroughness in Theatre* (1911) in Walton, 1983:97.

[9] He was influenced by Adolphe Appia, the Swiss designer who, realising that painted scenery was two-dimensional and the actor three-dimensional, proposed an unframed stage which used levels, stairs and, above all, light to create a flexible space providing a range of suggestive possibilities.

[10] Roose-Evans, 1984:53.

[11] Richard Eyre places physical theatre in the popular tradition of theatre as opposed to the verbal tradition, and asserts that as such, it has 'both flourished and languished' at various points in history. (Foreword to 'Moving into Performance, a report on the European and Physical Theatre Workshop Symposium', MAG 1994). Drawing a distinction between a physical and verbal tradition perpetuates the idea that one does not feed the other. Great periods of theatrical endeavour are born out of the marriage of the two. The Ancient Greek playwrights were actors and choreographers; Shakespeare was an actor, and so was Molière. George Devine, founder of the English Stage Company at the Royal Court in London, ran mask workshops for playwrights (including Edward Bond)

believing they needed some experiential understanding of acting if they were writing for the stage. Peter Brook and Jacques Lecoq both believe that when the verbal tradition is lack-lustre theatre seeks to renew itself by returning to the language of image and gesture.

[12]   Artaud, 1977:72.

[13]   Decroux codified the techniques necessary to the successful execution of the mime's *trompe l'oeil*. In particular, he and Barrault formulated the *contrepoids* technique: 'the basis for the modern mime's ability to conjure the existence of the intangible'. (Felner, 1985:67). Essentially this works on the principle that an imaginary object will appear real providing the body expresses the muscular tension imposed by the object. Think of lifting a suitcase, and how the *weight* of the suitcase creates tension, causing one shoulder to list to the side and that arm to lengthen, whilst the free arm lifts slightly. Without an actual suitcase, the mime replicates and accentuates this tension: spectators respond by 'seeing' the suitcase.

[14]   It was the actor Jean-Louis Barrault who first coined the phrase 'total theatre'. His work was influenced by the mime artist Etienne Decroux with whom he worked in the nineteen-thirties to codify the techniques of mime which enable him/her to create viable illusions on stage. Both zealot and high priest of mime, Decroux also championed the ideal of performers creating their own work, (and Barrault initially became famous for his one-man shows). In this sense, Decroux can be seen as the precursor of modern devising.

Total Theatre Network is the title of the UK umbrella organisation for physical-based, visual theatre and mime, and the journal which covers this field.

[15]   During more than forty years his *Ecole Internationale de Mime et de Theatre* in Paris admitted over 3,000 students from all over the world.

[16]   *Ecole Philippe Gaulier* offers courses in at least six European countries as well as New York and Australia. Gaulier studied with Lecoq from 1968-70, and taught there for the next nine years. Following an invitation from the Arts Council in 1990 to come and work in England for a year, he established his London school. Much of his work is centred on 'championing the clown's humanity in the face of an aggressive and self-seeking society'. Source: *Ecole Philippe Gaulier* Brochure 1996.

[17]   This was followed by a series of adaptations and original plays, all performed in the high-octane physical style for which Berkoff has become renowned: *The Trial* (1973), *Agamemnon* (1973), *The Fall of the House of Usher* (1975), *East* (1975), *West* (1977) and *Greek* (1980).

[18]   Rea,1987:5.

[19]   Berkoff, 1992:9.

[20]   Hodge, 2000:8.

[21]   Banu, 1991:272.

[22]   Barba, 1991:8.

[23]   Grotowski, 1968:121.

[24]   Brook quoted in Hunt and Reeves, 1995:72.

Section One

[25] Brook, 1993:2.

[26] Copeau quoted in Rudlin and Paul, 1990:49.

[27] Jacques Prénet's account of a visit to Copeau's School in Burgundy, quoted in Rudlin and Paul, 1990:49.

[28] Lecoq, 2000:67.

[29] Ibid.:69.

[30] Callery, D.: 'Skills Exchange' in *Total Theatre*, Vol.11 No.2 July 1999.

[31] Christofferson, 1993:79.

[32] Richards, 1995:125.

[34] Feldenkrais, 1977:50.

[34] Oida, 1997:18.

[35] Ibid.

[36] It is Etienne Decroux, the mime artist, who first codified the concept of articulation, through which the body becomes not only pliable but the instrument of expression: physical movements are not merely broken down into constituent parts, but rather the mime has to think about the inclination and rotation of an isolated unit of action. It requires understanding of, and an ability to separate, the head from the neck, the neck from the chest etc. – isolation of individual segments which, when practised, gives greater expressive control and range of movement possibilities. The result is an angularity and stylisation of movement that reflects the influence of Cubism on Decroux.

[37] Lecoq, 2000:79.

[38] Christofferson, 1993:150.

[39] Steven Berkoff talks of this effect with actors playing the Samsa family in *Metamorphosis*: 'By breaking down the movement to the ticks of the metronome I make the family appear not only to be ruled by the clock but to become more fascinating as the elements of the body are separated and laid bare. The watch casing is taken off and we see the springs and ratchets within. Far more interesting to watch than a slavish production of what those very actors have done that morning at home . . . The units of their movement, their signature, are broken down and we are able to see the family moving as a trio, cutting their food, raising a fork, munching until in a way they are like living paintings caught by a strobe, or a clock made of human flesh.' Berkoff, 1995:37-38.

[40] An adaptation of Boal's much-loved game where the loser wins. Boal, 1974:128.

[41] Barba, 1991:55.

[42] Grotowski, 1969:208.

[43] Watson, 1995:62.

[44] Christofferson, 1993:108.

[45] The notion of tapping a creative realm through physical discipline is endemic in Oriental performance traditions. Tadashi Suzuki has developed his modern performance training method which involves stomping (stamping the ground) in a position similar to the fixed-hip positions of

classical Japanese theatre on the premise that through this training the actor can tap the 'animal energy' which he regards as essential for performance. The strenuousness of Suzuki's method also fosters physical stamina.

46   Recent scientific evidence is emerging that a bundle of nerves in this area of the small intestine, (corresponding with the point identified as the 'chi', 2cm below the belly button and 2cm in) is a key centre for nerve activity, so much so that it is being referred to as 'the second brain'. BBC Radio 2. 11 November 2000.

47   Rea, 1984:15.

48   Yoshi Oida, 1997:21.

49   Rolfe, 1972:37.

50   Oida, 1997:26.

51   Brook, 1989:184.

52   Eldredge and Huston, 1995:121.

53   Leabhart,1989:28.

54   See Appendix for a list of Mask makers.

55   Felner, 1985:157.

56   Eldredge and Huston, 1995:127.

57   Houben, Jos *The Neutral Mask* Arts Archive Video,1997.

58   Lecoq, 2000:38

59   Ibid.

60   Interview with Andy Paget in Coombs, C. *An Exploration into Feldenkrais and Actor-Training Technique.* Unpublished dissertation, Liverpool John Moores University, 2000.

61   Since Pagneux's first visit to Britain, there are now several qualified Feldenkrais practitioners working in theatre, and both 'pure' Feldenkrais and Feldenkrais-inspired movement work is increasingly incorporated into actor-training workshops. If you find yourself learning new and efficient ways of coming from sitting to standing, or lying on the floor moving only your eyeballs, or being instructed to work out 'how your body organises itself' to do something, it is likely that the workshop leader is using Feldenkrais.

62   John Wright founded Trestle Theatre and went on to create the company Told By An idiot with Hayley Carmichael and Paul Hunter, whom he met when working at Middlesex University.

63   Interview with John Wright in Roberts, J. *The Influence of Feldenkrais on Physical Theatre.* Unpublished dissertation, Liverpool John Moores University, 1997.

64   'After a session with Laban you began to look at the world with different eyes, as if it had changed its colours or its shapes, or you could see neutrons and protons instead of mass. You watched for the slightest gesture which would give away a secret. After a while, with some degree of accuracy, you could tell what people did for a living, or analyse their state of mind as they passed you on the street.' Littlewood, 1994:772/773.

65   The Feldenkrais Method is a registered trademark of the Feldenkrais
      Guild. For a list of qualified practitioners in your area, or country, contact
      The Feldenkrais Guild UK, P.O.Box 370, London N10 3XA. The best
      way of learning about Feldenkrais is to do it with a qualified practitioner.
      Once experienced, never forgotten, is the response of most people. You
      can invite a qualified practitioner to lead an ATM session with a group.
      An accessible introduction to ATM is available in paperback: *Awareness
      Through Movement, Health Exercises for Personal Growth* by Moshe
      Feldenkrais, Arkana/Penguin 1990.
66   Feldenkrais, 1984: 38.
67   Ibid.: 39.
68   Schechner, 1966:117.
69   Ibid.:114.
70   Feldenkrais, 1984:111.
71   Schechner, 1966:121.
72   Feldenkrais, 1984:19 and 25.
73   Roberts, J. Unpublished interview with John Wright, op. cit.1997.

Section Two

74   George Bernard Shaw, quoted in Fo, 1991:37.
75   Cairns, 1989:266.
76   Felner, 1985:60.
77   Copeau in Rudlin and Paul, 1990:50.
78   Ibid.
79   Ibid.
80   Saint-Denis,1960:104.
81   Jean Dorcy quoted in Rudlin and Paul, 1990:239.
82   Rudlin, 1994:43.
83   Oida, 1997:26.
84   Levy, 1978: 51.
85   Ibid.:50.
86   Berkoff, 1995: 47.
87   'The only way to keep a straight face', by Georgina Brown. *The
      Independent*, 5 May 1993.
88   Fo, 1991:26.
89   Lecoq, 2000:38.
90   Jos Houben, *The Neutral Mask*, Arts Archive Video, Arts Documentation
      Unit Exeter University 1996.
91   See the Appendix for a list of Mask Workshop outlets
92   A chair inhibits movement, thereby encouraging the necessary stillness.
      Also, in the initial learning stages, people feel less exposed sitting in front
      of a group than standing.
93   Lecoq quoted by Huston, 1996:52.
94   Lecoq, 2000:41.
95   Huston, 1996: 52.

[96]   Jean Dasté writing of his debt to Copeau in Rudlin and Paul, 1990:237.
[97]   Rudlin, 1994:40.
[98]   Fo, 1991:13.
[99]   Cairns, 1989:246.
[100] Anderson, 1998:168.
[101] Fisher, 1992:11.
[102] Green and Swan, 1993:130.
[103] Lecoq, 2000:108.
[104] Ibid.: 108-9.
[105] Ibid.
[106] Ibid.: 111.
[107] Grantham, 2000:13.
[108] Fo, 1991:22.
[109] Lecoq, 2000:113.
[110] Grantham, 2000:115.
[111] Adapted from a workshop given by Mike Chase, London 1997.
[112] See Barry Grantham's *Playing Commedia* (2000) for a range of games and
       drills which equip actors with the skills to execute similar commedia gags.
[113] Lecoq, 2000:116.
[114] Grantham, 2000:16.

Section Three

[115] Meyerhold quoted in Gladhov, 1997:105.
[116] Gladhov, 1997:103.
[117] Richards,1995:84.
[118] Gladhov, 1997:162.
[119] Oida, 1997:25.
[120] Most backache in Britain arises from poor posture caused quite simply by
       sitting; children have perfectly good posture until they are required to sit
       all day in school. In cultures where squatting, kneeling and perching are
       preferred to sitting, the incidence of back problems is significantly less.
[121] Oida, 1997:9.
[122] Barker, 1977:94.
[123] Adapted from one of Guy Dartnell's workshops.
[124] Grotowski quoted in Kumiega,1987:119
[125] Oida, 1997:42.
[126] These exercises are derived from a workshop in Biomechanics led by
       Gennadi Bogdanov, who was taught by one of Meyerhold's pupils, at the
       International Workshop Festival (IWF), London, 1998.
[127] Ludwig Flaszen explains: 'Meyerhold was important not as a formulator
       of concrete exercises or techniques, but as the inspiration of the theme
       that 'Biomechanics exists in the fact that behind each gesture of the actor,
       the whole of his body stands'. This formula was a major discovery.'
       Quoted in Kumiega,1987:121.
[128] Meyerhold in Gladkov, 1997:108

129 Lecoq, 2000:89.

130 See Lecoq's *The Moving Body*, 2000:89-90 for a full explanation of his theory of the 'laws of motion'.

131 I learnt this brilliant version from Paul Hunter of Told By an Idiot.

132 Adapted from a workshop run by Paul Hunter from Told By An Idiot, Liverpool 1998.

133 Barba quoted by Watson, 1995:32.

134 Adapted from a workshop run by Annabel Arden from Theatre de Complicité at IWF 1999. Annabel was using this exercise in a workshop related to *Hamlet* to give actors some idea of the 'magnificence' necessary to convey the character of the Ghost. I have found it equally effective in expanding student actors' understanding of presence.

135 Banu, 1991: 273.

136 Brook, 1993:76.

137 Oida, 1997:40.

138 Ibid.

139 Ratcliffe is describing the stage presence of members of Theatre de Complicité, which he writes they acquired through studying with Lecoq. Programme note to *Three Lives of Lucie Cabrol* 1994.

140 Joan Littlewood, 'A Goodbye Note from Joan', *Encore* 1961, reprinted in Marowitz, 1965:132.

141 The founder members of Theatre de Complicité met at Lecoq's school and initially intended to base themselves in France and Europe, which was why they chose their French name.

142 See the sub-section 'AUDIENCE'

143 I learned this game from Sally Cook (one of the co-founders of Trestle Theatre). She played it with a new group over two days and presented an improvised performance based on the game and structured around the Seven Ages of Man on the evening of the second day.

144 Hayley Carmichael in an unpublished interview with the author.

145 Chambers Dictionary definition.

146 'Copeau's training stressed the importance of improvisation. Although now taken for granted in actor training, like so many of Copeau's innovations, improvisation was an unheard of technique of which there was no living tradition in the French theatre of the early 1900s.' Leabhart,1989:25.

147 From Copeau's *Resgistres* in Rudlin and Paul, 1990:39.

148 Rudlin and Paul, 1990:237,

149 Rudlin,1994.

150 Pinetti quoted by Arditti,1994:19.

151 McBurney, 1994:18.

152 Smith, 1972:36.

153 Adapted from Annabel Arden's workshop, IWF, 1999. Theatre de Complicité use bamboo sticks a great deal in their training and rehearsal process, as does Peter Brook. Photographs and exercises with bamboo sticks can be found in Complicité's 'Background Pack' for *Caucasian Chalk Circle*.

[154] Adapted from Lucy O'Rorke of Bouge-de-la: Workshop during Real Action, Liverpool 1999.

[155] Davis Robinson uses a similar game he calls Ping-Pong as the foundation for physical comedy work: see Robinson, 1999:50ff for a full explanation of how he uses it.

[156] I learnt this game from Annabel Arden of Theatre de Complicité.

[157] McBurney, 1994:23.

[158] Ibid.:15.

[159] Gladhov, 1997:106.

[160] Oida, 1997:52.

[161] McBurney, 1994:15.

[162] Annabel Arden in Taylor, 1994:40.

[163] McBurney, 1994:15.

[164] Banu, 1991:275.

[165] Heilpern, 1977:127-133.

[166] Brook, 1988:132.

[167] Banu, 1991:275.

[168] Adapted from a workshop run by Kenneth Rea at IWF, 1999.

[169] Berkoff, 1995:75.

[170] Robinson, 1999:41. Robinson offers some excellent ideas for generating physical comedy in his handbook, including an exercise from the Swiss clown Garde Hutte. 'Hutte's Points' as he calls it, is a highly technical method of developing soundless comic material through alternating the focus between your partner and the audience, pp.70-72.

[171] This is an adaptation of a demonstration used by Jos Houben in his 'Laughter Workshop' Liverpool, 1998.

[172] For information on the concept of the mask's 'gaze' see SECTION TWO (UN)MASKING THE ACTOR.

[173] Anecdote taken from Jos's 'Laughter Workshop', Liverpool 1998.

[174] After-show discussion, The Unity Theatre, Liverpool, October 1999.

[175] Brook, 1987:12.

[176] Grotowski, 1969:181.

[177] Grotowski quoted in Richards,1995:120.

[178] Innes, 1981:160.

[179] Richard Eyre 'Sharing the Space', in programme for The Caucasian Chalk Circle, Royal National Theatre, 1997.

[180] Simon McBurney, 'Watching Your Back, notes on The Caucasian Chalk Circle' in programme for The Caucasian Chalk Circle, Royal National Theatre, 1997.

[181] For a full exposition of Lecoq's 'balanced stage' see his book The Moving Body, 2000:132-136.

Section Four

[182] Brook, 1993:69.

[183] Cole and Chinoy, 1970:451.

[184] Dario Fo.

[185] In Gladkov, 1997:124.

[186] 'He eventually began calling his rehearsal books 'scores' . . . I think Meyerhold had the notion that he was creating a score you couldn't fuck with, and that the actors would have to perform the way musicians did.' Schmidt in Bates, 1998:82.

[187] Appia quoted by Lee Simonson 'The Ideas of Adolphe Appia' in *The Theory of the Modern Stage* ed. by Bentley, 1970:27.

[188] Dalcroze was a Swiss composer who developed a system of studying music through the body called Eurhythmics. This was used by Nijinsky to train dancers before negotiating his fiendishly difficult choreography for the first performance of Stravinsky's *Petrushka*.

[189] Suzanne Bing quoted in Rudlin and Paul, 1990:56.

[190] 'Have you ever considered why there is always music during the acrobatic numbers at the Circus? . . . Circus people need music as a rhythmic support, as an aid to keeping time . . . without it . . . catastrophe.' Meyerhold quoted in Schmidt, 1996:155.

[191] It is also translated as 'intention', which is misleading, as that implies a preconceived and intellectually-driven purpose leading the movement. In practice, learning this 'form' with Gennadi Bogdanov, there was never an avowed intention behind the *otkas*.

[192] You can see how this works in the final video of Gennadi Bogdanov's 1998 IWF workshop when he conducts a class in 'The Dagger Attack', Video Archive, 2000.

[193] For fuller expositions of *Jo-Ha-Kyu* see Heilpern, 1977:129, and Oida, 1997:30-33

[194] Oida, 1997:30.

[195] Oida, 1992:64.

[196] Adapted from Lucy O'Rorke from Bouge-de-la, who used this exercise in the Real Action workshop, Liverpool 1999. Lucy was not demonstrating Meyerhold's principle, but I found this exercise an extremely effective way of teaching it.

[197] Watson, 1995:48.

[198] Marowitz, 1967:174.

[199] Lecoq quoted in Robinson, 1999:111.

[200] Lecoq quoted in Felner, 1985:148.

[201] Lecoq, *Mime, Movement, Theatre*, trans. by Bari Rolfe, 1981:151.

[202] See Section Two: Working with Neutral Mask.

[203] Lecoq, 2000:84.

[204] Laban, 1980:10.

[205] Ibid.:82.

[206] This is a phrase used by Jos Houben in his workshop on 'Laughter'. The next two exercises are also adapted from that workshop.

[207] From Jos Houben, 'Laughter' Workshop, Liverpool Hope Street Actor's Centre, 1999.

[208] Ibid.

[209] Grotowski, 1975:153.

[210] Leabhart,1989:47.

[211] Newlove, 1993:99.

[212] This is one of Philippe Gaulier's *le jeu* exercises taught to me by Nick Kellington of Gooseberry Fools.

[213] The term 'vocal action' is used by Eugenio Barba, (Watson, 1995:66) but is a concept used by other practitioners.

[214] Rodenburg,1987:4-8.

[215] Grotowski recommends 'total respiration' which uses both abdominal and thoracic chambers, and his exercises for respiration and vocal training are recommended together with those for placing the voice and using the resonators (see *Towards a Poor Theatre*, 1975:115-141). Barba's actors at Odin used these in their early training and once they'd mastered them, moved on to individual voice training.Yoshi Oida also offers excellent exercises (1992:148). Actors should not be trained to breathe like opera singers, just as their bodies are not meant to operate like dancers or gymnasts; their voices are primarily for speaking, although singing is a valuable route to freeing the voice.

[216] Berkoff, 1989:4.

[217] Jenkins in Zarrilli, 1995:244.

[218] Hayley Carmichael, unpublished interview with the author, 1999.

[219] Grotowski, 1975:189.

[220] Roose-Evans,1984:181.

[221] Ibid.

[222] Ibid.:183.

[223] Martin,1991:65.

[224] Ibid.:67.

[225] Adapted from Guy Dartnell Workshop, Liverpool John Moores University, Spring 2000

[226] Brook, 1987:123.

[227] Ted Hughes quoted in Roose-Evans,1984:176.

[228] Brook, 1987:108-110.

[229] Ibid.

[230] Ibid.

[231] Hughes in Smith, 1972:45.

[232] Beale and Gayton, 1993:174-176.

[233] Fo, 1991:56.

[234] Ibid.:64.

[235] Watson, 1995:130.

[236] Leabhart,1989:47.

[237] Martin,1991:157.

[238] Saint-Denis,1982:116.

[239] Roose-Evans,1984:178.

[240] Goorney, 1981:167.

[241] Toporkov, 1998:157.

[242] Ibid.:163.

243   Ibid.:157.
244   Ibid.
245   Ibid.:159.
246   Ibid.:160
247   Ibid.:202 original emphasis.
248   Ibid.:170.
249   I learned this exercise from David Llewellyn, Head of Drama at Liverpool JMU.
250   Their essay 'Effector Patterns of Basic Emotions, a psychophysiological method for training actors,' in Zarrilli,1995:197-218 is an absorbing account of the whole process of the training and experiment. Susana Bloch is a trained psychologist based at the University of Pierre et Marie Curie in Paris, whose research into human emotion has fed this experiment.
251   Bloch *et al* in Zarrilli, 1995:205.
252   Ibid.:213-214.
253   Ibid.:215.
254   Ibid.:216.
255   Artaud, Collected Works vol.4, p.103 in Martin, 1991:61.
256   Kumiega,1987:12.
257   Laban,1980:19.
258   Kumiega,1987:119.
259   Grotowski, 1975:192.
260   Ibid.:196
261   Ibid.:192
262   Brook, 1987:233.
263   Ibid.
264   Susan Sontag interviewed by Sarah Dunant, BBC Radio 3, 8 June 2000.
265   Torgier Wethal in Christofferson,1993:44.
266   Oida, 1997:59.
267   Oida, 1992:150.
268   Artaud, 1977:53.
269   *Registres* quoted in Rudlin and Paul, 1990:77.

Section Five

270   Dario Fo believes actors should learn to make their own theatre as an antidote to the idea of theatre as 'staged literature': 'What is the purpose of improvisation? To weave and shape a script with words, with gestures and off-the-cuff situations, but above all to rid actors of the false and dangerous notion that theatre is no more than literature that happens to be staged, acted and adapted, rather than simply read.' Fo, 1987:183.
271   Leabhart,1989:46.
272   Frost and Yarrow, 1990:33.
273   The position is different in many university drama departments where students are frequently required to devise their own work. In A Level and BTEC courses, devising is part of the assessment process.

274 Lecoq, 2000:18
275 Leabhart,1989:101.
276 Lawrence Wylie quoted in Leabhart, 1989:95.
277 McBurney, 1995:17.
278 O'Rorke, 1992:17.
279 Ibid.:18.
280 Berkoff's *East* (1975) which represents the birth of the physical theatre impetus in Britain is one of few Berkoff plays which is not an adaptation.
281 Picasso quoted in Fo, 1987:52.
282 Simon McBurney interviewed in Giannachi and Luckhurst, 1999:68-71.
283 Picasso quoted in Fo, 1987:52.
284 John Wright: course leaflet for *A school for devisers*, Summer 2000.
285 For a fuller exposition of writing for performance see my chapter 'Writing for Stage' in Newman, Jenny (*et al*) *The Writers Workbook*, Arnold, 2000.
286 Mackey, 1997:79.
287 This tripartite process is not exclusive to physical-based theatre work; Joint Stock are a prime example of a company who developed a sophisticated approach to devising in the 1970s and '80s, particularly in their collaborations with Caryl Churchill, under the direction of Max Stafford-Clark. However, they were working principally from political ideas or themes, and generated material through more traditional (psychological) improvisatory routes rather than from a somatic base. A detailed account of some of their early productions is available in Rob Ritchie's entertaining *The Joint Stock Book,*1984.
288 I developed this scenario from a newspaper article by Edward Bond in which he mentioned this game. Unfortunately I no longer have the source.
289 McBurney, 1995:17.
290 O'Rorke, 1992:34-35.
291 Annabel Arden quoted by Jane Edwardes, 'Directors: The New Generation' in Shank,1994:214-5
292 These are sometimes also called 'scales of escalation'. They are originally a Lecoq exercise, but many companies use them who have not been Lecoq trained.
293 Davis Robinson has a very useful section on scales of escalation in his *Physical Comedy Handbook*, p.105-110.
294 Adapted from a a workshop run by Jos Houben (who has directed The Right Size).
295 Probably the earliest example of deign-led devising is with The People Show, founded in 1966, who develop performances from images, impulses, musical compositions, art works or ideas, usually unified by ideological theme. In many instances, the set is active and interactive with the performers. This is exemplified in *The People Show 100*, where performers entered and exited through a dry-cleaning machine which also revolved to reveal alternative perspectives. Interestingly, the original members of The People Show were 'visual artists brought together [in

1966] by sculptor and jazz pianist Jeff Nuttall to stage a 'happening' involving motor bikes, fishing nets and very fat women in Notting Hill'. Their shows are sparked by the preoccupations of those involved, an itinerant medley of artists, musicians and performers. Sobrieski, in Shank, 1994:72

[296] The two strands of the L.E.M. course are: 'Movement work which brings the *miming body* into play, and creative work [in] building scenographic structures'. Lecoq, 2000:155.

[297] Bouge-de-la, unpublished interview with the author, September 1999.

[298] Ibid.

[299] Ibid.

[300] Jon Hough, After Show Discussion, The Unity Theatre, March 1999.

[301] Tim Hibberd interviewed in Mackay, 1997:126.

[302] Ibid.:125.

[303] Hayley Carmichael and Paul Hunter, unpublished interview with the author.

[304] David Benedict 'Precision Playing', *The Independent*, 30 November 1996, p.5.

[305] Naomi Cooke of Foursight Theatre, unpublished interview with the author, December 1999.

[306] *The Street of Crocodiles* Information Pack 1999:17.

[307] Bim Mason, unpublished interview with the author, December 1998.

[308] Jos Houben, *The Neutral Mask* Arts Archive Video.

[309] Watson, 1995:78.

[310] Adapted from Herbert Blau's concept of ideographs which 'not only carry concentrated meaning but also become icons of a sort, a theatrical sign language', from Blumenthal and Taymor, 1999:12. The concept of ideographs seem closely related to Barba's way of working with actors to access gestural images.

[311] Adapted from a workshop by Kate Hale of Foursight Theatre as part of Real Action, Liverpool Unity Theatre, 1999.

[312] It is important to get in the habit of writing things down, to create an *aide memoire* for yourself in this way whether working alone or collaboratively. It is easy to forget what happened in improvisation, and not only frustrating but time-wasting trying to remember. Your work journal will act as a useful trigger.

[313] Richards, 1995:12.

[314] Wethal in Christofferson, 1993:44.

[315] Ibid.:45.

[316] Laukvik in Christofferson, 1993:86-87.

[317] Rasmussen in Christofferson, 1993:98.

[318] Christofferson, 1993:124.

[319] Attributed Meyerhold, source unknown.

[320] Frank Zappa, source unknown.

[321] The Russian formalists separated story (or *fabula* as they called it) from narration (which they called *sjuzhet*) in the 1920s. This formed the basis of

the structuralist approach to literary criticism which has been developed
into post-sixties deconstruction. See Terence Hawkes *Structuralism and
Semiotics* 1977 for an account of Russian formalism and structuralism.
[322] You may be familiar with Tarantino's *Pulp Fiction* (1994) which also plays
with time-structure in a fascinating and quite theatrical way.
[323] If you are trying to develop a plot with your own characters it is worth
remembering that there are a limited number of plot structures. Analysing fairy tales and myths to reveal the functions of characters enables you
to see how plots work.
[324] Esslin, 1978:44.
[325] Simon McBurney, programme note to *Mnemonic* 1999.
[326] Ibid.
[327] Stein, *Plays* in *Look at Me Now and Here I Am, Writings and Lecture 1919-1945*, 1971:75
[328] Ibid.:78
[329] Bouge-de-la, unpublished interview with the author, September 1999.
[330] Ibid.
[331] Ibid.
[332] Albert Hunt in Williams, 1988:81.
[333] The Russian film-maker Eisenstein coined the word 'montage' to indicate
how any two pieces of film stuck together inevitably combine   to
create a new concept born of juxtaposition, cutting and rearranging of
snippets of sensation and experience in order to create dramatic effects.
[334] Mark Wheatley, in *The Street of Crocodiles* information Pack, 1999:17.
[335] Meyerhold quoted in Gladhov, 1997:128.

Section Six

[336] Berry, 2000:22.
[337] Berkoff, 1989:101.
[338] Non-verbal sound, in the Artaudian sense, is predominantly used for
decorative or atmospheric purposes (the Georgian songs of Theatre de
Complcité's production of *The Caucasian Chalk Circle*, and the operatic
chants of the Kaos *Renaissance*).
[339] Berkoff, 1989:3.
[340] Clive Mendus in *The Caucasian Chalk Circle* education pack, Theatre de
Complcité, 1997:31.
[341] Grotowski, 1969:58.
[342] Ibid.:57.
[343] Simon McBurney in Gannachi and Luckhurst, 1999:70.
[344] Berry, 2000:10.
[345] Simon McBurney in Gannachi and Luckhurst, 1999:74.
[346] This exercise is based on a workshop run by Annable Arden of Theatre
de Complicité at the IWF, 1999.
[347] Reading and re-reading a play is a far better way to familiarise yourself
with it than simply reading the sections you may be cast in. Every actor in
every part, however small, needs a knowledge of the whole play.

348 Berkoff, 1989:202. Berkoff's *I am Hamlet* is an extremely detailed account of the process of rehearsal and virtually a moment-by-moment account of the play in production. It is full of ideas for solving problems through physical means, in addition to containing some of Berkoff's forthright views on theatre.

349 Berkoff, 1989:201.

350 Grotowski, 1969:193.

351 Brook, 1968:12.

352 Berkoff, 1992:9.

353 Berry, 2000:52.

354 This was used by Nigel Charnock during his workshop entitled 'Four Days in a Hot Room', Nottingham, September 1998.

355 Smith, 1972:157.

356 Oida, 1997:101.

357 Ibid.

358 On a recent trip to New Zealand I realised that this is Maori, but I do not have a translation.

359 See Peter Hall's illuminating book *Exposed by the Mask, Form and Language in Drama*, Oberon Press, 2000.

360 Berkoff, 1995:23.

361 Lecoq, 2000:61.

362 Brook, 1998:32.

363 Fo, 1991:144.

364 Berkoff, 1995:27.

365 Berkoff, 1995:26.

366 In Lecoq's LEM course, which relates movement to architecture, colour is explored in this way. Students work with colours in a similar way to working with masks, seeking the 'blue of all blues' in much the same way as the mask might seek the 'fear of all fears'.

367 Artaud, 1977:43.

368 Ibid.:60.

369 Adapted from Annabel Arden's Workshop at IWF, September 1999.

370 Lecoq, 2000:65.

Select Bibliography

Arditti, Michael (1994) 'Making a Scene: Joan Littlewood talks to Michael Arditti', in *The Independent Magazine*, 26th March:17-20.

Artaud, Antonin (1977) *The Theatre and its Double*, trans. by Victor Corti, London: John Calder.

Banu,Georges (1991) 'Brook's Six Days, Theatre as the Meeting Place Between the Visible and Invisible', in *Peter Brook and The Mahabharata, Critical Perspectives*, edited by David Williams, London: Routledge.

Barba, Eugenio and Savarese, Nicole (1991) *A Dictionary of Theatre Anthropology, The Secret Art of the Performer*, edited and compiled by Richard Gough, translated by Richard Fowler. Centre for Performance Research, London: Routledge.

Barber, Stephen (1993) *Antonin Artaud, Blows and Bombs*, London: Faber.

Barker, Clive (1975) *Theatre Games*, London: Methuen.

Beale, G. and Gayton, H. (1998) 'The Drive to Communicate, The Use of Language in *Commedia dell'arte*', in *Theatre Research International*, 23(2): 174-178.

Bentley, Eric (ed.) (1970) *The Theory of the Modern Stage*, London: Penguin.

Berkoff, Steven (1989) *I Am Hamlet*, London: Faber.

——— (1995) *Meditations on Metamorphosis*, London: Faber.

——— (1992) *The Theatre of Steven Berkoff*, London: Methuen.

Berry, Cicely (2000) *The Actor and The Text*, revised edition, London: Virgin Publishing.

——— (1973) *Voice and the Actor*, London: Harrap.

Blumenthal, Eileen and Taymor, Julie (1999) *Julie Taymor: Playing With Fire: theater, opera, film*, revised edition, New York: Harry N. Abrams Inc.

Braun, Edward (1982) *The Director and the Stage from Naturalism to Grotowski*, London: Methuen.

Brook, Peter (1968) *The Empty Space*, London: Macgibbon and Kee.

——— (1988) *The Shifting Point*, London: Methuen.

——— (1993) *There Are No Secrets*, London: Methuen.

——— (1988) *Threads of Time, a Memoir*, London: Methuen.

Buckland, Fiona (1995) 'Towards a Language of the Stage: theWork of DV8 Physical Theatre', in *New Theatre Quarterly* 11: 371-380.

Cairns, Christopher (ed.) (1989) *The Commedia Dell'Arte from the Renaissance to Dario Fo*, Lewison: Edwin Mellen Press.

Christoffersen, Erik Exe (1993) *The Actors Way*, translated by Richard Fowler, London: Routledge.

Cole,T. & Chinoy, H.K. (eds.) (1970) *Actors on Acting*, New York: Crown Publishing Co.

Esslin, Martin (1978) *An Anatomy of Drama*, London: Sphere Books.

Feldenkrais. Moshe (1990) *Awareness Through Movement*, London: Arkana, Penguin Books

――――― (1984) *The Master Moves*, California: Meta Publications.

Felner, Myra (1985) *Apostles of Silence, The Modern French Mimes*, London: Associated University Presses.

Fisher, James (1992) *The Theatre of Yesterday and Tomorrow: Commedia Dell'Arte on the Modern Stage*, Lampeter: Edwin Mellen Press.

Fo, Dario (1992) *The Tricks of the Trade*, London: Methuen.

Frost,Anthony and Yarrow, Ralph (1990) *Improvisation in Drama*, Basingstoke: Macmillan.

Giannachi Gabriella and Luckhurst, Mary (eds.) (1999) *On Directing: Interviews with Directors*, London: Faber.

Gladkov, Aleksandr (1997) *Meyerhold Speaks / Meyerhold Rehearses*, Netherlands: Harwood Academic Publishers.

Goorney, Howard (1981)*The Theatre Workshop Story*, London: Methuen.

Grantham, Barry (2000) *Playing Commedia, A Training Guide to Commedia Techniques*, London: Nick Hern Books.

Green, Michael and Swan (1993) *The Triumph of Pierrot, The Commedia dell'Arte and the Modern Imagination*, revised edition, Pennsylvania: Pennsylvania State University Press.

Grotowski, Jerzy (1975) *Towards a Poor Theatre*, London: Methuen.

Hall, Peter (2000) *Exposed by the Mask, Form and Language in Drama*, London: Oberon Press.

Heilpern, John (1977) *The Conference of Birds, The Story of Peter Brook in Africa*, London: Faber.

Hodge, Alison (ed.) (2000)*Twentieth Century Actor Training*, London: Routledge.

Hunt, Albert and Reeves (1992) *Peter Brook, Directors in Perspective*, London: Macmillan.

Huston, Hollis (1996) 'Flavors of Physicality', in *Journal of Dramatic Theory and Criticism*, 11(1):35-54.

Kumiega, Jennifer (1987) *The Theatre of Grotowski*, London: Methuen.

Kustow, Michael (2000) *Theatre @ Risk*, London: Methuen.

Laban, Rudolf (1980) *The Mastery of Movement*, fourth edition, revised by Lisa Ullmann, Plymouth: Macdonald and Evans.

Leabhart, Tom (1997) 'The Man Who Preferred to Stand: Etienne Decroux – Megalomaniac or Genius?" in *Total Theatre*, 9(2):16-17.

――――― (1989) *Modern and Post-Modern Mime*, London: Macmillan.

Leask, Josephine (1995) 'The Silence of the Man, an essay on Lloyd Newson's physical theatre', in *ballet international*.

Lecoq, Jacques (2000) *The Moving Body (Le Corps Poetique)*, trans. by David Bradby, London: Methuen.

Levy, Alan (1978) 'A Week Avec Lecoq', in *Mime, Mask and Marionette* 1(1): 45-62.

Littlewood, Joan (1994) *Joan's Book, Joan Littlewood's Peculiar History As She Tells It*, London: Methuen.

McBurney, Simon (1994) 'The Celebration of Lying, an interview with Simon McBurney', in *Food for the Soul*, edited by David Tushingham, London: Methuen.

Mackey, Sally (ed.) (1997) *Practical Theatre ; A Post-16 Approach*, London: Stanley Thorne.

Marowitz, Charles (1967) 'Notes on the Theatre on Cruelty' in *Theatre at Work, Playwrights and Productions in the Modern British Theatre*, edited by Charles Marowitz and Simon Trussler, London: Methuen.

Marowitz, Charles (ed.)(1965) *New Theatre Voices of the Fifties and Sixties, Selections from Encore Magazine, 1956-1963*, London : Methuen.

Mazzone-Clementi, Carlo (1979) 'Commedia and the Actor', in *Drama Review*, 18(1):159-64.

Meisner, Nadine (1992) 'Strange Fish, Lloyd Newson talks to Dance and Dancers about his new work', in *Dance and Dancers* :10-12.

Mitchell, Jaqueline (1991) *Voice in Modern Theatre*, London: Routledge.

Mitter, Shomit (1992) *Systems of Rehearsal: Stanislavsky, Brecht, Grotowski and Brook*, London: Routledge.

Newlove, Jean (1993) *Laban for Actors and Dancers, Putting Laban's Movement Theory into Practice: a Step-by-Step Guide*, New York : Routledge; London: Nick Hern Books, 1993.

Oida, Yoshi with Lorna Marshall (1992) *An Actor Adrift*, London: Methuen.
——— (1997) *The Invisible Actor*, London: Methuen.

Rea, Kenneth (1984) 'The Physical Life of the Actor', in *New Theatre Quarterly*, 153(2).

Richards, Thomas (1995) *At Work with Grotowski on Physical Actions*, London: Routledge.

Robinson, Davis R. (1999) *The Physical Comedy Handbook*, Portsmouth USA: Heinemann.

Rodenburg, Patsy (1997) *The Actor Speaks, Voice and the Performer*, London: Methuen.

Rotté, Joanna (1998) 'Feldenkrais Revisited: Tension, Talent, and the Legacy of Childhood', in *New Theatre Quarterly*, 15(4) XIV.

Rudlin, John (1994) *Commedia dell'Arte, An Actor's Handbook*, London: Routledge.

Rudlin, J. & Paul, N.H. (eds.) (1990) *Copeau: Texts on Theatre* London: Routledge.

Saint-Denis, Michel (1982) *Training for the Theatre*, New York: Theatre Arts Books.

Schechner, Richard (1966) 'Image, Movement, and Actor: Restoration of Potentiality: an interview with Moshe Feldenkrais', in *Tulane Drama Review*, 10(3):117.

Schmidt, Paul (ed.) (1996) *Meyerhold at Work*, New York: Applause Books.

Shank, Theodore (ed.) (1994) *Contemporary British Theatre*, London: Macmillan.

Smith, A.C.H (1972) *Orghast at Persepolis, An Account of the Experiment in Theatre*, London: Methuen.

Stein, Gertrude (1971) *Look at Me Now and Here I Am: Writings and Lectures 1909-45*, edited by Patricia Meyerowitz, London: Penguin.

Taylor, Hilary (1994) 'Language in their Gesture: Theatre de Complicité', in *The European English Messenger*, 2(2).

Toporkov, Vasily Osipovich (1998) *Stanislavski in Rehearsal: the final years*, trans. Christine Edwards. New York & London: Routledge.

Trewin, J.C. (1971) *Peter Brook, A Biography*, London: Macdonald.

Wardle, Irving (1975) *The Theatres of George Devine*, London: Methuen.

Watson, Ian (1995) *Towards a Third Theatre*, London: Routledge.

Williams, David (ed.)(1988) *Peter Brook, a Theatrical Casebook*, London: Methuen.

Wright, John (1994) 'Monika Pagneux, some thoughts on her teaching and unique approach', in *Total Theatre*, 6(1):11.

Zarrilli, Phillip B.(ed.) (1995) *Acting (Re)Considered, Theory and Practice*, London: Routledge.

Videography

Biomechanics with Gennadi Bogdanov. Arts Archive, Arts Documentation Unit, 1999.

Les Deux Voyages de Jacques Lecoq with English subtitles produced by Jean Noel Roy and Jenn-Gabriel Carosso Le Sept Arte – On Line Productions ANRAT 1999. On Line Productions, 33 av. MacMahon 75017 Paris, France.

A Lesson in the Feldenkrais Method with Garet Newell. Arts Archive, Arts Documentation Unit, Exeter University, 1996.

The Neutral Mask with Jos Houben. Arts Archive, Arts Documentation Unit, Exeter University 1996.

Index